THE MINISTRY OF GOVERNANCE

Partiũ nauis εἰκοσόρου,quæ pagina 13.præceſſit, nomēclatura Latina & Græca.

A Gubernator, κυβερνήτης.
B Remiges, Nautæ, ἐρέται.
C προρεὺς καὶ προρεώτης, Latinis Proreta, qui prorá regit. Iurecóſ.in lege, Cotem·§·Dominus.ff.De publicanis.
D Acroteria.
E Thronus.

WITH OARS AND SAILS

Governance is derived from the Latin term, *gubernare*, to steer. It originally applied to the person who steered the ship, controlling the tiller and, in ships with sails, the set of the sails. The *gubernator* could determine the direction and speed of the vessel.

The illustration above is taken from Cardinal Lazarus Baysi, *Annotationes in L. II. De captivis, & postliminio reversis: in quibus tractatur de re navali* (Lutetiae: Ex officina Roberti Stephani, typographi Regii, M.D.XLIX).

Illustrations are courtesy of Carolyn Lee, curator of rare books at the John K. Mullin of Denver Memorial Library, The Catholic University of America, Washington.

WITH OARS AND SAILS
BOOK ONE

THE MINISTRY OF GOVERNANCE

Edited by

James K. Mallett

Canon Law Society of America
Washington, DC 20064

Library of Congress Cataloging-in-Publication Data

The Ministry of governance.

  (With oars and sails ; bk. 1)
  Includes bibliographical references.
  1. Catholic Church—United States—Government—
Congresses. 2. Catholic Church—Government—Congresses.
3. Dioceses—United States—Congresses. 4. Dioceses—
Congresses. 5. Canon law—Congresses. I. Mallett,
James K., 1941–   . II. Canon Law Society of America.
III. Series.
BX1407.D54M56 1987   262'.0273   87-5121
ISBN 0-943616-31-X
SAN 237-6296

TABLE OF CONTENTS

INTRODUCTION

James K. Mallett

When Pope John XXIII called for a revision of the Code of Canon Law and opened the Second Vatican Council, the Canon Law Society of America was almost 25 years old. The members of the Society responded enthusiastically to the papal call for church renewal. Many American canonists saw the mid-sixties as a time for a collegiate responsibility to the whole Church, a time for the Canon Law Society of America to set into motion a positive plan that would contribute to the world-wide process of renewal. The Society initiated cooperation with individuals and organizations doing research in the other church sciences, and committed itself to the service of the bishops on canonical matters with the pledge to participate in the constant renewal of the law by canonical research and proposals for revision.

In 1974 the Canon Law Society of America gathered together a select group of leaders representing a cross-section within the Church for a three-day "think tank" situation to look ahead for a decade to identify goals and means by which they might be achieved.

> The goals agreed upon fell into three broad areas: the Church as an ordered *communio*, the Church in dialogue with secular society, and within the Church an expanded concept of ministry. Goals undergirding these general areas related to the role of law and the process and dynamics of governance. The realization of all the goals was seen to involve research and development, legal reform, technical assistance, and massive education. (*Origins*, August 15, 1974.)

In addressing itself to the question of governance the report noted that Vatican II had "taught us to look at authority as service exercised through subsidiarity and coresponsibility," but ignorance of administrative and legislative dynamics and obsolete structures had acted against this.

> Laity, clergy and bishops alike need to be informed of the science and art of government. They need to have some grasp of the

process involved in formulating policy, solving problems, making decisions, shaping organization, maintaining communication, resolving conflict, deploying personnel, and establishing laws. Present structures should be evaluated to determine their effectiveness in the exercise of an authority understood as functional and diffused among the people of God. Where necessary new structures must be designed. (*Origins*, August 15, 1974.)

The recommendations of the think tank generally were accepted and acted upon by the Canon Law Society of America, which held a follow-up three-day consultation the next year with somewhat broader participation of key persons from various national organizations and associations. Because of the priority given to tribunal procedures and advocacy in the revision of law, however, it was not until 1981 that the Board of Governors of the Canon Law Society of America commissioned a study to develop a proposal for a Symposium on Diocesan Governance. The proposal was approved in October 1981, and a director of the symposium was appointed in January 1982.

The tremendous impact of the Second Vatican Council on the diocesan church is obvious. There has been an extraordinary proliferation of councils, offices, service agencies, commissions, and myriad experiments in coordinating old and new institutes in various organizational structures. These years of experimentation have certainly been profitable for the Church in this country, but as the CLSA think tank recognized eleven years ago, there is a serious need to learn from the results of these experiments and to promote governance in the Church as a special ministry. This need is heightened by the promulgation of a revised Code of Canon Law. There is a notable emphasis in the new law on the coordination of the various operational and participative institutes of diocesan governance, reflecting a growing appreciation for this need.

The proliferation of diocesan agencies and specialized ministries has occasioned the organization and growth of national associations for professional sharing and collaboration. These are most notably the National Pastoral Planning Conference, the National Federation of Priests' Councils, the National Association of Church Personnel Administrators, the National Organization for Continuing Education of Roman Catholic Clergy, and the Diocesan Fiscal Managers' Conference. The need for better communication among these associations has been felt in recent years. All of these associations, together with older groups such as the National Catholic Educational Association and the National Conference of Catholic Charities, are related to the practice of diocesan governance and should be involved in any effective attempt to study the implementation of the revised code and to promote a common understanding of the principles and dynamics of diocesan governance.

These needs are among those which prompted the Canon Law Society of America to initiate a symposium on diocesan governance, in the tradition of former symposia which have made important contributions to the Church in the United States. The major objectives of the symposium were to publish studies on diocesan governance. A secondary objective, promoted in the process of the symposium, was to promote better communication and cooperation among the Canon Law Society of America and other professional associations concerned with diocesan governance. The following organizations were invited to appoint one representative to participate in the symposium: the National Pastoral Planning Conference, the National Association of Church Personnel Administrators, the National Federation of Priests' Councils, the Diocesan Fiscal Managers' Conference, the National Catholic Educational Association, the National Organization for Continuing Education of Roman Catholic Clergy, the National Catholic Charities Conference, and the Center for Applied Research in the Apostolate. These eight persons were joined by canon lawyers and experts in each of the following areas: patristics, history, theology, sociology, research, and psychology.

During the first phase of the symposium the participants gathered for extended conversation on the problems of governance from the viewpoint of each organization and discipline, and planned the future of the symposium by mutual agreement on the studies and tasks to be accepted by the participants. Two publications resulted from these efforts: this volume of studies entitled *The Ministry of Governance*, and a Workbook for diocesan organization and governance entitled *The Governance of Ministry*. More specific information concerning the development of *The Governance of Ministry* can be found in the introduction to that volume.

The first drafts of most of the articles contained in this volume were presented and discussed at a meeting of all symposium participants in November 1984. Revisions were made by the authors in light of these discussions. The paper by Roland-Bernard Trauffer, O.P. was not presented or discussed at this meeting. The paper by James H. Provost was developed after the meeting in response to concerns expressed by the symposium participants.

The studies which comprise *The Ministry of Governance* might be divided into three categories: the diocesan church in the world, in mission, and in experience.

The first three studies concern the diocesan church in the world. We have learned from the Second Vatican Council that the Church is a living body in constant interaction with the cultural, political and economic realities of the world. The study by Thomas Curry shows how the American Church developed a style of diocesan governance which was influenced by the circumstances of American society and history. In order to combat anti-Catholic sentiment American Catholics demonstrated their loyalty to country by an excessive adherence to the characteristics and values of American culture which are compatible with our religion. Another perspective on the history of the American Church is given by Gerald P. Fogarty, S.J., who examines the internal factors which shaped diocesan structure and governance.

John Lynch examines the history of the reformation churches in America; from his study we learn more about the religious milieu in which American Catholicism developed, and in this process we are taught some valuable lessons concerning church governance.

The next three studies deal with the diocesan church in mission. Any study of diocesan governance should consider the biblical roots of governance and the relation of governance to the mission of the Church. Agnes Cunningham, S.S.C.M., has contributed a study of power and authority in the Church as these concepts developed in the Judeo-Christian tradition and were gradually modified by historical, social and cultural influences. John M. Huels, O.S.M., has contributed a study of the role of canon law in light of *Lumen gentium*, providing a broader understanding of law in the Church and the relation of law to governance. Michael J. Fahey, S.J., provides a theological investigation of diocesan governance in the revised Code of Canon Law.

The next set of three studies concern the diocesan church in lived experience. The experience of diocesan governance at this time in the history of the American Church involves many considerations. The other publication which has resulted from our symposium, *The Governance of Ministry*, focuses on the principles and dynamics of diocesan governance. Several authors in the present volume have dealt with concrete canonical, empirical, and psychological issues. Eugene Hemrick has contributed a survey of what can be learned concerning diocesan governance from research. Robert Willis studies the issue of personal development as it relates to the ministry of governance in an interpersonal context. Finally, Rolland-Bernard Trauffer, O.P., has provided us with a study of diocesan governance in European dioceses since the promulgation of the revised code.

The concluding article, by James H. Provost, explores several issues related to diocesan governance. This study complements his more expository report on provisions of the code found in the companion volume, *The Governance of Ministry*.

In conclusion, a word of gratitude is due to those who participated in the development and completion of the Symposium on Diocesan Governance. A list of participants may be found at the end of this volume. Many hours of careful study, reflection, and open discussion contributed to this project. Although the studies themselves are the work of individual scholars, the symposium which identified the tasks and provided a forum for discussion and criticism has produced in this volume the result of a unique collaborative effort.

THE EMERGENCE AND DEVELOPMENT OF A STYLE OF AMERICAN DIOCESAN GOVERNANCE IN RESPONSE TO EXTERNAL FACTORS

Thomas Curry

Until the mid-twentieth century the assumption, usually tacit but often explicit, on the part of large numbers of Americans that Catholicism was alien, un-American, and a threat to the nation's institutions proved a constant source of frustration for American Catholics. In order to refute this accusation and to reassure themselves that they were as compatible with American ways as any other group, Catholics proclaimed the significant contributions they had made to the growth of American institutions. In the American Catholic ethos the history of colonial Maryland took pride of place. The Calverts' devotion to religious toleration proved to Catholics that they, too, were pioneers in the development that led to the formation of the First Amendment. Indeed, they could point to the fact that Catholic tolerance fell victim to Protestant intolerance. Catholic scholars also propounded the notion that Thomas Jefferson had quarried the building blocks of American liberty in the writings of Robert Bellarmine. Many of their less scholarly co-religionists exhibited assorted brands of super-patriotism in an effort to demonstrate to the nation at large that they were second to none in their love of country.[1]

The election of a Catholic president in 1960 seemed to Catholics the long-delayed vindication of what they had always proclaimed, that their ways were compatible with American institutions. In this assertion they were correct. Catholics had never wanted to eradicate the First Amendment and overthrow the Constitution. However, in another sense, they had posed a definite threat to American ways and understanding. From colonial times until well into the twentieth century, they challenged

---

[1] Gaillard Hunt, "Cardinal Bellarmine and the Virginia Bill of Rights," *Catholic Historical Review* 3 (1917) 276; Merrill D. Peterson, *The Jefferson Image in the American Mind* (New York: Oxford University Press, 1960), p. 500; William M. Halsey, *The Survival of American Innocence: Catholics in an Era of Disillusionment, 1920–1940* (Notre Dame: Notre Dame University Press, 1980), p. 70.

the self-image and national definition adhered to by the dominant American culture and the majority of the population and played a major role in shattering it. This challenge helped shape America as we know it. It also shaped the organization and governance of the American Catholic Church.

Colonial America

Many early English settlers came to the New World in order to build the true biblical church, whose emergence in England Charles I and Archbishop Laud were preventing by their "Popish" machinations. The prolific writings of New England Puritans gave this vision its classic and most celebrated expressions, but virtually every American settlement saw itself as staking a claim for the Protestant Reformation.[2] In a world as ideologically divided as our own, Protestants viewed their colonies as bastions of true religion, liberty, and enlightenment. "Popery," for them, represented corruption, tyranny, ignorance, and the antithesis of America as they perceived it.

Samuel Mather, in his condemnation of the "Popish" Church of England, synopsized the Puritan perception of Catholicism and the style of religion Puritans wanted eliminated:

> The Doctrine Condemns and cashieres at once all the Ceremonies, and whatever other Inventions of men have been introduced into the worship of God by the Spirit of AntiChrist, and reteined, and continued by some reforming Magistrates, who have made but incomplete and imperfect Reformations. As who knows not, that almost all the Ordinances of Christ have been polluted and corrupted by them. The Gospel might not be preached without a Surplice, nor Baptisme administered without the sign of the Cross, So likewise kneeling at the Sacrament, bowing to the Altar, and to the name of Jesus, Popish holy days, holiness of places, Organs and Cathedral Musick, The Books of Common prayer, Prelacy or Church Government by Bishops. . . . They are nothing else but reliques of Popery, and remnants of Baal, and

---

[2] Perry Miller, "Religion and Society in the Early Literature of Virginia," in *Errand into the Wilderness* (Cambridge, Mass.: Harvard University Press, 1956), p. 99; Babette M. Levy, "Early Puritanism in the Southern and Island Colonies," *American Antiquarian Society Proceedings* 70 (1960) 69.

therefore when the Kingdome of Christ is come, they shall perish from off the Earth, and from under these Heavens.[3]

Puritans and American Protestants generally, therefore, were not simply prejudiced against Catholics. They were diametrically and ideologically opposed to them, for true biblical religion as Puritans defined it and Catholicism could not coexist.

In such a world the Calverts' largely unexplained plans to combine Catholics and Protestants peaceably in a commercially successful colonial venture proved quixotic. In an era when Catholics and Protestants still saw each other as mutually incompatible, neither side could draw on experiences or examples of peaceful coexistence. Protestants did not carefully consider and reject the Maryland plan. Rather, they were baffled by it and incapable of grasping it. They could not transcend their perception of Catholics as a fifth column in their midst, ready to open the door to an annihilating enemy.

By 1700, with the suppression of all Catholic public influence in Maryland, the American colonies had become completely Protestant-dominated. By the same date the intense religious fervor of the preceding century had subsided, and the emergence of a multitude of sects had shattered any possibility for uniformity of belief in American Protestantism. As described by Samuel Mather, however, Puritanism constituted more than doctrine: it was perhaps primarily a liturgy, a religious practice, a way of being religious that utterly rejected the style and content of Catholic practice and substituted its own self-consciously opposing practices. In doctrinal and theological matters, Puritanism splintered hopelessly; in the manner of being religious, the non-sacramental, non-ritualistic, anti-hierarchical Puritan style dominated—even in the Anglican settlements—the form of American religion. Throughout the English colonies the forms, language and habits of Protestantism as influenced by Puritanism entwined themselves with colonial culture, thought patterns, and legal systems and came to be identified by the inhabitants as the truly "American" religion. From the vantage point of Protestantism, colonial America was filled with diversity; from the perspective of Catholicism, it formed a unified whole.[4]

Colonial Americans throughout the different colonies assumed that America was Protestant, and all the colonies restricted Catholics from

---

[3] Samuel Mather, *A Testimony from the Scriptures* (Cambridge, MA: 1672), p. 25.

[4] Mary Augustina Ray, *American Opinion of Roman Catholicism in the Eighteenth Century* (New York: Columbia University Press, 1936).

participating in public life. In the 1750's William Livingston of New York, a man determined to fight for an open educational system against the monopolizing tendencies of Anglicans, took it as axiomatic that government would "always, for political reasons, exclude Papists."[5] Although the liberal spirit of the revolutionary period somewhat broke down the inherited anti-Catholicism, the majority of the states still restricted officeholding to Protestants.

First Amendment to the Constitution

In 1790 Congress, in one of the amendments that constituted the Bill of Rights, decreed that "Congress shall make no law respecting an establishment of religion, or prohibiting the free exercise thereof." Commentators often assume that the First Amendment created the substance of modern American Church-State relations, the "separation of Church and State," to employ that imprecise but durable phrase, and that Catholics and other immigrants who came here adjusted themselves to and assimilated themselves into the pre-existing system. For instance, Canon Stokes, in his monumental work on American Church-State relations, dealt with Catholicism in a chapter entitled "The Roman Catholic Adjustments to American Church State Conditions."[6] It denigrates not, however, the achievement of colonial and revolutionary Americans to say that while they did create extraordinary structures for the advancement of constitutional government and religious liberty, they did not create the present system of Church and State. That system was not simply created in the First Congress. It came into being over the course of America's history, and it is still in the process of formation.

The enactment of the First Amendment did not of itself bring about a "separation of Church and State." The very Congress that enacted it appointed a day of prayer in thanksgiving for the "many signal favors of Almighty God," thereby demonstrating how much its members were still wedded to the forms of their Protestant culture.[7] The states preserved this culture, and during the early years of the republic and throughout the nineteenth century local governments interfered, formally and informally, in a multitude of religious matters.

[5] Francis X. Curran, *Catholics in Colonial Law* (Chicago: Loyola University Press, 1963); *The Occasional Reverberator* 4 (October 5, 1752).

[6] Anson Phelps Stokes, *Church and State in the United States*, 3 vols. (New York: Harper & Brothers, 1950), 1:784.

[7] *The Debates and Proceedings in the Congress of the United States* (Washington, DC, 1834), 1:914.

James Madison, a chief architect of the Constitution, had originally opposed the addition of a Bill of Rights as useless. Repeatedly he argued that liberty would be guaranteed by a balance of interests, not by constitutional amendments. In *The Federalist* he wrote: "In a free government the security for civil rights must be the same as that for religious rights. It consists in the one case in the multiplicity of interests, and in the other in the multiplicity of sects." To Jefferson, he wrote:

> The same security seems requisite for the civil as for the religious rights of individuals. If the same sect form a majority and have the power, other sects will be sure to be depressed. *Divide et impera*, the reprobated axiom of tyranny, is under certain qualifications, the only policy, by which a republic can be administered on just principles.[8]

Madison doubted the effectiveness of what he termed "parchment barriers" against a determined majority and placed his hope for liberty in the mutual checking and balancing of competing interests.

Much of America's subsequent religious history can be read as an elaboration and illustration of Madison's Federalist argument. No one sect gained a majority, but a number of denominations united in common sentiments combined to impose a non-denominational Protestant ethos on nineteenth-century America. Catholics would constitute the single most numerous and most powerful competing religious interest, a role that shaped not only American Catholicism but America itself.

Religious Equality and Protestant Nation

The United States embarked on an experiment new in history, a nation without an aristocracy or established church. To many Americans, especially after the ideas of the French Revolution reached these shores, their society seemed endangered by deism and "infidelity." Without the traditional sources of authority, they had therefore to organize a society whose control came not from above but from the citizens themselves, one wherein voluntarism took the place of deference. In this reordering of society, religion played a central role.

Church-State developments during the American Revolution provided

---

[8] *The Federalist*, no. 51; "James Madison to Thomas Jefferson, October 1787," in *The Papers of James Madison*, ed. Robert A. Rutland et al. (Charlottesville, VA: University of Virginia Press, 1977–), 11:214.

the basis for the reorganization of American religion. Protestantism in its different forms had pervaded colonial America, but not on a basis of equality. In the colonial period southern colonies maintained establishments of religion; Baptists and Quakers lived as second-class citizens in New England; and all non-Anglicans feared the pretensions of the Church of England. The Revolution removed all danger of Anglican dominance and most of the establishments of religion. Unable to resort to government power either to support churches or coerce citizens, Protestants found themselves obliged to convert and hold a pluralist nation on the basis of voluntary church membership. However, in the absence of establishments of religion or conflicting claims to dominance on the part of particular denominations, American Protestants could focus on their commonality. This organization of religion based on voluntarism, rather than state coercion or support, had to rely on the presence of certain agreements or suppositions among the members of society.

The laws decreed the equality of all denominations, and the major Protestant denominations came to accept this in fact. Members of the different Protestant groups, while retaining their traditional theological beliefs and customs, accepted each other's legitimacy, recognizing each other as authentic expressions of Christianity. Such cooperation came about largely by deemphasizing, in favor of action, theology and the importance of adherence to proper doctrine. Reform or "benevolence" became the watchword of nineteenth-century Protestantism. Henry Commager has written that during the nineteenth century, "religion prospered while theology went slowly bankrupt."[9] Whereas before the Revolution the First Great Awakening had revived Calvinist theology, with its fiercely introspective search to discern one's election by God, the Second Awakening of the 1820's became an exercise in voluntarism, an urging of the members of the meeting to come forward and accept God.

The early nineteenth century saw the emergence of a Protestant nation that shared an evangelical Protestantism based on a "common Christianity" which contemporaries distinguished from "sectarian beliefs," i.e., tenets peculiar to each denomination. They shared a common interpretation of history that went back to Foxe's *Book of Martyrs* and gave a special place to England in the Reformation. They shared a common bible and, increasingly, common hymns and prayers. Revivalism, associated today with fundamentalist or marginal groups, acted as the dynamic force in

---

[9] Henry Steele Commager, *The American Mind. An Interpretation of American Thought and Character since the 1880's* (New Haven: Yale University Press, 1950), p. 165.

nineteenth-century Protestantism. It appealed to mainstream America and provided a common language and approach for the churches.

Tocqueville observed Americans' love of equality even over liberty, and this passion for equality extended to religion.[10] Pressing no claims to be the one true church, Protestant denominations could live in competition but equality. Their desire to reform society, their hopes for Christian perfection, and the belief that they were the "grand experiment of Protestantism" united them more than their individual sectarian differences separated them.[11] Moreover, all subscribed to an essentially democratic form of governance. The last great religious controversy of colonial times, a dispute between the Anglican clergy and the rest of the colonists over the introduction of bishops into America, had renewed and heightened Americans' prejudice against hierarchical and centralized churches. In revolutionary and post-revolutionary America, the churches generally followed and the states generally mandated a congregational form of organization.[12]

During the nineteenth century Protestants not only constituted the majority of the population, they dominated both state and society, forming what was in fact a Protestant nation. This situation came about not because Protestant Americans wished to tyrannize minorities or to impose their ways on others, but because despite their diversity, they were able to sink many of their differences and agree informally on a non-denominational Protestantism common to all. Sharing similar mores, a common outlook, bible, and view of history, they saw their way in Church and State not as the imposition of a religion on the nation, but as the marrow of civilized living and the path to progress. Commentators repeatedly affirmed that America was a Christian—by which they usually meant Protestant— nation, and as late as 1931 the Supreme Court made its third affirmation of that belief.[13]

---

[10] Alexis de Tocqueville, *Democracy in America*, ed. Phillips Bradley, 2 vols. (New York: Vintage Books, 1945), 2:98.

[11] Martin E. Marty, *Righteous Empire. The Protestant Experience in America* (New York: The Dial Press, 1970), pp. 67, 88; Winthrop Hudson, *Religion in America* (New York: Charles Scribner's Sons, 3rd ed. 1981), p. 151.

[12] Patrick J. Dignan, *A History of the Legal Incorporation of Catholic Church Property in the United States, 1784–1932* (Washington, DC: Catholic University Press, 1933), pp. 51–66; Mark DeWolfe Howe, *The Garden and the Wilderness. Religion and Government in American Constitutional History* (Chicago: University of Chicago Press, 1965), pp. 32–60.

[13] *Vidal v. Girard's Executors* 2 How 127 (1843); *Church of Holy Trinity v. U.S.* 143 U.S. 457 (1892); *U.S. v. Macintosh* 283 U.S. 605 (1971). James Fulton Maclear, " 'The True

Non-denominational revivalist Protestantism demonstrated a superb ability to assimilate—to harmonize mainstream American Protestants in an overall culture. Revivalism conquered the frontier and then returned the forms of belief and worship developed there back to more settled areas, thereby uniting East and West.[14] So dominant was Protestant evangelical religion in nineteenth-century America that Martin Marty has written:

> Legal disestablishment meant instant establishment in the national ethos. Years before, they [evangelicals] had given up the idea of receiving much financial support or privilege, even where vestigial establishment remained. They now had little more to lose. They had much to gain: parity, prestige, privilege, the absence of anticlericalism and of public resentment. They could achieve what the contenders for the national church wanted in England, but they needed no legal support.[15]

This fact of the Protestant nation was of paramount importance in shaping the American Catholic church, including its governance. Some Protestant denominations, such as the Lutheran, lived on the fringes of the dominant consensus. Other groups, such as Unitarians, Mormons, and the many utopian communes like the Shakers existed beyond its boundaries. Catholics increasingly came to represent the largest and the most visible

American Union' of Church and State: The Reconstruction of the Theocratic Tradition,'' *Church History* 28 (1959) 41–62; Leo Pfeffer, "The Deity in American Constitutional History," *Journal of Church and State* 23 (1981) 215–239.

[14] Timothy L. Smith, *Revivalism and Social Reform in Mid-Nineteenth Century America* (Nashville: Abingdon Press, 1957), p. 9.

[15] Martin E. Marty, "Living with Establishment and Disestablishment in Nineteenth-Century Anglo-America," *Journal of Church and State* 18 (1976) 73. On the Protestant nation, see Robert T. Handy, *A Christian America. Protestant Hopes and Historical Realities* (New York: Oxford University Press, 2nd ed. 1984); Martin E. Marty, *Righteous Empire*; Perry Miller, *The Life of the Mind in America* (New York: Harcourt, Brace & World, Inc., 1965), pp. 3–95; Paul E. Johnson, *A Shopkeeper's Millennium. Society and Revivals in Rochester, New York, 1815–1837* (New York: Hill and Wang, 1978); Lawrence B. Davis, *Immigrants, Baptists and the Protestant Mind in America* (Urbana, IL: University of Illinois Press, 1973); Elwyn A. Smith, "The Voluntary Establishment of Religion," in *The Religion of the Republic*, ed. Elwyn A. Smith (Philadelphia: Fortress Press, 1971), pp. 154–87; James C. Carper, "A Common Faith for the Common School? Religion and Education in Kansas, 1861–1900," *Mid-America* 60 (1968) 147; Timothy L. Smith, "Protestant Schooling and American Nationality," *Journal of American History* 53 (1967) 679; David Tyack, "The Kingdom of God and the Common School. Protestant Ministers and the Educational Awakening in the West," *Harvard Educational Review* 36 (1966) 447; James Bryce, *The American Commonwealth*, 2 vols. (New York: The Commonwealth Publishing Company, 1908), 2:650.

exception to the national religious ethos. As a small minority during the colonial and early national periods, they remained largely invisible to the dominant society. Conscious of their minority and tenuous status, they had always been careful not to give offense. Unlike Quakers or, later, Baptists, they had not organized to combat religious discrimination but had rather worked quietly, depending upon influential leaders for the amelioration of restrictive legislation. In 1633, Lord Baltimore had instructed his Catholic colonists to offer no offense to Protestant settlers and ordered that "all Acts of the Romane Catholique Religion . . . be done as privately as may be."[16] Few in numbers, they had to be careful lest they antagonize the majority. John Carroll, a century and a half later, remained conscious that his appointment as a bishop might stir up resentment.[17]

The legal disestablishments that took place during the revolutionary period, however, together with the liberal spirit that pervaded that era, brought Catholics considerable relief. Their participation in the Revolution even won them a certain amount of respect. To an extent, "The Era of Good Feeling" describes the relationships between Catholics and Protestants during the early years of the republic.[18] Both the smallness of American Catholicism and its composition, often respectable middle-class citizens or powerful landowners, as in Maryland, masked its difference from the majority of the population. Given the rise and progress of the Protestant nation, Catholicism, like other unassimilated religious groups, could expect toleration and a measure of accommodation so long as it remained insignificant and posed no threat or competition to the dominant ethos.

Trustee Controversy

During the early decades of the nineteenth century, the trustee controversy, a crisis of governance, signaled the Catholic rejection of the majority religious consensus. In their efforts to secure control over church property and the appointment of pastors, lay trustees saw themselves as

[16] *The Calvert Papers*, 3 vols. (Baltimore: Maryland Historical Society, 1889–1899), 1:133.

[17] Thomas O'Brien Hanley, ed., *The John Carroll Papers*, 3 vols. (Notre Dame: University of Notre Dame Press, 1976), 1:162–163.

[18] Joseph Agnito, "Ecumenical Stirrings: Catholic-Protestant Relations during the Episcopacy of John Carroll," *Church History* 45 (1976) 358–375; Joseph P. Chinnici, "American Catholics and Religious Pluralism, 1775–1820," *Journal of Ecumenical Studies* 16 (1979) 727.

adapting "the European Catholic Church to American culture by identifying that Church with American republicanism."[19] From another aspect, however, the trustee controversy can be seen as a crisis of survival, whether American Catholicism would continue to maintain its own strong separate identity or whether it would take its first major step toward assimilation into the dominant Protestant culture.

John Carroll understood the significance of what the trustees were advocating. To a group of them in New York he wrote that if their proposals were accepted, "the unity and Catholicity of our Church would be at an end; and it would be formed into distinct & independent Societies, nearly in the same manner, as the Congregational Presbyterians of your neighbouring New England states." Some trustees agreed with this interpretation and were explicit in their desire for a "National American Church."[20]

At work here was not only the desire of Catholics to adjust their church to local circumstances, but the assimilative genius of the evangelical Protestant nation—homogenizing different groups and bringing them under a huge umbrella. In attempting to democratize the Church, trustees were responding to societal pressures. Contemporary American society looked with disfavor on hierarchical churches as authoritarian, as a violation of the passion for equality that pervaded society, and as incompatible with the basic consensus that held together in unity the larger denominational society. Contemporary American law regarding incorporation and property holding assumed and mandated that churches follow a trustee, congregational type of government. In adhering to a different approach, Catholics risked the antipathy of their Protestant neighbors.[21]

Many of Catholicism's bitterest opponents agreed with the proponents of lay trusteeism that they were Americanizing the Church. Indeed, several states threatened or attempted to impose a congregational form of government on it. According to the reasoning that underlay the First Amendment, however, government had no power in religious matters at all. As Madison had insisted, the State "had not a shadow of right" to interfere in religious matters. America had, therefore, in law created a structure in which

---

[19] Patrick Carey, "The Laity's Understanding of the Trustee System, 1785–1855," *Catholic Historical Review* 64 (1978) 358. On the trustee controversy, see Dignan, pp. 60–140, and Patrick W. Carey, "Republicanism Within American Catholicism, 1785–1860," *Journal of the Early Republic* 3 (1983) 413–437.

[20] Hanley, 1:203, quoted in James Hennessey, S.J., *American Catholicism* (New York: Oxford University Press, 1981), p. 77.

[21] Carey, pp. 363–366, 375.

churches might be what they chose to be—congregational or hierarchical. Yet popular opinion arrogated the title of "truly American" to the form of church government most acceptable to the majority of the population, and it was to this definition of "American" that the lay trustees were responding. Madison had predicted that "no one sect" would be able to "outnumber and depress" the rest. During the nineteenth century, however, a combination of denominations was able to dominate public opinion and to define their ways in Church and State as the American way.

Nineteenth-Century Immigration

The refusal to accept trusteeism signaled Catholicism's determination to reject the assimilating thrust of non-denominational Protestantism, but not until the advent of large-scale Catholic immigration did the extent of that rejection become evident. Catholics in the early republic did not stand out in glaring contrast to the rest of the native population. They did so only after substantial numbers of their coreligionists began to arrive, especially from Ireland and Germany, in the 1820's and 1830's.

Poor and in many cases non-English speaking, these immigrants brought immense social problems to the cities where they settled and, in turn, encountered intense hostility from the native population. The presence of such large numbers of poor Catholic immigrants in their midst brought out Americans' latent fear of Catholicism and seemed to confirm all their inherited stereotypes—that Catholicism bred ignorance, that its adherents were superstitious, priest-ridden, and manipulated by an international conspiracy led by the Vatican to reduce the Protestant world to slavery. Although early immigrants had come from rather lax, culturally-Catholic milieus, they found themselves upon their arrival in America bearing the brunt of accusations that were the accretions of centuries of religious invective. Protestant America saw Catholic immigrants not as they were, but as a whole inherited culture told them they should be.[22]

Driven back on themselves by the fierce opposition they encountered in Protestant America, Catholics developed a heightened sense of their ethnic identity and their religion. They did not so much bring with them a foreign

---

[22] Ray Allen Billington, *The Protestant Crusade 1800–1860. A Study of the Origins of American Nativism* (Chicago: Quadrangle Books); Jay Dolan, *The Immigrant Church. New York's German and Irish Catholics* (Baltimore: The Johns Hopkins University Press, 1975); David Miller, "Irish Catholicism and the Great Famine," *Journal of Social History* 9 (1975) 81–89; Emmet Larkin, "The Devotional Revolution in Ireland, 1850–1875," *American Historical Review* 72 (1972) 625–652.

church as create one in order to shelter themselves from a barrage of
hostility. The more the dominant society stereotyped and rejected them,
the greater strength they found in uniting against a common enemy. Just as
in politics Catholics often identified with the Democratic Party not so much
because they adhered to its platforms as because its enemies were their
enemies, so also in religion they found their identity by defining themselves against a clear opposition.[23]

Catholicism, in turn, provided Protestant America with a clear backdrop
against which it could continually define itself. The Protestant nation could
unite in a crusade to defend the common schools, to save the West from
"Popery," and to rescue the country from the Catholic conspiracy to
destroy American liberties.[24] In the argument that the Catholic Church did
not accept the separation of Church and State, Protestant apologists found
a powerful rallying cry, while ignoring the fact that they themselves
defined the nation as Protestant and used the power of government to
impose their own mores and ethos on society at large. Thus by their mutual
opposition, American Catholicism and American Protestantism intensified
each other's self-perception and helped recreate, define, and strengthen
each other.

Large-scale immigration precluded the possibility of American Catholics' achieving accommodation with the population at large by keeping a
low profile. Despised and stereotyped by the dominant society, they fought
back by rejecting it and attacking some of its most cherished symbols.
Open warfare between Catholics and Protestants, mostly verbal but
sometimes physical, absorbed much of the religious energy of nineteenth-
century Americans. In such an atmosphere the combativeness of John
Hughes inevitably replaced the diplomacy of John Carroll as the guiding
force in American Catholicism.[25]

Catholic incompatibility and opposition to the dominant ethos took
several forms. At its most fundamental level, the conflict manifested itself

[23] Thomas T. McAvoy, "America's Cultural Impact on Catholicism," in *The Religion
of the Republic*, p. 48; Lee Benson, *The Concept of Jacksonian Democracy* (Princeton:
Princeton University Press, 1961), pp. 186–192.

[24] Tyack, p. 459; Billington, pp. 32, 142; David Brion Davis, ed., *The Fear of
Conspiracy. Images of Un-American Subversion from the Revolution to the Present* (Ithaca:
Cornell University Press, 1971).

[25] John B. Hughes, *A Discourse . . . is the Roman Catholic and Presbyterian Religion
inimical to Civil and Religious Liberty* (reprint ed., New York: Da Capo Press, 1970); John
Coleman, *An American Strategic Theology* (New York: Paulist Press, 1982), p. 156.

as a rejection of the underlying consensus of the denominational society, the agreement that each group represented an equal and authentic expression of Christianity. Like Mormonism, Catholicism laid claim to exclusive truth, thereby rendering impossible its absorption into the non-denominational consensus, and—again as in the case of Mormonism—the larger society reacted with frenzied hostility.

Furthermore, whereas Protestants looked to the bible as the source of all religious teaching and guidance, Catholics looked first to the Church. Despite their division into a multiplicity of denominations, Protestants still believed that the bible held the authoritative answer to all religious questions. Familiarity with its writings gave them a common language and culture that Catholics, with their scanty biblical knowledge, could not share. Whereas Puritans, on setting up the first printing press in the English colonies, had printed the psalms, Catholics first issued not a bible (granted, a tall order for any printer) but a volume of devotional prayers. These seemed to Protestants the essence of ignorance and superstition. Before the development of the theory of evolution and subsequent fundamentalism, the bible was for Protestants the source book of civilization. Despite their varied theological traditions, they still possessed a core of Reformation optimism in the feeling that putting the bible in the hands of all people would bring about the triumph of true Christianity.

These divergent approaches to religion first surfaced in the public schools. The common schools not only prescribed bible reading and Protestant devotional exercises, but permeated their education with an interpretation of history that viewed England and Protestantism as having saved the world from Catholicism, tyranny, and Spain. Catholics most often opted to challenge the use of the King James version of the bible. For purposes of controversy, they endowed the Douay version with an importance that it probably did not possess in their own devotional lives. Nevertheless, their demand to be allowed to read their own version, while suitably controversial, was eminently defensible.

On observance of the Sabbath Catholics again ran headlong into one of the cherished symbols of the Protestant nation. The strict observance of Sunday (which coincided well with the needs of an increasingly industrializing society), though often associated with Puritanism, had permeated the colonies and the custom carried over into the republic. Perhaps because it provided a clear topic of agreement, the observance of the Sabbath took on a symbolic importance that was central to Protestant America, and ministers proclaimed that it served as a test for the presence of Christian civilization.[26] They regarded Catholics as corrupted by "the demoralizing influence of the continental Sunday, and . . . not yet sufficiently naturalized to appreciate the habits of the land of their adoption."[27] The nation's attachment to the Sabbath proved strong enough to withstand even the notorious economic conservatism of the Supreme Court. In 1905 the justices contemptuously dismissed social legislation limiting the number of hours bakers could work in New York as a violation of "freedom of contract." However, five years previously, in a case dealing with a Minnesota law closing barbershops on Sunday, the court had shown considerable solicitude for the health and welfare of barbers and their working hours.[28]

In the program of reforms by which Protestant Christians in the antebellum period hoped to bring about the triumph of a Christian America, the temperance movement worked its way to the center. This campaign showed yet another stark contrast between those who regarded themselves as the proponents of progress and Christian civilization and Catholic immigrants, be they Irish in Eastern cities or German settlers in the Midwest.[29]

Anti-Catholicism

Anti-Catholicism provided American society with a vehicle for venting an assortment of frustrations and grudges. The genre of writing typified by Maria Monk's *Awful Disclosures* legitimized for respectable citizens the perusal of salacious literature. Know-Nothingism transformed the expression of prejudice in its grossest form into patriotism. However, to limit the interpretation of nineteenth-century anti-Catholicism to naked bigotry would be to underestimate its significance. These hysterical forms only carried to extremes what were the sentiments of the nation at large.

Catholics constituted the principal group that the genius of non-denominational evangelical Protestantism could not assimilate. The dom-

[26] Handy, pp. 42–45, 73–77; William Addison Blakely, ed., *American State Papers Bearing on Sunday Legislation* (Washington, DC, 1911; reprint ed., New York: Da Capo Press, 1970).

[27] Philip Schaff, *Church and State in the United States* (New York, 1888; reprint ed., New York: Arno Press, 1972), p. 72.

[28] *Lochner v. New York* 198 U.S. 45 (1905); *Petit v. Minn.* 177 U.S. 164 (1900). For other cases favoring Sabbath legislation, see *Soon Hing v. Crowley* 113 U.S. 703 (1884); *Burcher v. Cheshire* 125 U.S. 555 (1886); *Hennington v. Georgia* 163 U.S. 299 (1896).

[29] Billington, pp. 195, 323; Johnson, p. 57.

inant culture promoted social control by means of its common religious culture, through the inculcation of self-discipline and restraint; but in doing so it did not limit its objective to the cultivation of unity, uniformity, and equality. American Protestants came increasingly under the influence of the perfectionist millennial impulse, the hope that America's free institutions and religion would bring about the triumph of Christian civilization. Catholics sometimes scoffed at these efforts, dismissing mainstream reformers and faddists together as people who had "infected our whole society and turned a large proportion of our citizens into madmen."[30]

As the depth and extent of Catholics' rejection of the vision of the Protestant nation became more and more evident, hostility to them increased. Catholics not only repudiated the cherished symbols of American religion, they proceeded to construct and proclaim a rival vision and structure. They not only demanded a different version of the bible in public schools, they began to build their own schools, hospitals, and institutions. To the Protestant vision, they offered their own opposing vision of a triumphantly Catholic America.

Confronted with such opposition, Protestant leaders viewed Catholics not only as a retrograde disruptive force in society, but as a hindrance to the emergence of their cherished dreams for the future. Catholics were un-American as such leaders defined that term, and consequently, they saw themselves engaged in a life and death struggle to save American liberty and Christian civilization. Catholics' rejection of biblical religion and free institutions in favor of an authoritarian, foreign, and "Babylonian" church appeared to them explicable only by the presence of a giant conspiracy. The more Catholics challenged the mores of Protestant America, the more frenzied the reaction became. Nativism and anti-Catholicism in their various forms represented the reactions of a people whose national definition was being attacked, whose self-image was being challenged, and whose deepest aspirations for the future seemed to them to be frustrated by a rising Catholicism.

For their part, the struggle to preserve their identity marked and shaped American Catholics and the form and governance of their Church. Under attack by the larger society, they developed the skills of siege warfare: unity of command, loyalty, obedience, a deep sensitivity to criticism, and a strong adherence to tradition. These were the qualities reflected in the governance of their Church. The more society demanded that the governance of churches be congregational, the more Catholic bishops insisted on

---

[30] Oscar Handlin, *Boston's Immigrants* (New York: Atheneum, 1975), p. 132.

the hierarchical nature of the Church. They prized and insisted upon uniformity in devotion, discipline, and practice. Not trusteeism but the corporation sole became the hallmark of Catholic Church property tenure.[31]

Apart from the unrelenting pressure from the dominant society, other features of American culture helped cement Catholic unity and strength. The Church grew and prospered in industrializing America and imitated the business world with its emphasis on consolidation, centralization, and rationalization. Church leaders, too, absorbed the mores of the Victorian age—sobriety, respectability, and discipline. Members of their flock, especially those most upwardly mobile, and consequently most influential, shared the same ethic. Moreover, the rank and file, especially those involved in patronage politics, learned the overarching virtue of loyalty.[32]

Like American Protestantism with its different and often competing sects, American Catholicism embraced a number of competing and frequently mutually hostile ethnic populations. Although these remained in many cases remarkably separate, they did nevertheless adhere to similar beliefs and practices. For both Catholics and Protestants, however, there were limits to the consensus. Whereas the Protestant non-denominational society could not embrace such groups as the Mormons who demanded exclusivity of truth, Catholicism was unable to integrate such groups as Oriental Rite Catholics, whose practice in the matter of clerical celibacy especially breached the Catholic consensus.[33]

Redefinition of America: 1865–1960

After the Civil War the introduction of the higher criticism, debates over evolution, and the growth of the social gospel movement brought new divisions to American Protestantism. Catholicism, however, continued to be regarded as the common enemy. In 1885 Josiah Strong, a man who bridged several of the rifts in late nineteenth-century Protestantism, identified immigration, "Romanism," intemperance, and the city—all

[31] Joseph Chinnici, "Organization of the Spiritual Life: American Catholic Devotional Works, 1791–1866," *Theological Studies* 40 (1979) 229, 231; Dignan, p. 179.

[32] Dennis J. Clark, "The irish Catholics. A Postponed Perspective," in *Immigrants and Religion in Urban America*, ed. Randall M. Miller and Thomas D. Marzik (Philadelphia: Temple University Press), pp. 49–68; Emmet Larkin, *Historical Dimensions of Irish Catholicism* (Washington, DC: The Catholic University Press), p. 11.

[33] See Gerald P. Fogarty, *The Vatican and the American Hierarchy from 1870–1965* (Stuttgart: Anton Hierseman, 1982), pp. 61–64.

associated with Catholicism—as four of the "seven perils" endangering the nation.[34]

During the course of the nineteenth century the dominant self-image of America shifted somewhat in emphasis. As the religious intensity of the earlier part of the century decreased, the vogue of Anglo-Saxonism replaced it. Previous generations had viewed America as a Protestant nation and seen liberty and Protestantism moving hand in hand. As the twentieth century came closer, many less religiously oriented Americans tended to equate Americanism with Anglo-Saxonism, and to identify the Anglo-Saxon race as the originator and bearer of free political institutions. James Bryce wrote:

> If the people of New England, rural New York, and New Jersey had been left unpolluted by the turbid flow of foreign immigration, they would be the fittest of any in the world for a pure democratic government.

This heightened consciousness of race coincided with the beginnings of massive waves of heavily Catholic immigration from southern and eastern Europe, people who were seen as both religiously and racially undesirable. The new immigrants brought considerable internal division to American Catholicism, but external forces continued to unify Catholics in the eyes of the larger society.[35]

World War I, restrictive legislation in the 1920's, and the Depression decreased the flow of immigration. For the first time in a century, the Catholic Church did not have to absorb large numbers of new immigrants. Ironically, during the 1920's, at the very time it was rejecting the ideals of Protestant America, the nation at large was experiencing in Prohibition— the measure that generations of reformers had seen as a prerequisite of triumph—the fulfillment of one of them. In the same decade, in the 1928 presidential campaign, three of the seven perils previously identified by Josiah Strong seemed to come together in Al Smith's Catholicism, anti-Prohibitionism, and big-city background—all elements that large numbers of Americans still regarded as un-American. Smith's defeat drove Catholics back upon themselves and heightened in them their perception of a hostile dominant society.

Following the election of Franklin D. Roosevelt in 1932, however,

---

[34] Handy, p. 74.

[35] John Higham, *Strangers in the Land. Patterns of American Nativism 1860–1925* (New York: Atheneum, 1975), pp. 9–11; Bryce, 2:270.

Catholics came to play an increasingly important role in American political and national life. As their acceptance grew, so did their confidence. Catholics had in the past countered Protestant hopes for a Christian America with their own vision of a Catholic civilization. During the 1930's and 1940's, some Catholics even began to draw up blueprints for its implementation.[36]

Even though circumstances had changed, church authorities continued to receive a great deal of obedience and to exercise the strong centralized power they had acquired in Catholicism's long battle for survival over the course of a century. As institutions sometimes reach their apogee and their most stylized expressions after they have served their usefulness, so perhaps American Catholicism in the 1950's reached its apex of centralization, uniformity, and confidence. It now turned on itself the power it had developed to meet the challenge from outside and attempted to preserve almost as an absolute the form and style that had been intended to meet the needs of particular historical circumstances. During that decade the Church's dilemma was reminiscent of the one that Lincoln had articulated when he asked: "Must a government, of necessity, be too strong for the liberties of its own people, or too weak to maintain its own existence?"[37] The governance strengths developed in a war for survival brought about an extraordinary degree of centralization and control when they were turned upon the Church itself.

The election of John F. Kennedy in 1960 proved that the acceptance of Catholics as Americans had become a reality. It also coincided with a crisis within Catholicism itself. Heretofore, outside hostile forces had to a great extent provided Catholics with their identity and held them together. Now, with the collapse of that opposition, Catholicism had to find its primary identity from within. Like all opposition groups after they have achieved power or joined the mainstream, Catholics had to rediscover themselves and experienced considerable confusion in the process.

An Evaluation

Catholic commentators often choose to locate the golden age of the American Church in the early republic. They tend to see this enlightened

---

[36] George Q. Flynn, *American Catholics and the Roosevelt Presidency 1932–1936* (Lexington: University of Kentucky Press, 1968); Halsey, *The Survival of American Innocence.*

[37] Roy P. Basler, ed., *The Collected Works of Abraham Lincoln*, 9 vols. (New Brunswick, NJ: Rutgers University Press, 1953), 4:426.

church, symbolized by John Carroll, as swamped by the "immigrant church," and to view the history of Catholicism in America from the early nineteenth century until Vatican II as a series of missed opportunities to "Americanize" the Church. These include failure to heed the call of the lay trustees for shared responsibility in the Church and the failure to become truly American of Catholics who insisted on sheltering themselves from the mainstream of American life in ghettoes of their own making.[38]

To see the past as a series of failures, however, and to see the present as a time of catching up on missed opportunities distorts both. It posits the possibilities of options not available to previous generations, and it fails to appreciate their legacy to the present. As far as the governance of the Church is concerned, this inheritance is principally a society wherein Catholics are free to define the Church according to their own religious and theological understanding, without having to conform to given definitions of what is compatible with "American" religion.

Within the context of the Protestant nation, the small Catholic Church of the early republic could only have continued to live on sufferance and with deference to the dominant culture. As Madison anticipated, the First Amendment was not self-defining or self-enforcing. Something akin to the possibility he envisioned actually happened. A majority of Americans who shared a common religious ethos appropriated title to America and identified American values as their values in both Church and State. Thus Catholics, when they refused to be assimilated, became by definition un-American. Catholics refused to become "American" because in order to do so they would have had to shed their identity. The manner in which the nation defined itself in practice did not leave open the possibility of an hierarchical church being truly American.

Catholics, as Philip Schaff, the noted church historian, admonished them in the 1880's, would have had to "learn to appreciate Protestant Christianity, which has built up this country and made it great, prosperous, and free.[39] When lay trustees called for the Church to adopt American ways, or when later Americanists called for Catholics to become American, they were both to some extent responding to pressures to accommodate themselves to definitions of America as Protestant congregationalist or Protestant Anglo-Saxon. By refusing to be assimilated, however, Catholics provided

---

[38] See Coleman, p. 157, and such popular works as William Bausch, *Pilgrim Church: A Popular History of Catholic Christianity* (Notre Dame: Fides Publishers, 1973), pp. 468, 497; Don Brophy and Edythe Westenhaver, eds., *The Story of Catholics in America* (New York: Paulist Press, 1978), p. 25.

[39] Schaff, p. 73.

the greatest obstacle to the homogenizing tendencies of non-denominational
Protestantism. They supplied the strong element necessary to check and
balance the power of the majority, thereby making possible, as Madison had
foreseen, a truly pluralistic society and an open secular state.

What Robert Handy has called the "Second Disestablishment"—the
process of disentangling Protestantism and American culture and civilization in the decades following the First World War, a process participated
in by many Protestant leaders—confirmed in both society's practice and
later in constitutional form the demise of the Protestant nation. When
America elected its first Catholic President, that event came about not
because Americans had tardily decided Catholics were no longer a threat,
but because Catholics themselves had helped re-fashion the definition of
America, so that by the 1960's they were able to take their place in a nation
they had helped to create.

In the nineteenth century the dominant culture demanded that religions
conform to certain prerequisites if they were to be truly American. Now the
American way is understood—as the constitution envisaged—to be that
each religion defines its own identity. In the last century the pressure to
promote more democratic control or adjustment to society at large came
from outside, often from the sharpest critics of Catholicism. Now the same
pressure comes from inside the Church, from the reflections of Catholics
and from their own self-definition as Church. Catholics seek shared responsibility not because they wish to bring their Church into line with
American republicanism, but because they wish to bring it into line with
Vatican II.

This transformation of society and Catholicism's contribution to it came
at a price. Catholics, perhaps because they rejected many of the characteristics defined as "American" by a dominant and hostile culture, often
attempted to demonstrate their loyalty to country by an excessive adherence
to those they could embrace. Ironically, the very qualities that enabled the
Church to broaden America's self-definition are the ones that render it
difficult for the Church itself to take advantage of the freedom it helped
create. Cohesiveness came at the price of defensiveness, and unity was
purchased by means of authoritarianism. The struggle left its mark on many
Catholics, e.g., a deep bitterness and an inability to image the Church as
anything but a warrior armed for combat. As they struggle with these
inheritances from the past, modern American Catholics need to balance
them against Catholicism's contribution to American secular and religious
society; i.e., as it continues the struggle to redefine itself, the Church is now
free to do so according to its own inner needs rather than in response to
outside pressures.

DIOCESAN STRUCTURE AND GOVERNANCE IN THE UNITED STATES

Gerald P. Fogarty, S.J.

The American Catholic church developed within an unusual environment. Far from Rome, it was frequently misunderstood because it flourished in the midst of religious pluralism. It existed in a nation whose people may have harbored anti-Catholicism, but whose government neither accorded the Church legal privilege nor placed any legal restriction upon the exercise of its authority. The situation of distance from Rome and religious liberty provided a milieu in which it expressed its own identity. The bishops in the early nineteenth century developed a strong sense of collegiality, which in turn reflected a distinct theological outlook. They were initially quite conscious of the distinctive legal tradition of the United States. By mid-century, however, they had lost sight of that tradition and became almost absolutist in their approach toward the pastoral government of their immigrant flocks. This was evident in the Third Plenary Council in 1884 when they granted priests canonical rights only under Roman pressure. Shortly afterward, some began a conscious reflection upon the tradition of religious liberty and the British and American common law which underlay that tradition, and which had enabled their predecessors to develop their collegial tradition. Unfortunately, this conscious reflection on the American tradition led to misunderstanding in Rome and to the Romanization of the hierarchy in the twentieth century.

John Carroll and Selection of Bishops

John Carroll, the first bishop of Baltimore, had distinct notions about the type of bishop appropriate for the United States and the manner of his selection. He and the other priests in the thirteen original states had been members of the Society of Jesus until its suppression in 1773. He chafed when the Congregation of Propaganda, without any consultation of the clergy, approached the United States government concerning the appointment of a vicar apostolic. This prompted one of his reflections on the nature of a bishop and his authority. If the new nation were to have a

21

bishop, he wrote a friend, "he shall not be *in partibus* (a refined political Roman contrivance), but an ordinary national bishop, in whose appointment Rome shall have no share: so that we are very easy about their machinations."[1] For Carroll, the American church was not a mission. It should, therefore, have an ordinary bishop with his own diocese and he should be chosen by his priests. On this point he was reflecting the influence not of the new American republic, but of a much older ecclesiastical tradition according to which priests did nominate their bishop. He was, to use James Hennessey's phrase, "an eighteenth century bishop."[2]

Carroll's notions on episcopal authority did not stop with the nature and manner of choosing a bishop. In 1784 he engaged in a refutation of a pamphlet written by a cousin and former Jesuit who had become an Anglican, Charles Wharton. Wharton had stated that "all Roman catholics are bound to admit an infallible authority; yet few of them agree, where or in whom it resides." Carroll responded that "I will venture to assert, that he cannot cite one catholic divine, who denies infallibility to reside in the body of bishops united and agreeing with their head, the bishop of Rome."[3] Carroll's sense of episcopal authority, then, was horizontal rather than vertical. An "ordinary national bishop" was to be nominated by his clergy and he was, in union with the pope, constituted a member of the infallible body of the bishops.

Carroll was elected bishop by his fellow priests in 1789 and met with them in the First Synod of Baltimore in 1791. In a letter to Cardinal Lorenzo Antonelli, Prefect of Propaganda, he proposed a method for the election of future bishops. He suggested the designation of fifteen priests, ten of whom had served in the American church for the longest time and five chosen by the bishop, who were to nominate future bishops.[4] Two years later, he wrote the cardinal that, after seeking "the counsel of the older and more worthy workers in this vineyard of the Lord," he was proposing that the Holy See name Lawrence Graessl as his coadjutor. At the same time he recommended that he be given the authority "to organize

[1] Archives of the Maryland Province of the Society of Jesus, 202 B 6, Carroll to Plowden, April 10, 1784. See Thomas O'Brien Hanley, ed., *The John Carroll Papers*, 3 vols. (Notre Dame: University of Notre Dame Press, 1976), 1:145–147, which unfortunately omits the phrase in parenthesis.

[2] James Hennesey, "An Eighteenth Century Bishop: John Carroll of Baltimore," *Archivum Historiae Pontificiae* 16 (1978) 171–204.

[3] Hanley, 1:104–105.

[4] Archives of the Archdiocese of Baltimore, Carroll to Antonelli, April 23, 1793 (draft).

ten or twelve priests who are in charge of the principal congregations in this diocese into a sort of chapter, an advisory body for the bishop; and this position should be enjoyed by their successors."[5] Graessl was appointed Carroll's coadjutor, but died before being consecrated. It is uncertain, however, whether Carroll did, in fact, gain the type of cathedral chapter he requested. In any event, Carroll's plan for bishops to be nominated by their priests fell by the wayside as other issues confronted the infant American church.

By 1808 Carroll had become a metropolitan with the suffragan sees of Boston, New York, Philadelphia, and Bardstown. The growth of his church was due not to natural increase but to immigration. The relative homogeneity of Anglo-Marylanders and Germano-Pennsylvanians gave way to ethnic pluralism. In 1790 Catholics numbered 35,000 out of a total white population of 3,172,006. By 1850 Catholics were 1,606,000 in a white population of 19,553,068.[6] With immigration, the Church experienced new tensions, among the first of which was lay trusteeism.

Lay trustees in Philadelphia, New York, Norfolk, and Charleston—almost all educated Irish immigrants—presented a series of arguments for their right to call or reject a priest. Some asserted that just as in a monarchy the Holy See signed a concordat with the king, in a republic the Holy See should enter a concordat with the people.[7] Sometimes the trustees simply wanted a priest who spoke their language. The Church which Carroll had envisioned had begun to fade. By 1817, two years after his death, there were six dioceses, four occupied by Frenchmen, one by an Irishman, and the other, Philadelphia, vacant. Partially in response to trusteeism, in 1820 the Holy See established the two new dioceses of Richmond and Charleston and appointed Irish bishops to both. The see of Charleston received one of the most creative bishops in the history of the American church, John England.

John England and Role of the Laity

England already had experience in Ireland in attempting to preserve the freedom the Irish church had wrested from the British government. With

---

[5] Hanley, 2:93–98, Carroll to Antonelli, June 17, 1793.

[6] Gerald Shaughnessy, *Has the Immigrant Kept the Faith? A Study of Immigration and Catholic Growth in the United States: 1790–1920* (New York: The Macmillan Company, 1925), pp. 73, 134.

[7] Patrick Carey, *An Immigrant Bishop: John England's Adaptation of Irish Catholicism to American Republicanism* (Yonkers, NY: U.S. Catholic Historical Society, 1982), pp. 63–65.

Daniel O'Connell he had helped organize the laity and the clergy against the Holy See's attempt to give the crown the right to veto Irish episcopal appointments. In the United States he found ready-made the situation in which to develop his vision of the Church. Instead of condemning all forms of lay participation in the Church, in 1823 he issued a constitution for his diocese. The preface to the constitution indicated his affinity with many of Carroll's notions of the episcopate. "The portions of our church government," he wrote,

> are very like to those of the government of this Union. The entire consists of dioceses, the bishop of each of which holds his place, not as the deputy of the Pope, but as a successor to the Apostles; as the governor of each state holds his place not as the deputy of the President, but as vested therewith by the same power which vests the President with his own authority. And as all the states are bound together in one federation of which the President is the head, so are the dioceses collected into one church, of which the Pope is the head. Each state has power to make its own laws, provided they do not contravene the general Constitution of the United States; so in each diocese there exists the power of legislation, provided the statutes made therein be not incompatible with the faith or general discipline of the Catholic Church.[8]

Like Carroll, England envisioned a collegial relationship between the pope and bishops.

In what pertained more directly to the laity, England divided his diocese into districts with vestries, composed of the priest and elected laymen, who were to have a say in the temporalities of each church. Every year there was to be a convention of the diocese consisting of a house of clergy—all the priests of the diocese—and a house of laity, composed of delegates elected from each district according to its Catholic population. The convention was "not to be construed as a portion of the ecclesiastical government of the church; but the two houses are to be considered as a body of sage, prudent, and religious counsellors to aid the proper ecclesiastical governor of the church in the discharge of his duty" in financial matters. The convention was not to have any authority in the strictly spiritual affairs of the Church, but

In those cases where the convention has no authority to act,

---

[8] Ignatius Reynolds, ed., *The Works of the Right Rev. John England, First Bishop of Charleston*, 5 vols. (Baltimore: John Murphy & Co., 1849), 5:92.

should either house feel itself called upon by any peculiar circumstances to submit advice, or to present a request to the bishop, he will bestow upon the same the best consideration at the earliest opportunity; and as far as his conscientious obligations will permit, and the welfare of the church will allow, and the honour and glory of Almighty God, in his judgment require, he will endeavour to follow such advice or to agree to such request.[9]

With the latter clause, England's constitution came close to the *consilium pastorale* adopted by the Second Vatican Council.[10]

First Provincial Council of Baltimore

England's vision for the Church extended beyond the boundaries of his diocese. From his arrival, he argued with Ambrose Marechal, the archbishop of Baltimore, that there was need for uniform discipline in the American church if there was to be an end to lay trusteeism. He, therefore, began a long campaign to hold a provincial council. His arguments were numerous. The Council of Trent had decreed that within one year of the council and every three years thereafter, each metropolitan was to convoke a council of his suffragans. England noted, moreover, that "the usual mode of a Synod is more in accordance with the spirit of our National institutions, and . . . is the mode which will best please the flock and insure their support of its regulations." For the archbishop to refuse to hold a council appeared to him to be "an encroachment upon the rights of Diocesan Bishops, and an attempt to reduce them to the level of Vicars-Apostolic." It destroyed, he concluded, "what Cardinal Bellarmine calls the republican part of church government, and properly states to be one of its characteristics, and is calculated in this country to create a great moral obstacle to the continuance and progress of our Faith."[11] In short, England's view of being a diocesan bishop meant concern for the whole American church and collaborating with his fellow bishops.

England was unsuccessful in having Marechal call a council. He had to wait for the archbishop's death. Immediately upon the appointment of Marechal's successor, James Whitfield, England wrote both to complain

[9] Ibid., 104–105.
[10] Christus Dominus, 27.
[11] Peter Guilday, *The Life and Times of John England, First Bishop of Charleston: 1786–1842* (New York: The America Press, 1927), 2:109.

about not having been invited to his consecration and to urge that he call a council. On December 18, 1828, Whitfield issued the call for the council to meet on October 1, 1829. The council condemned lay trusteeism, stated that trustees could not be considered the heirs to the *patronato real*, but exempted the arrangement England had made for the Diocese of Charleston.[12]

But England saw the further relationship between a lay voice and priests having tenure in office. The bishops decreed that priests were to accept the mission assigned to them by the bishop, if he ''judges that there could be there sufficient subsidy for a decent sustenance of life.'' But they were careful to add that this was not to be construed as the establishment of parishes in the full canonical sense, only one of which, New Orleans, did they acknowledge. They argued that they were frequently faced with priests who came to the United States with letters of dismissal from their bishops without any honest evaluation of their character. While acknowledging this problem, England argued that one way of combatting the abuses of trusteeism was to establish at least some canonical parishes with irremovable pastors. In this, he had the support of Francis P. Kenrick, present at the council as a theologian for Bishop Benedict Joseph Flaget of Bardstown, who sent a lengthy report to Propaganda in favor of England's proposal.[13] Kenrick was appointed the coadjutor Bishop of Philadelphia in 1830, but made no effort to implement the establishment of canonical parishes. England was the sole bishop who argued for priests' rights in the nineteenth century.

Episcopal Collegiality

Trusteeism was not the only issue with which the council dealt. In the pastoral letter, drafted by England probably with the assistance of Kenrick, the developing collegial tradition of the bishops was evident. In speaking of Scripture, the pastoral said:

> We know not that it is the word of God, except by the testimony of that cloud of holy witnesses which the Saviour vouchsafed to establish as our guide through this desert over which we journey towards our permanent abode. Together with the book they gave

[12] *Collectio Lacensis*, 3:27.

[13] Thomas F. Casey, *The Sacred Congregation De Propaganda Fide and the Revision of the First Provincial Council of Baltimore (1829–1830)* (Rome:Gregorian University, 1957), pp. 55–63.

to us the testimony of its meaning. . . . Thus the recorded
testimony of those ancient and venerable witnesses, who in every
nation and every age, proclaimed in the name of the Catholic
Church, and with its approbation, the interpretation of the Holy
Bible, whether they were assembled in their councils or dispersed
over the surface of the Christian world, is an harmonious
collection of pure light, which sheds upon the inspired page the
mild lustre which renders it pleasing to the eye, grateful to the
understanding, and consoling to the heart.[14]

Underlying the language of the pastoral was the theology of Francis
Kenrick, based not upon the scholastics but upon the fathers. In his
Theologia Dogmatica, which he was then writing, he took as the norm for
the interpretation of Scripture the consensus of the fathers; the norm for the
determination of doctrine was the consensus of the bishops reflecting on
the tradition. He would later recommend to his readers the theory on
tradition of Johann Adam Mohler of Tübingen.[15]

At the First Provincial Council, the bishops with England's urging were
trying to develop a practice of episcopal collegiality, already implicit in
their pastoral. Their final decree stated that "the next provincial council
should be held in three years unless for grave reason it should seem good
to the Archbishop to defer it."[16] Archbishop Whitfield decided he had
"grave reason" for not holding a council. In 1832, Propaganda asked him
to circulate his suffragans on their diocesan boundaries. England curtly
sent Whitfield a description of his diocese and expressed his "perfect
dissent from your prorogation of the provincial council." Unless the
council was canonically postponed, England assured the archbishop that he
would feel obligated to be present in the Baltimore cathedral on October 1,
1832, to attend the council.[17]

England did not show up in Baltimore as he threatened. Instead, he took
his case personally to Rome. There he explained that "the people of the
United States are wonderfully attached to their form of government; but they
are very sparing and reserved in their praise of others." Too many of the
clergy who came to the United States, he continued, "not only have not

---

[14] Hugh J. Nolan, ed., *Pastoral Letters of the American Hierarchy, 1792–1970*
(Huntington, IN: Our Sunday Visitor, 1971), pp. 51–52.

[15] Francis Patrick Kenrick, *Theologia Dogmatica*, 2nd ed., 4 vols. (Baltimore: John
Murphy & Co., 1858), 1:288, 365–370.

[16] *Collectio Lacensis*, 3:33.

[17] England to Whitfield, June, 1832, quoted in Guilday, 2:244.

wished to be subject to the United States and to be enrolled as citizens, but they did not hesitate to openly avow their predeliction for the governments of Europe.'' More importantly, England saw the relationship between American legal practices and the normal mode of procedure of the Holy See:

> the people of the United States are accustomed to have all their affairs transacted in accordance with fixed laws, and not according to the dictates of the will of an individual. They observe that nothing is done by the Holy See without previous consultation and deliberation. They know that in the Catholic Church the power of legislation resides in the Pope and the Bishops; and they would be greatly impressed if they would see the Church in America regulated in accordance with laws emanating from a Council of Bishops with the approbation of the Holy Father. The conformity of this mode of procedure with their own principles and practice is so striking, that it would easily gain not only their obedience but also their attachment. But they will never be reconciled to the practice of the bishops, and oftentimes of the priest alone, giving orders without assigning any reasons for the same.[18]

England, then, saw the compatibility of the American mentality and traditional church practice. Writing to Joseph Rosati, bishop of St. Louis, he noted that American Protestants held regular meetings and thus profited from unity of action and gained influence in American society. ''Whilst they by adopting this catholic principle of ancient discipline were daily & yearly growing compact, soothing their jealousies & collecting large means which they applied to common objects after common consultation, we were a parcel of disunited congregations, having no practical union.''[19]

England was ultimately successful in having Whitfield convoke the Second Provincial Council, but the conflict between him and the archbishop was both nationalistic and ecclesiological. Whitfield complained bitterly to Nicholas Wiseman, rector of the English College in Rome, about England and Kenrick. ''These two bishops are both warm-headed Irishmen,'' he wrote,

> and have, it seems, strong Irish predelictions in favour of Irish Bishops & Irish discipline for the U. States. They have both

---

[18] ''Papers Relating to the Church in America, from the Portfolios of the Irish College at Rome,'' *Records of the American Catholic Historical Society of Philadelphia*, 8 (1897) 461–462.

[19] England to Rosati, Rome, January 14, 1833, quoted in Guilday, 2:244.

recommended for the vacant see of Cincinnati, Irishmen, & I believe the three names on each list were all Irish Priests. They both have united in using every effort, even by publications in their newspapers, to make me hold another Provincial Council, which, notwithstanding all they have exposed before the public, I have not consented to convoke, because such is the agitating position of Dr. England, that he would be restless in proposing changes in our discipline until it were reduced to the standard of Ireland or reformed according to his republican notions. Before I knew that Dr. England was going to Rome, I wrote to the Cardinal Pref. of Prop. some of my reasons for not complying with their wishes, adding however I would not, until commanded by the S. Cong. I am sorry that any more Irish bishops are added to our Hierarchy, as I fear their increase in number will have power to have others of their countrymen nominated hereafter & bring over to this country a great number of Irish Priests whilst I wish, with a few exceptions, they would all stay at home.[20]

Whitfield and his predecessor, Marechal, indeed had problems with Irish priests who were not suited for their ministry, but his opposition to England was also theological.

Second Provincial Council of Baltimore

Whatever may have been Whitfield's misgivings, on August 6, 1833, he acted on orders from Propaganda and convoked the Second Provincial Council to meet on October 22, 1833. When the council convened, some of his fears of England's republicanism were realized. He announced the appointment of two promotors of the council. England immediately protested that, canonically, they were to be elected by the bishops.[21] The council passed a complicated decree which gave the bishops a consultative voice in drawing up a *terna* of candidates for the episcopacy to be submitted to Propaganda.[22] The bishops also took no chances of leaving it to the archbishop to find ''grave reason'' to defer subsequent councils. In their final decree, they stated: ''the fathers decree that the next council is

---

[20] Archives of the English College, Rome (microfilm, Notre Dame), Whitfield to Wiseman, Baltimore, June 6, 1833.

[21] Guilday, 2:260–261.

[22] *Collectio Lacensis*, 3:41. See also John Tracy Ellis, ''On Selecting Catholic Bishops for the United States,'' *The Critic* (June-July, 1969) 45.

to be held on the third Sunday after Easter in the year of our Lord 1837.''[23] At the third council in 1837, the fourth in 1840, the fifth in 1843, and the sixth in 1846, the final decree each time set the date for the next council.[24] The bishops thus modified Trent's decree calling for each metropolitan to hold a council every three years and took upon themselves the right to set a date. The American bishops, together with their metropolitan, constituted a regular legislative assembly in which the archbishop was a member. Just as England had earlier drawn the analogy in his constitution between, on the one hand, the president of the United States and the state governors, and on the other, the pope and bishops, now the bishops seemed to envision themselves as analogous to the Senate, which convened regularly and not at the discretion of the president.

When the Seventh Provincial Council convened in 1849, there were actually already three metropolitan provinces in the United States— Baltimore, St. Louis, and Oregon City. All the metropolitans, however, were in attendance. The bishops petitioned that New Orleans and New York be elevated to metropolitan status, that a Plenary Council be convoked by the Holy See in 1850, and that the archbishop of Baltimore be declared the primate of the American church.[25] Having the archbishop of Baltimore declared primate was a means for the bishops to preserve their now developed sense of collegiality and of relative autonomy from Rome. Historically, a primate had the right to convoke and preside over a plenary or national council, but by the nineteenth century most primates retained only the right to preside over such a council.[26] While Rome would thus have to convoke any future national council, the archbishop of Baltimore would preside.

Paradoxically, because the American bishops acted according to the Council of Trent in holding regular provincial councils, they fell under Roman suspicion. The Holy See refused the title of primate to the archbishop of Baltimore. In 1852 it convoked the First Plenary Council and did name Francis P. Kenrick, who had been transferred from Philadelphia to Baltimore, as the apostolic delegate to preside over the council—a right he would have had *de jure* had he been named primate. The council introduced the first innovations in diocesan structure. Each bishop was to appoint consultors and seek their opinion in the administration of his diocese. The council commended the practice of holding monthly consul-

---

[23] *Collectio Lacensis*, 3:42.
[24] Ibid., 58, 71, 88, 102.
[25] Ibid., 115, 117.
[26] Francis X. Wernz, *Ius Decretalium* (Rome, 1906), 2/2:498, 728.

tors' meetings to discuss the affairs of the diocese. The bishops also decreed that each bishop should appoint a chancellor "for the easier administration of ecclesiastical affairs, and for achieving a stable norm of acting in those matters."[27] While in theory the chancellor was only the archivist and keeper of the records, he would subsequently become of greater significance in American dioceses.[28]

The First Plenary Council petitioned to hold a Second Plenary Council in 1862. The Holy See, however, was still suspicious of the independent spirit of the American bishops. In June 1853, Archbishop Gaetano Bedini, nuncio to Brazil, began a visitation of the American church without any consultation of the American hierarchy. Bedini linked the refusal of primacy to Baltimore with the fear of too much freedom. While the bishops were loyal to Rome, he wrote,

> would not the exceptional condition in which they find them-
> selves, and the ocean that divides them, the unbridled liberty of
> their civil institutions, might all of these later form some pretext
> for independent action. The Holy See has very wisely refused
> them their request for a Primatial See. Experience has given too
> may proofs of the abuse which an individual can do who was
> invested "ad vitam" and who never knew how to divest himself
> of nationalistic feeling, when it goes beyond the just and honest,
> or when it endangers Catholic unity, which because it is unique,
> cannot suffer any difference of nationality, since every nation is
> centered and founded in it.

Bedini acknowledged that the American request for a primate had been motivated by the desire "to have a constant local and authoritative vigilance for preserving this unity against the innovations, the plots or interests, which either the Government, the Bishops or the people might present." But he was convinced that a permanent nunciature, the occupant of which would be periodically changed and who would not be imbued with any nationalistic spirit, would be more appropriate to "bring about their complete unity."[29]

---

[27] *Collectio Lacensis*, 3:146.

[28] See John Edward Prince, *The Diocesan Chancellor: An Historical Synopsis and Commentary*, Canon Law Studies, 167 (Washington: The Catholic University of America Press, 1942), pp. 38–39.

[29] Given in James F. Connelly, *The Visit of Archbishop Gaetano Bedini to the United States of America (June, 1853–February, 1854)* (Rome: Università Gregoriana, 1960), pp. 275–277.

Second Plenary Council

Because of the Civil War the American bishops could not meet in council in 1862, but they came together in a display of national unity for the Second Plenary Council in 1866. Between the first and second plenary councils, however, there had been some further canonical developments. In 1855 the Eighth Provincial Council of Baltimore, applying the legislation of the First Plenary Council in regard to diocesan consultors, decreed that they were to number between ten and twelve. On the death of the bishop they were to give their opinions on candidates to the metropolitan or senior suffragan.[30] Though this was merely a consultative vote, it was the first reintroduction of a priests' voice in the selection of bishops since the time of Carroll. In 1859, moreover, Propaganda demanded that each metropolitan write his views on nominations to vacant metropolitan sees.[31]

When the Holy See convoked the council, it delegated Archbishop Martin J. Spalding of Baltimore to preside as Kenrick had done before him. In preparation for the council he sounded out the other bishops on a number of matters. Probably reflecting the Baltimore council of 1855, he stated he was personally in favor of allowing diocesan consultors an actual vote in the nomination of bishops. He was thus attempting to raise consultors to the status of cathedral chapters as they existed in Europe. Though the bishops discussed the issue at the council, they failed to make any provision for a priests' voice in the selection of a bishop.[32]

Though England and Francis Kenrick were then dead, the tradition of collegiality still flourished. In their decree on the episcopal office the bishops stated:

> Bishops, therefore, who are the successors of the Apostles, and whom the Holy Spirit has placed to rule the Church of God, which He acquired with His own blood, agreeing and judging together with its head on earth, the Roman Pontiff, whether they are gathered in general councils, or dispersed throughout the world, are inspired from on high with the gift of inerrancy, so that their body or college can never fail in faith nor define anything against doctrine revealed by God.[33]

---

[30] *Collectio Lacensis*, 3:162.

[31] Ellis, "On Selecting Catholic Bishops," p. 46.

[32] Ibid.

[33] *Concilii Plenarii Baltimorensis II. In Ecclesia Metropolitana Baltimorensi a die VII.*

The bishops now stated explicitly what had been implicit in the First Provincial Council—that the bishops constituted a college with the pope. With John Carroll they affirmed that it was the body of the bishops, united with the pope, which enjoyed infallibility. This would have repercussions at the First Vatican Council. But there were other issues more pertinent to episcopal authority.

Unfortunately, the bishops did not extend their collegial concepts to their priests. Every council since 1829 had reaffirmed the condemnation of lay trusteeism and restated that there was only one canonical parish in the United States. There was, therefore, an anomaly in the American church. Whereas there was a regularly established hierarchy of ordinary bishops, priests were officially "rectors" of missions who had only delegated authority from the bishop. The First Plenary Council had decreed that the bishops should establish ecclesiastical districts in their dioceses, but it was careful to state that these were not to be canonical parishes.[34] There were numerous valid reasons for not establishing parishes—the mobility of the American population and the shift in ethnic composition of regions, to name but two. But the problem remained that priests had no canonical rights. While the bishops were developing a strong sense of collegiality among themselves and toward Rome, some were in danger of exercising absolutism over their priests. In 1855 the First Provincial Council of St. Louis adopted a decree to provide a disciplinary procedure for priests. Should a priest protest his removal or transfer, he was to be suspended from exercise of his ministry and the bishop was to appoint two of his consultors to hear his case. Between them, the consultors had one vote. If both voted in the priest's favor, the bishop was to appoint a third consultor. If all three voted against the bishop, the case was to go to the metropolitan or senior suffragan, whose decision was final, save for appeal to the Holy See.[35] The Second Plenary Council adopted this procedure for the entire American church.[36] This would be one source of friction between bishops and their priests and of further Roman suspicion.

The council also adopted other legislation pertaining to episcopal authority. It repeated the decree of the First Plenary Council urging each bishop to appoint a chancellor. It also described the office of vicar general—he was to have precedence over the rest of the clergy, but could

---

ad diem XXI., Octobris A.D. MDCCCLXVI. Habiti et a Sede Apostolica Recogniti Acta et Decreta (Baltimore: John Murphy, 2nd ed. 1894), no. 50, p. 41.

[34] *Collectio Lacensis.*, 3:145, no. 2, and 146, no. 10.

[35] Ibid., 308, 311–312.

[36] *Concilii Plenarii Baltimorensis II . . . Acta et Decreta*, no. 108, p. 75.

not exercise the extraordinary faculties delegated to him by the bishop
unless the bishop were absent for an entire day.[37] In subsequent practice,
the vicar general became largely honorific while the chancellor became the
actual delegate of the bishop.

Vatican I

Priest-bishop tension would carry over for several more decades. Of
more immediate importance was the notion of episcopal collegiality in
relationship to the pope, particularly in regard to infallibility. The
American hierarchy from John Carroll to the Second Plenary Council had
been quite clear that infallibility resided in the whole body or college of
bishops, united with the Roman Pontiff. This tradition was brought into
question with the First Vatican Council in 1869–1870. Most American
bishops thought that it was inopportune to define papal infallibility as a
doctrine. Some, most notably Peter Richard Kenrick, archbishop of St.
Louis, Edward Purcell, archbishop of Cincinnati, and Bernard McQuaid,
bishop of Rochester, were outright opponents to the doctrine. Kenrick,
who reflected the theology of his brother, Francis, became the most
prominent among them because of both his speeches at the council and his
failure to submit to the definition until six months after the council. At the
council he argued that the role of bishops was to reflect upon what had
always and everywhere been taught by the Church. What did not belong to
the constant tradition of the Church was merely theological opinion and
could not become doctrine, even if a council or pope so defined it. Kenrick
relegated to mere theological opinion not only papal infallibility but also
the Immaculate Conception of the Virgin Mary, which had been defined by
Pius IX in 1854.

Most of the opponents to papal infallibility obtained permission to
absent themselves from the solemn definition of the doctrine on July 18,
1870. Only after his return to his diocese on January 2, 1871, did Kenrick
submit to the definition "simply and singly [upon] the authority of the
Catholic Church." Nevertheless, it was not to be until the following July
that the Holy Office formally accepted Kenrick's submission and pulled
back from compelling him to retract what he had spoken at the council.[38]

Vatican I seemed to sound the death-knell of the American tradition of

[37] Ibid., nos. 71–72, pp. 54–55.
[38] For this confusing episode, see my "Archbishop Peter Kenrick's Submission to Papal
Infallibility," *Archivum Historiae Pontificiae* 16 (1978) 205–222.

episcopal collegiality. Bishop McQuaid said it well in an address in his
cathedral after his return from Rome. "I have now no difficulty in
accepting the dogma," he said, "although to the last I opposed it; because
somehow or other it was in my head that the Bishops ought to be
consulted."[39] What was occurring, however, was not only the response to
what was seen as a new doctrine but also a different theological method.
The theology of England and Francis Kenrick, premised upon the fathers,
was giving way to a particular school of Thomism. The older theology was
compatible with the general tradition of the British and American common
law, which provided the basis for the American notion of the separation of
Church and State and which enabled the tradition of collegiality to develop
and flourish. The new theology, which would be encouraged under Leo
XIII, stressed objective truth and the formation of a concept rather than the
act of judgment of what was truth; it provided a milieu in which a more
vertical rather than horizontal concept of authority began to develop.[40] The
Americans had already had some experience of the new theology with
Johann Baptist Franzelin, S.J., who helped draft the Vatican Council's
schema on faith. They would have more direct contact with him when he
was designated the cardinal *ponens* in preparation for and approval of
the Third Plenary Council.

Priests' Rights

Between Vatican I and the Third Plenary Council, the principal issue
between the American church and the Holy See was priests' rights. In
1878, Bishop George Conroy, Bishop of Ardagh, Ireland, and apostolic
delegate to Canada, paid an official visit to the American church. Jealous
of their relative autonomy from Rome, the American bishops had been
highly suspicious of Roman visitors. Conroy began his American visitation
on February 10, 1878, at the investiture of James Gibbons as archbishop of
Baltimore. Perhaps to assure that Conroy did not fall under the wrong
influences, Gibbons arranged for the bishop to be accompanied on his trip
by Father Denis J. O'Connell, newly ordained in Rome for the Diocese of
Richmond. Conroy's visit lasted until late April and took him through the
Mid-West to California. If O'Connell's companionship on the journey was
intended to filter his vision of the American church, the ploy was

[39] Frederick J. Zwierlein, *The Life and Letters of Bishop McQuaid*, 3 vols. (Rochester:
The Art Print Shop, 1926), 2:63.
[40] For the type of Thomism which developed under Leo XIII, see Gerald A. McCool,
Catholic Theology in the Nineteenth Century (New York: Seabury Press, 1977), pp. 13, 234.

only partially successful. Conroy's report was a devastating critique in some areas.

Conroy praised the progress of the American church, but noted that it was heavily in debt. This produced four problems. First, the priests were constantly asking the people for money. Second, this led to secular rather than religious criteria being used for the appointment of bishops. In Conroy's words:

> In the selection of bishops priority is given to financial, rather than pastoral, abilities. . . . Whenever there is a deliberation to choose a candidate for the episcopacy, the bishops of a province feel constrained to seek, at all costs, a man skilled in financial administration. Indeed, it has too often happened that the most valued gifts in a candidate proposed to the Holy See were properly those of a banker, and not of a Pastor of Souls.

The third difficulty was that bishops frequently used the same criteria in appointing priests to a given mission. Finally, the need to place the church on a firm financial footing led one bishop—Archbishop Edward Purcell of Cincinnati—to establish a bank from which he loaned out money to the churches of his diocese at higher rates of interest than he paid his depositors.

Conroy then addressed the place which the Church had in American society. Anti-Catholicism was still a factor in American life, but he thought the bishops had exercised great prudence in tempering it. Nevertheless, he thought there was a danger that "in order to demonstrate that Catholics are good Americans, some would shape the Church along American lines." This led some to "claim that the disciplinary customs of the Church in other countries and even the dispositions of canon law do not apply to them; and they affect a kind of ecclesiastical independence which, if the faith were to fail among the clergy or the people, would not be without damage to the very unity of the Church." The bishop here voiced one of the abiding fears of the Holy See about the American church. To lessen that spirit of independence, Rome began discussing the appointment of an apostolic delegate. Conroy had investigated the possibility of such an appointment. Of the nineteen archbishops and bishops and several priests he consulted, only a few bishops thought a delegation necessary, but none opposed it. In his opinion, an Italian should not be appointed, and if an American could not be named, then the delegation should not be permanent.

The appointment of a delegate was intended to alleviate one of the problems which Conroy had been sent to investigate—the relations between priests and bishops. He singled Gibbons out for praise for the harmonious relationship between him and his priests, but he was critical of the situation elsewhere. There were two main points to the clergy's complaints: both the manner in which bishops were selected, and the failure of bishops to observe canon law in regard to priests' rights. Though there were norms from the Second Provincial and Second Plenary Councils for the nomination of bishops, Conroy reported the secrecy surrounding these proceedings produced cynicism among the priests. For them, "it is enough . . . to cast a glance at the American Episcopate! Of the total number of 68 bishops, there are hardly ten distinguished in talent of any kind. The others hardly approach a decent mediocrity, and in theological knowledge they do not reach even mediocrity!" Conroy, therefore, suggested that pastors have a consultative voice in the nomination of bishops. Though there was already legislation pertaining to clerical discipline, he felt that both bishops and priests appealed only to part of it. The priests were not denying episcopal authority, he argued, but they did feel a bishop should not remove them from their missions without cause. Propaganda, he recommended, should devise some practical procedures for preserving the mutual rights of priests and bishops.[41]

Conroy's report provided the agenda for the Holy See's concerns for the American church for the remainder of the century. It is doubtful, however, if it reached Propaganda in time to influence its decision in regard to clerical discipline. In 1878 it issued an *Instructio* on clerical trials. It decreed that every bishop, preferably in a diocesan synod, was to appoint a commission of five or at least three priests, trained in canon law, to examine the evidence, collect testimony, and interrogate witnesses in order to assist the bishop in rendering his decision. If a priest protested his removal from a mission the bishop had to have the advice of at least three members of this commission. In the event of an appeal, the metropolitan or senior suffragan was to proceed in the same manner and his investigating commission was to have access to the records of the trial in the first instance.[42] Here was precisely the type of Roman intervention into the American church which the bishops had long sought to prevent.

Bishop McQuaid of Rochester protested to Cardinal Giovanni Simeoni, Prefect of Propaganda, that the new system substantially altered the

---

[41] Archives of the Congregation de Propaganda Fide (hereafter abbreviated as APF), SCAmerCent 36 (1882) 194–217, George Conroy, "Relazione sullo stato presente della Chiesa Cattolica negli Stati Uniti dell'America."

[42] *Acta Sanctae Sedis* 12 (1878) 88–89.

legislation of the Second Plenary Council without any consultation of the bishops. McQuaid was particularly concerned with the rumor that Propaganda would issue an interpretation of the *Instructio* requiring that bishops consult their commission in every case of a priest's removal or transfer. This would effectively introduce irremovable rectors, an essential change in the legislation of the American church. Reporting on his campaign in Rome, he wrote Bishop Michael A. Corrigan of Newark:

> I have learned one thing in Rome, that it is useless to batter your head against a stone wall. So I was very deferential apparently, but stuck firmly to my main point. All my aim was to keep them from legislating without consulting us.[43]

Propaganda ultimately did not make consultation of the commission a prerequisite for the transfer or removal of a rector, but it was clear that the Holy See was concerned with the lack of harmony between American and universal canon law. McQuaid, for his part, still clung to the earlier collegial tradition of the American hierarchy. Paradoxically, just as this tradition was beginning to die out, Rome resurrected it by calling the Third Plenary Council.

Third Plenary Council

There were several reasons for the Holy See's decision to convoke the Third Plenary Council—the continuing problem of immigration; the existence of a Catholic population in a pluralistic society, which led many to join suspect secret societies and send their children to public schools; the continuing priest-bishop tension; the division among the bishops themselves about holding a council; and finally, the desire to test the loyalty of the bishops, so many of whom had opposed papal infallibility. To prepare for the council, the archbishops or their representatives were summoned to a meeting in Rome in November 1883. Prior to that meeting the cardinal members of Propaganda held their own meetings.

Johann Baptist Franzelin, S.J., then a cardinal, was deputed to draw up the *ponenza* or outline of the problems for the other cardinals to discuss. He had at hand Conroy's report. His *ponenza* was sprinkled with references to Romanizing the American church. In regard to seminaries, for example, he praised those in Baltimore, Philadelphia, Troy, and Milwaukee, but especially noted Philadelphia for "Roman instruction."

---

[43] Quoted in Zwierlein, 2:183. See also pp. 175–192.

While many of the priests were poorly educated, he continued, there were some in Baltimore, Boston, New York, Philadelphia, and Cincinnati who were especially distinguished in learning and piety, but the last three sees named were outstanding because "graduates of Rome are in good number." Franzelin noted, however, that many bishops felt that Roman alumni showed ambition for better assignments, were disloyal to the Holy See, and were disedifying in telling "scandals and stories to the discredit of the Roman Curia."[44]

The cardinal then turned to other issues. The *Instructio* on clerical discipline, he wrote, "was received with joy by the priests and was greeted by the more advanced as a magna charta which put an end to their slavery."[45] He also dealt with the issues of parochial schools, the conversion of Negroes, and the administration of church property.[46] Finally, he treated at length of the necessity of having an apostolic delegate to provide detailed information on candidates for the episcopacy, keep Propaganda better informed on priest-bishop relations, and to encourage bishops to proceed more regularly in dealing with their priests.[47] Curiously, Franzelin's *ponenza* said nothing of the fact that Bishop Luigi Sepiacci, a consultor to the congregation, had already been named the delegate to preside and elevated to the rank of archbishop the previous August.[48] But his proposals virtually set the agenda for the meeting with the archbishops.

On November 13, 1883, the archbishops began their meetings with Propaganda. They were confronted with a series of schemata, distinctly Roman in origin, and destined to give American dioceses the shape they would have in the twentieth century. The original schemata called for the establishment of cathedral chapters, for which the Americans gained the substitution of diocesan consultors. Analogous to cathedral canons, consultors in this version were to give their advice on calling diocesan synods, dissolution of parishes, or assigning churches to religious orders; their consent, however, was required for the appropriation or alienation of any church property valued at over $300. The Americans also acquiesced in agreeing to name irremovable rectors and to establish diocesan curias—an outgrowth of the *Instructio* of 1878 establishing an investigating commis-

---

[44] APF, Acta, 252 (1883) 1088–1089.

[45] Ibid., 1092.

[46] Ibid., 1096–1099.

[47] Ibid., 1106–1108.

[48] Ibid., 1080, Audience, August 26, 1883.

sion.[49] But the Americans were still intent on maintaining their relative autonomy from Rome. When they learned of Sepiacci's appointment as delegate, they protested and had Archbishop Gibbons named as the delegate to preside over the council, as the archbishops of Baltimore had done in 1852 and 1866.

On November 9, 1884, the American bishops assembled for the Third Plenary Council. In what pertained to diocesan administration and episcopal authority, they tried to strengthen their position over the Roman schema. In treating diocesan consultors the bishops decreed that there were ordinarily to be between four and six consultors; the bishop was to choose half that number himself and the other half from a list submitted by the priests. But in designating the sphere of competence of consultors, the council moved further away from the original proposal of cathedral chapters. Only their advice, but not their consent, was required for the dissolution of a mission, giving a church to a religious order, and in acquiring or alienating church property if the value exceeded $3000. They were to serve a term of three years and could not be removed except for grave reason and with the advice of the other consultors. They did not, however, have the right to administer a vacant see, as a cathedral chapter would, but the administrator of the diocese was bound to accept their advice.[50]

The bishops displayed their determination to maintain their authority on the issue of priests' rights as well. In a lengthy discussion about appointing irremovable rectors, Bishop John Ireland of St. Paul asked the opinion of Gibbons, who replied that the Holy See was so intent on their appointment that, if the bishops failed to adopt the legislation themselves, they would be "compelled to do it by the authority of the Holy See, not without some

---

[49] The document presented to the archbishops was *Capita praecipua quae Emi. Cardinales S.C. de Propaganda Fide censuerunt a Rmis. Archiepiscopis et Episcopis Foederatorum Statuum A.S. Romae congregatis praeparanda esse pro futuro Concilio.* From this there came the *Capita proposita et examinata in collationibus, quas coram nonnullis Emis. Cardinalibus Sacrae Congregationis de Propaganda Fide ad praeparandum futurum Concilium plenarium habuerunt Rmi. Archiepiscopi et Episcopi foederatorum Statuum Americae Septentrionalis Romae congregati.* This latter document was then submitted by chapters to the various metropolitan provinces for preparation of the final *Schema Decretorum* presented to the council.

[50] *Acta et Decreta Concilii Plenarii Baltimorensis Tertii in Ecclesia Metropolitana Baltimorensi habiti a die IX. Novembris usque ad diem VII. Decembris A.D. MDC-CCLXXXIV* (Baltimore: John Murphy, 1884), nos. 18–22, pp. 7–8. This was the version of the decrees as adopted at the council, before the Holy See's approval.

shame to the episcopate.''[51] The designation of consultors and irremovable rectors had yet further significance. Under pressure from the Holy See, the council decreed that when a diocese fell vacant, they were to draw up a *terna* for the diocese. The bishops of the province were then to meet and draw up their own *terna*, but only after giving their opinion on the priests' list. In the case of a metropolitan see, the two lists were then to be submitted to the other archbishops for comment.[52] Finally, the bishops requested that the St. Louis form of clerical discipline be retained, at least in those dioceses which found it difficult to implement the *Instructio* of 1878.[53]

Once the council ended the decrees had to meet Roman approval. Again Cardinal Franzelin was deputed as the *ponente*. The Americans who went to Rome to gain approval of the conciliar decrees were Denis J. O'Connell, Gibbons' confidante, and Bishops Joseph Dwenger of Fort Wayne and John Moore of St. Augustine. Later, Richard Gilmour of Cleveland joined them. They soon found Roman opposition to requiring only the consultors' advice, but not their consent, to the alienation or acquisition of church property. Moore expressed his distaste for Franzelin in an audience with Leo XIII. As he recounted his conversation for Gibbons, he told the pope that Franzelin

> has a hard head, he is full of speculative theology, abstract principles, and scholastic distinctions, whereas our matters not being questions of dogma but of discipline and practice require, in order to judge of them correctly, a knowledge of the habits and customs of the people and the dispositions of the priests, of the laws of the several States and of the Constitution of the United States, of the decisions pronounced in the courts all over the country in cases similar to those which may be expected to arise between the priests and their bishops, and from the government of temporalities of the church.[54]

When the decrees finally gained Roman approval, the American bishops failed to retain the St. Louis form of clerical discipline. They also compromised on the issue of needing their consultors' consent in financial matters. The approved decree stated that the bishops did not need the

---

[51] Ibid., xlvii; see also xl–xlii and xlviii–xlix. The minutes of this part of the debate at the council are translated in Zwierlein, 2:313–315.

[52] Ibid., no. 15, p. 6.

[53] Ibid., nos. 301, 302, pp. 100–101.

[54] AAB 79 0 5, Moore to Gibbons, Rome, July 6, 1885.

advice of their consultors on financial negotiations for sums less than $5000. For sums in excess of that amount, the advice of the consultors was required; if it was lacking, the bishops needed the permission of the Holy See.[55]

From the convocation of the council until the approval of its decrees, it was obvious that Rome was suspicious of the American church and its canonical tradition, particularly in regard to priests' rights and episcopal independence. Yet the council also passed legislation which resulted in preserving a vestige of the older collegial tradition. Suspect secret societies then plagued the American church. To provide some form of uniform discipline in the matter, the council decreed that the case of each society was to be submitted to the judgment of all the archbishops. If they failed to reach a unanimous decision in favor of the society, the case was to be referred to Rome.[56] This decree, together with the right of the archbishops to be consulted about vacant metropolitan sees, led them to begin holding annual meetings in 1890. These meetings continued until 1919 when, as will be seen, the National Catholic Welfare Council was formed.

Ethnic Concerns

The Third Plenary Council remained fundamentally Roman in its agenda and its legislation. It did not treat the pressing issues then beginning to emerge in the American church. It did not legislate for the various ethnic groups within the church, although a postconciliar interpretation of the decree on irremovable rectors allowed them to be appointed for specific language parishes.

In the Spring of 1885 Bishop Kilian Flasch of LaCrosse, Wisconsin, wrote Propaganda to ask whether a national parish could have an irremovable rector and whether children born of parents of a particular nationality were to be obliged to attend the national parish as long as they remained under the supervision of their parents.[57] The Holy See polled those bishops in whose dioceses there were national as well as territorial

---

[55] *Acta et Decreta Concilii Plenarii Baltimorensis Tertii in Ecclesia Metropolitana Baltimorensi habiti a die IX. Novembris usque ad diem VII. Decembris A.D. MDCCCLXXXIV* (Baltimore: John Murphy and Co., 1886), no. 20, p. 15. For an account of the Roman approval of the conciliar decrees, see my *Vatican and the Americanist Crisis: Denis J. O'Connell, American Agent in Rome, 1885–1903* (Rome: Università Gregoriana, 1974), pp. 48–60.

[56] *Acta et Decreta*, no. 254, pp. 143–144.

[57] APF, SOCG, 1026 (1887) 943–944, Flasch to Simeoni, La Crosse, April 7, 1885.

parishes, and all responded in the affirmative to both questions.[58] The American bishops and Propaganda had already agreed that both English and non-English speaking priests were to be equal, when the superficial harmony between ethnic and language groups was shattered with the petition of Father Peter Abbelen late in 1886.

Abbelen arrived in Rome with a petition on behalf of a number of German priests in Milwaukee, Cincinnati, and St. Louis. It had the explicit endorsement of his ordinary, Archbishop Michael Heiss of Milwaukee. In addition to Flasch's original questions, it called for a German vicar general in dioceses with large German-speaking populations where neither the bishop nor the vicar general spoke German, and for the written consent of a rector of a national church before children of immigrants could attend a territorial church.[59]

Abbelen's memorial gave rise to a heated controversy. Irish-Americans, led by John Ireland, who was soon to become the first Archbishop of St. Paul, were intent on proving that the Church was not foreign. They saw Abbelen's memorial in terms of a German attempt to resist Americanization. The recently opened archives of the Congregation of Propaganda, however, reveal that the German-American bishops were also split. Frederick Katzer, Bishop of Green Bay and later successor to Heiss in Milwaukee, wrote Simeoni of his full approval of Abbelen's memorial and said that "this entire question" was simply one of conflict "between the congregations and priests" of Irish birth or ancestry and "the congregations and priests of other nations." If Propaganda did not accept Abbelen's proposals, all who were not "Irish" would be reduced to second-class citizenship.[60] Bishops Joseph Rademacher of Nashville and Henry J. Richter of Grand Rapids, both German-born, however, repudiated the memorial and Heiss' approval.[61]

In the midst of this controversy Propaganda met, not on Abbelen's memorial, but on Flasch's two questions. Gibbons, then in Rome to receive his red hat, had been named to the congregation. He, too, was in attendance. Cardinal Camillo Mazzella, S.J., former dean of Woodstock College, was designated to draw up the *ponenza*. The congregation voted that missions for different nationalities could coexist within the same

[58] Ibid., 884–902, 1003–1024.

[59] Ibid., 927–942. The petition is printed in Colman J. Barry, *The Catholic Church and German-Americans* (Milwaukee: The Bruce Publishing Co., 1953), pp. 289–296.

[60] APF, SOCG, 1026 (1887) 1085–1086, Katzer to Simeoni, Green Bay, January 3, 1887.

[61] Ibid., 1068–1081, Ireland and Keane, "La question allemande. . . . "

territory, that they could have irremovable rectors, and that children were to attend their parents' church until reaching their majority. It further requested that Simeoni have Gibbons communicate its response to the other archbishops "so that there may be removed every hope in the future of accepting the petitions of Father Abbelen in any way whatsoever."[62]

It was not so much the content of Abbelen's petition—many of the issues had already been settled before he arrived in Rome—as the way in which he ignored the ordinary channels of episcopal authority, which antagonized the majority of English-speaking bishops. Jealous of their authority within their own dioceses and adamant against overlapping jurisdictions, they reacted all the more strongly against the issues raised by Cahenslyism.

Peter Paul Cahensly, a devout Limburg merchant and member of the Center Party, had founded the St. Raphaels-Verein for the care of emigrants from Germany. Soon the organization spread to other nations. In 1890 the boards of directors of most of the various branches met in Lucerne and drafted a memorial which raised many of Abbelen's demands. It called for national parishes, for parochial schools where the immigrants' native language would be taught, and for immigrant priests to have the same rights as native ones. In addition it contained a proposal calculated to arouse the ire of the Americanizing bishops—that "it seems very desirable that the Catholics of each nationality, wherever it is deemed possible, have in the episcopate of the country where they immigrate, several bishops of the same national origin."[63] Such a proposal served, in the minds of the Americanizing bishops, to increase the charge that the Church was foreign to American society. They also falsely accused Cahensly and German-Americans of attempting to have the German government influence the Vatican. Propaganda ultimately rejected the suggestions. Moreover, the American archbishops, including Archbishop Frederick Katzer of Milwaukee, repudiated this foreign intrusion into American ecclesiastical affairs.[64]

Cahenslyism and the "German Question" have drawn most of the attention of historians of ethnic tension in the nineteenth century. But the question of some type of representation of each nationality in the hierarchy extended also to the Italians, Poles, and Oriental Rite Catholics.

The Italians' sense of national identity led some of them to call for a bishop with jurisdiction over the Italians in the United States. This demand

[62] APF, Acta, 257 (1887) 187–198.

[63] Barry, p. 136; the entire text of the memorial is given on pp. 313–315.

[64] See my *The Vatican and the American Hierarchy from 1870 to 1965* (Stuttgart: Anton Hiersemann Verlag, 1982), pp. 55–60.

coincided with the Lucerne memorial and resulted in friction between Bishop Giovanni Battista Scalabrini and Archbishop Corrigan, who were otherwise close friends. Scalabrini was not supporting a separate jurisdiction for Italians, but could not see that the suggestion of bishops representing various ethnic groups implied to many Americans that the Church was foreign.[65] The Italians, far more than the Germans, became victims of the American reaction to Cahenslyism. Though there were Italian-born bishops in the American hierarchy in the nineteenth century, these were mainly missionaries. It was well into the twentieth century before Italian-Americans received a bishop, Joseph M. Pernicone, auxiliary bishop of New York, and this was to help mobilize them to influence their relatives in Italy to vote against the Communists.[66]

While the Italians faced prejudice from their co-religionists in the new world, Catholics from eastern Europe confronted still greater problems of assimilation. Oriental Rite Catholics brought with them unique traditions, among them a married clergy. Resistance to them was one thing on which Ireland and Archbishop Michael Corrigan of New York could agree. Ireland refused to see Father Alexis Toth, a widower, and give him faculties for the Archdiocese of St. Paul—his argument was that he had a Polish priest who could minister to Ruthenian Catholics who had settled there. Toth left the Catholic Church and became an apostle of the Russian Orthodox Church; he was ultimately responsible for the conversion of over 200,000 Oriental Catholics to Orthodoxy.[67]

For the American bishops the question of having a separate jurisdiction for Oriental Rite Catholics was analogous to, but more divisive than, the one which Cahensly had raised. In the 1890s the discussion of Oriental Rite Catholics occupied more space than Cahenslyism in the minutes of the archbishops' meetings. Ireland led an unsuccessful campaign to have the Holy See make all Oriental Rite Catholics in the United States conform to the Latin Rite. Although he had falsely accused German-Americans of negotiating with the German government about their situation, he himself accepted a protest about Ruthenians from the Austro-Hungarian ambassador to the Holy See and tacitly ignored the visitor the Holy See sent, at the emperor's request, to examine the state of Ruthenian immigrants to the

---

[65] Silvano M. Tomasi, *Piety and Power: The Role of Italian Parishes in the New York Metropolitan Area, 1880–1930* (Staten Island, N.Y.: Center for Migration Studies, 1975), pp. 86–92.

[66] See my *Vatican and the American Hierarchy*, p. 338–340.

[67] Keith S. Russin, "Father Alexis G. Toth and the Wilkes-Barre Litigations," *St. Vladimir's Theological Quarterly* 16 (1972) 128–149.

United States. In 1907 the Holy See compromised on establishing a separate jurisdiction and appointed Bishop Soter Stephan Ortynsky, who was to receive delegated jurisdiction from the Latin-rite ordinaries in whose dioceses Eastern Catholics resided. Only in 1924 did the Holy See establish eparchies for Ruthenian and Ukrainian Catholics.[68]

Within the Latin Rite, Polish Catholics presented a variation on the now familiar theme of assimilating to American culture. For them, language was not only a means of preserving religion, as it was for the Germans, but religion had also been an expression of nationalism, for it had been a point of resistance to both Russian and Prussian partition. Like the Irish, their religion was a further source of national identity. While they won the praise of American bishops for their zeal in contributing to the support of the Church, their assimilation was a painful one. In the late 1890s schisms broke out in Chicago, Buffalo, and Scranton and led to the formation of the Polish National Church.[69] Perhaps to prevent further schism the Holy See, early in the century, appointed a number of Polish-American bishops.[70]

But this did not assuage the feelings of alienation of some Poles. In 1920 a group of Polish-American priests protested directly to the Polish government about their treatment. The Polish Legation to the Holy See forwarded the protest to Cardinal Pietro Gasparri, the Secretary of State. The priests had called for a Polish auxiliary bishop in those dioceses with large Polish populations and for Bishop Paul P. Rhode of Green Bay, a native of Prussian Poland, to be made an archbishop. They also accused Archbishop George Mundelein of Chicago of mistreating Poles. It was a replay of the Cahensly dispute, but this time some of the principals had some ironic roles. At the annual meeting of the hierarchy in September 1920, the bishops protested against the interference of a foreign government in American affairs and chastised the Polish-American priests for making their protest. Cardinal James Gibbons then appionted a committee to draft a response to Gasparri. The committee consisted of Mundelein, Archbishop Dennis Dougherty of Philadelphia, and Archbishop Sebastian Messmer of Milwaukee. Messmer, who had been an opponent of Ireland

---

[68] Fogarty, *Vatican*, pp. 61–64, 184–185, and "The American Hierarchy and Oriental Rite Catholics, 1890–1907," *Records of the American Catholic Historical Society* 85 (1974) 17–28.

[69] William Galush, "The Polish National Church: A Survey of Its Origins, Development and Missions," *Records of the American Catholic Historical Society of Philadelphia* 83 (1972) 131–149.

[70] James Hennesey, *American Catholics: A History of the Roman Catholic Community in the United States* (New York: Oxford University Press, 1981), p. 209.

and the Americanizers thirty years before, now said: "It is of the utmost importance to our American nation that the nationalities gathered in the United States should gradually amalgamate and fuse into one homogeneous people and, without losing the best traits of their race, become imbued with the one harmonious national thought, sentiment, and spirit, which is to be the very soul of the nation. This is the idea of Americanization."[71] German-Americans could now stand firm with Irish-Americans in resisting outside influence. But their stance derived, in part, from the homogenization of the various ethnic groups within the American church and one way this was accomplished was first to Romanize them.

Romanization of the American Hierarchy

Ethnic tension was but one of the issues which divided the American church in the 1890s and ultimately shaped the style of diocesan governance in the twentieth century. But there were other issues, more theoretical and theological ones, which divided the hierarchy into two parties within a few years of the Third Plenary Council. The liberal or Americanizing party took a more aggressive stance toward American society. It began consciously to reflect upon the uniqueness of religious liberty in the United States, which had enabled the hierarchy to develop its former sense of collegiality. Running through the thought of the liberal bishops was the benefit to the Church of British and American common law. Ultimately their program would arouse Roman suspicion and be defeated. With that defeat came increased Romanization of the hierarchy.

Few Roman observers could distinguish between American liberty and license. One exception was Monsignor Germano Straniero, who brought the red biretta to Cardinal James Gibbons of Baltimore in 1886. In the United States, he reported, there was truly "a free Church in a free State," for "there the Church was born and has remained separate from the State. It was born free and such it has always remained. In Europe, on the other hand, Church and State were born, in a manner of speaking, from the ruins of paganism."[72] Cardinal Gibbons himself stated the same position when he took possession of his titular church of Santa Maria in Trastevere. The Church, he said, had "often . . . been hampered in her divine mission and has had to struggle for a footing wherever despotism has cast its dark shadow like the plant excluded from the sunlight of heaven, but in the

[71] Fogarty, *Vatican and the American Hierarchy*, pp. 211–213.
[72] Archivio Segreto Vaticano, SS 280 (1902), fasc. 10, fol. 26.

genial air of liberty she blossoms like the rose!'' He proclaimed ''with a deep sense of pride and gratitude . . . that I belong to a country where the civil government holds over us the aegis of its protection without interfering in the legitimate exercise of our sublime mission as ministers of the Gospel of Jesus Christ. Our country has liberty without license, authority without despotism.''[73]

But other issues were dividing the American bishops. Among the liberals, John Ireland, who became an archbishop in 1888, urged a controversial accommodation with public schools and antagonized the German-American bishops on that issue and on his program of Americanization. The liberals, too, began to shift in their attitude toward priests' rights. Ireland had opposed the appointment of irremovable rectors at the council. On the issue of upholding episcopal authority, the liberal bishops initially supported the suspension and subsequent excommunication in 1887 of Father Edward McGlynn by Archbishop Michael A. Corrigan of New York. But gradually they worked for his reconciliation.[74] It was somewhat ironic that to shore up their many-faceted program, they had to agree to introduce what their own program seemed to exclude—the establishment of a permanent apostolic delegation to the American hierarchy. Under the guise of escorting maps and mosaics from the Vatican Museum to the Columbian Exposition in Chicago in October 1892, Archbishop Francesco Satolli was spirited into the country past the suspicious eyes of Archbishop Corrigan. He then met with the archbishops in November to discuss Ireland's school plan and the religious education of children in public schools. He also asked them for their opinion on establishing a delegation. All, except Ireland, gave a negative response. In December he reconciled McGlynn to the Church without any consultation of Corrigan. The following month, the Holy See announced that the delegation was established and Satolli was the first delegate.[75] In less than two years, however, Satolli turned against the liberals.

The establishment of the apostolic delegation would, in time, have tremendous influence on the structure of American dioceses through the delegate's role in the nomination of bishops. Perhaps the dramatic restructuring of the American church in the twentieth century would not

[73] Given in John Tracy Ellis, ed., *Documents of American Catholic History*, 2 vols. (Chicago: Henry Regnery Co., 1967), 2:461–463.

[74] For the best treatment of the McGlynn case, see Robert Emmett Curran, *Michael Augustine Corrigan and the Shaping of Conservative Catholicism in America, 1878–1902* (New York: Arno Press, 1978), pp. 168–256.

[75] Fogarty, *Vatican and the American Hierarchy*, pp. 118–126.

have occurred if the division in the American hierarchy had not erupted in Europe in the issue known as Americanism. The problem arose not so much from the mistranslation into French of Walter Elliott's *Life of Father Hecker*, as the inability to translate the American experience into a European context. As the French church became embroiled in the controversy, Denis O'Connell, who had been dismissed as rector of the American College in Rome in 1895, sought to clarify true Americanism in a speech in Fribourg, Switzerland, in 1897. He distinguished between political and ecclesiastical Americanism. The former he identified with the "order of ideas" contained in the Declaration of Independence, which represented the flowering of the common law. This form of law recognized "that dignity which in creation God conferred upon His image" and promoted "the dignity of 'adoption' conferred by Baptism, and the 'participation of the divine nature.'"

In treating ecclesiastical Americanism, O'Connell entered the thicket of the argument of thesis and hypothesis in regard to the separation of Church and State. He accepted that the thesis meant the union of Church and State, but then he went on to argue that the American hypothesis

> seems to work as well as any other actual system we are acquainted with. Nowhere is the action of the Church more free, and the exercise of Pontifical authority more untrammelled. The Church lives entirely under her own freely made laws; the relations of the bishops with the Holy See are direct and unhampered, and the exercise of the authority is immediate and uncontrolled. And though the Church enjoys no patronage under the law, she receives unbounded support from the warm sympathy of a Christian people and from the majestic strength of a favorable public opinion.[76]

Leo XIII finally took action on Americanism in his apostolic letter *Testem benevolentiae*, issued on January 22, 1899. While he stated that the controversy arose over the translation of the life of Hecker into French, he addressed his letter to Cardinal Gibbons.

But the Holy See not only spoke to the American church; it also acted to restructure it. The first sign of the wave of the future came in 1901. The diocese of Portland, Maine, was vacant. The canonical *ternae* of the consultors and irremovable rectors of the diocese and of the bishops of the province of Boston were submitted to Rome. Because of a canonical

[76] *Ibid.*, pp. 153–156.

irregularity on the priests' *terna*, the Holy See requested more information on the candidates through the apostolic delegate, Sebastian Martinelli. When Propaganda again met, it rejected all names and nominated William H. O'Connell, rector of the American College. Three years later Archbishop John Williams of Boston summoned the eligible priests of the archdiocese and the bishops of the province to draw up lists for a coadjutor. O'Connell was secretary to the bishops' meeting. Commenting on the *ternae*, he wrote his friend Cardinal Raffaele Merry del Val that both the priests and bishops had "one frank and avowed motive"—"to keep off the *terna* at all costs any name which stood for Rome, for Roman views and for Roman sympathies."[77] O'Connell's own name was not on the lists, but on January 22, 1906, Propaganda presented his name to Pius X for confirmation as coadjutor archbishop of Boston.[78] O'Connell had few friends in the American hierarchy. His appointment represented a new trend in the American Church—appointment through a powerful Roman patron rather than canonical nomination by American bishops and, after 1884, some priests.

In 1908 the American church was removed from the supervision of the Congregation of Propaganda and placed under the Consistorial Congregation, but this was the result of a reorganization of the curia rather than a recognition of a definitive change in the status of the American church. After 1908, however, the next major see to fall vacant was Chicago in 1915. In this case the bishops of the province totally rejected the priests' *terna* and submitted their own. Rumors began circulating in Chicago that the Holy See would reject the *ternae* and transfer Bishop Dennis Dougherty from Jaro in the Philippines to Chicago. In the meantime, the see of Buffalo was also vacant and Rome intended to name George Mundelein, auxiliary bishop of Brooklyn, when the British Foreign Office protested at having a bishop of German ancestry on the border between the United States and Canada during World War I. The Holy See, therefore, appointed Dougherty to Buffalo with the promise of being named to the first vacant metropolitan see. It then named Mundelein archbishop of Chicago. He owed his rise to prominence in part to his close friendship with Archbishop Giovanni Bonzano, the apostolic delegate, with whom he had become acquainted while a student at the Urban College of Propaganda.[79]

---

[77] O'Connell to Merry del Val, Portland, April 17, 1904, quoted in James Gaffey, "The Changing of the Guard: The Rise of Cardinal O'Connell of Boston," *Catholic Historical Review* 59 (1973) 230.

[78] Ibid., p. 235.

[79] For the succession to Chicago, see James P. Gaffey, *Francis Clement Kelley & the*

Because of a number of factors, the Holy See was choosing to ignore the method of nominating bishops decreed in the Third Plenary Council. In 1916 the Consistorial Congregation introduced a new method for the nomination of bishops. Every two years, each bishop was to submit to his metropolitan the names of one or two priests whom he thought worthy of the episcopate. To arrive at his two names he was to seek the opinion of his consultors and irremovable rectors, but he was to speak with them individually under the bond of secrecy, not in a group. The bishops of each province were then to gather to discuss the names submitted to the metropolitan and determine the ones to be forwarded to the Consistorial Congregation through the apostolic delegate. When a see was actually vacant, the Holy See would then seek the opinion of the bishops on the most likely candidates, "through the Most Reverend Apostolic Delegate or in some other manner."[80] The Holy See thus removed from the consultors and irremovable rectors the voice in nominating bishops, which it had demanded the Third Plenary Council grant them. It also removed from the bishops the right to submit *ternae* for a vacant see, which had been the custom since 1834. The apostolic delegate now received an increasing role in the naming of American bishops. To gain promotion to the episcopate, a priest depended directly or indirectly on a Roman patron. A vertical concept of episcopal authority replaced the more horizontal notion of collegiality.

National Catholic Welfare Conference

The new concept of episcopal authority can best be illustrated by the reaction to the National Catholic Welfare Council, originally organized in 1919 to implement Benedict XV's request that the hierarchy unite to work for peace. The NCWC consisted of annual meetings of the hierarchy and of a standing secretariat, appointed by the bishops, to coordinate activity between meetings.[81] Unfortunately, the death of Cardinal Gibbons on March 24, 1921, left William O'Connell as the senior cardinal in the

---

American Catholic Dream, 2 vols. (Bensenville, IL: The Heritage Foundatio , Inc., 1980), 1:151–155. See also Hugh J. Nolan, "Native Son," in *The History of the Archdiocese of Philadelphia*, ed. James F. Connelly (Philadelphia, 1976), pp. 343–344.

[80] *Acta Apostolicae Sedis* 8 (1916) 400–404.

[81] John Tracy Ellis, *The Life of James Cardinal Gibbons*, 2 vols. (Milwaukee: The Bruce Publishing Co., 1952), 2:298–309. Fogarty, *Vatican and the American Hierarchy*, pp. 214–216.

American church with the right, according to the *Codex Iuris Canonici* to preside over meetings of the hierarchy.

O'Connell was not a man for whom either humility or collegiality were values. His own diocese had been wracked with the scandal of his retaining his nephew, Monsignor James P.E. O'Connell, as his chancellor, though he had been married for several years. The cardinal, nevertheless, presided at the annual meeting of the hierarchy in the fall of 1921. Soon afterward, he poured out his soul to Merry del Val, who had been dismissed as Secretary of State in 1914 by Benedict XV. "There is," wrote O'Connell,

> all around about an intangible something which would seem to emanate from too much politics, diplomacy and intrigue—too much mingling with affairs which don't concern us. But thank God it does not exist around me. How different in the wonderful days of Pio X when the chief concern was God and when cheap politics and free-masons were kept in their place. The memory of those days is a rare possession—conditions then were as near ideal as they ever can be. Will they ever return? For one thing I shall live in the spirit of that holy time and rate intrigue at its true value—just zero.[82]

Merry del Val shared O'Connell's dim view of Benedict XV and his Secretary of State, Cardinal Pietro Gasparri. "We are drifting," he replied, and only hoped that the Church would "refrain from the tactics of human politics."[83] O'Connell and Merry del Val soon had an opportunity to recreate the Church of Pius X. On January 22, 1922, Benedict died.

There were at the time only two cardinals in the American church: O'Connell and Dougherty, who had been transferred to Philadelphia in 1918. Both arrived too late for the conclave, which elected Pius XI. But O'Connell, assisted by Dougherty, immediately sought to reverse the trends begun under Gibbons and to have the NCWC suppressed. As Dougherty left Rome, he was handed a decree of the Consistorial Congregation, signed by Cardinal Gaetano de Lai, the secretary and a known friend of O'Connell's. The decree ordered the NCWC to disband immediately. The other bishops, however, were prepared for this maneuver. By May, eighty-five percent of the hierarchy had petitioned Rome not to publish the Consistorial's decree until a delegation could be sent to

---

[82] Archives of the Archdiocese of Boston, M-850, O'Connell to Merry del Val, Boston, sometime after October 24, 1921 (copy).

[83] Ibid., Merry del Val to O'Connell, Rome, November 24, 1921.

Rome. While Dougherty voiced his opposition to the NCWC to the apostolic delegate, Archbishop Bonzano, O'Connell continued his protests directly to Rome. His letter to Cardinal de Lai revealed his own concept of the episcopacy. Condemning those of the administrative committee of the NCWC, who were working most feverishly to preserve the organization, O'Connell wrote:

> Now they are taking a "plebiscite" among the bishops in order to annul the force of the decree. The customary maneuver demonstrates again more evidently the wisdom of the decree. Today we are in full "Democracy, presbyterianism, and Congregationalism."
>
> If this maneuver succeeds, good-by to the authority of the Roman congregations. We will make all the laws and decrees through means of "plebiscites," a method which naturally has more popularity, the idol of the day.
>
> And now it seems more than ever that this N.C.W.C. shows more clearly that not only does it tend little by little to weaken hierarchical authority and dignity, but also wishes to put into operation the same tactics against the Consistorial.
>
> It is incredible that Rome does not see the danger of conceding today in order to have to concede *much more tomorrow*.[84]

It was quite clear that O'Connell envisioned any collegial structure as endangering episcopal authority. For O'Connell, proper authority in the Church was not dialogue or shared responsibility, but a direct dependent relationship with a highly centralized curia, with whose personnel he was on good terms. He regarded himself almost as a *legatus natus* for Pius X and those cardinals close to him, but he could not transfer his loyalty to any other pontiff or consider entering into consultation with his fellow bishops as his equals. He symbolized a dramatic change from the tradition of Carroll, England, Ireland, and Gibbons.

Despite O'Connell's efforts, the petitions of the majority of the other bishops prevailed. The delegation to Rome won the support of Cardinal Gasparri, who remained Secretary of State. The pope, too, was won over and ordered the Consistorial Congregation to reconsider the condemnation. On June 22, 1921, the congregation met and decreed that the NCWC could continue and that the bishops could proceed with their annual meeting as

---

[84] AABo, O'Connell to De Lai, Boston, May 10, 1922 (copy). He also wrote a similar, though briefer, letter to Merry del Val.

scheduled for September, in accordance with instructions, which were soon to be issued. The new instructions suggested that the bishops not hold annual meetings, that attendance be voluntary, that decisions of the meetings not be binding and not be in any way construed as emanating from a plenary council, and that the name "Council" in the title of the organization be changed to something like "Committee." O'Connell continued his attack on the NCWC and suggested that the change of the name to "Welfare Conference" was nothing short of another sign of disloyalty to Rome.[85]

Though the NCWC was to continue the American tradition of collegiality in practice, the theory and even the term was forgotten in the minds of the American bishops who attended Vatican II. The Romanization process which had begun with the rise of William O'Connell had as one side-effect provincialism or, at most, regionalization. As each bishop saw himself depending more and more upon Roman patronage and authority, he saw himself independent of the other bishops and supreme in his own diocese. Diocesan structure took the form not only of the canon law of either the American church or the code, but also of the personality of the bishop who presided over it. A further effect of Romanization was that it meant an American bishop's influence depended on the status of his Roman patron. If a Roman patron fell from power, so did his American client. Such was the case with O'Connell. After 1922, he restricted his activities to his own diocese and did not seek to dominate the American church. Different men rose up with different Roman patrons. Ironically, just as O'Connell was thrust upon Archbishop Williams as coadjutor in 1906, he had thrust upon him Francis Spellman, as auxiliary bishop, in 1932. Spellman's patron, of course, was the most powerful of all, Eugenio Pacelli, who was elected Pope Pius XII.

An Evaluation

In the history of the American church there have been a number of internal factors which have shaped diocesan structure and governance. But the extensive conciliar legislation of the nineteenth century was due to the American church's experience of religious liberty. Whenever the bishops consciously reflected on the basis for this liberty in common law, they provided for both priest and lay participation in the Church and attempted to adapt universal law to American circumstances. Their reflection, in

---

[85] Fogarty, *Vatican and the American Hierarchy*, pp. 223–228.

turn, was influenced by the theology they were taught. Thus Carroll, England, and Francis Kenrick shared a certain collegial concept. A bishop was not only the ordinary of a diocese; he was also acting in collaboration with other bishops for the good of the whole Church. They also shared a theology premised more on the fathers than on the scholastics. Whenever the collegial concept began to fade, the bishops exhibited absolutism toward their priests. The refusal of the bishops to establish canonical parishes and to grant priests tenure as pastors, however, has to be seen also in the context of lay trusteeism.

Though the concept of collegiality was beginning to fade at the end of the nineteenth century, Rome's response to Americanism hastened the process. The provincialism and individualism which flowed from Romanization did not so much change the canonical structure of a diocese, as stamp the personality of a particular bishop upon it. The expression of episcopal authority which resulted bore little resemblance to the tradition of Carroll, England, and Gibbons.

CHURCH GOVERNMENT: THE PROTESTANT EXPERIENCE

JOHN E. LYNCH, C.S.P.

The Second Vatican Council, in adjusting to social change, reversed the policy of centralization and the exclusion of the laity from church government which had prevailed since the 11th-century Gregorian Reform. The council not only enhanced the role of the bishop vis-à-vis the papacy but also encouraged within the diocese a more responsible participation of the presbyterate and the laity in decision making. The revised code has attempted to structure these policies through presbyteral and pastoral councils. This symposium seeks further implementation of the conciliar objectives.

Since Protestantism from its inception has assumed greater freedom in organization and has legitimated a broader-based authority, its history provides a rich fund of experience for the Catholic Church as it plans to meet contemporary needs. The Reformation churches are commonly classified as congregational, presbyterian or episcopal according to the degree of local autonomy practiced. The Baptists, for example, vest complete control of all ecclesiastical matters, whether of faith or of discipline, in the local congregation. In principle they acknowledge no higher government.[1] In the Presbyterian Church, on the other hand, the local congregations in a given area are gathered into a presbytery made up of all the ordained ministers and elected elders from each congregation. The presbytery exercises functions comparable to a Catholic diocesan bishop, but "ministerial and lay representatives at the middle and national levels form a complex structure of checks and balances to give democratic

---

[1]Lukas Vischer, for many years engaged in the work of the Secretariat of the Faith and Order Commission of the World Council of Churches, notes that "in recent times we have come to realize clearly the extent to which the forms and manners of decision-making in all the Churches have been the fruit of historical development. This even applies to the ancient Church." He continues, "The synodical and congregational order established in many Churches in the centuries following the Reformation cannot simply be presented as the biblical pattern. We must see it rather as a historical development; on the one hand, in reaction against an over-emphasis on Church authority and, on the other hand, as a rediscovery of the role not only of the individual Christian but, above all, of the whole people of God in fulfilling God's mission in the world." "Visible Unity—Realistic Goal or Mirage?" *One in Christ* 18 (1982) 23–24.

representation.''[2] The Episcopal Church, though insisting on the necessity of a formal hierarchy, does provide for a House of Deputies composed of presbyters and laity elected from each diocese. All legislation must be passed by both the House of Bishops and the House of Deputies. Some churches, such as the Lutheran, do not fit exactly into any single category.

Sociologists have been accustomed to differentiate the three polities on the formally defined power or authority of the local church to hire and fire its ministers. A fully autonomous local church would be congregational, a church without that authority would be episcopal. A presbyterian denomination was defined as one ''whose ministers and elders in the presbytery control the local church pastor from one side, while the congregation reserved the right of endorsement from the other.''[3] The form of polity has obviously influenced the structuring of a denomination but, as will be seen, all the larger Protestant churches today are organized along remarkably similar lines.

HISTORICAL OVERVIEW

Before considering contemporary patterns a brief survey of American Protestantism will be helpful. Three main stages of development may be identified: the colonial period through the Civil War, the era of Progressive Reformers (1876 to the end of World War I), and 1929 to the present.[4]

---

[2]K. Peter Takayama and Lynn W. Cannon, ''Formal Polity and Power Distribution in American Protestant Denominations,'' *The Sociological Quarterly* 20 (1979) 326. Howard Grimes in surveying the place of the laity in American church history notes that from the earliest times laymen assumed control of religious life in the Protestant colonies. ''Nor was it only in New England that this lay control emerged. In Virginia the Vestries of the Anglican churches assumed such powers in relation to the clergy that the Archbishop of Canterbury is reported as expressing surprise, in 1697, that clergymen might 'be removed like domestic servants by a vote of the Vestry.''' *The Layman in Christian History*, ed. Stephen C. Neill and Hans-Ruedi Weber (Philadelphia: The Westminster Press, 1963), p. 241.

[3]Takayama and Cannon, p. 326.

[4]For this section of the paper I am heavily dependent upon Ben Primer, *Protestants and American Business Methods* (Ann Arbor: UMI Research Press, 1979). For a general study see Kenneth S. Latourette, *Christianity in a Revolutionary Age*, Vol. 3 *The Nineteenth Century Outside Europe: the Americas, the Pacific, Asia and Africa* (New York: Harper and Brothers, 1961), Chap. IV, ''The United States of America: the Development of Ecclesiastical Organization and Leadership,'' pp. 84–111; Vol. 5 *The Twentieth Century Outside Europe: the Americas, the Pacific, Asia, and Africa: the Emerging World Christian Community* (New York: Harper & Row, 1962), Chap. II, ''The Complex, Multiform Record of Christianity in the United States of America,'' pp. 4–135. See also Sidney E. Mead, *The Lively Experiment: the Shaping of Christianity in America* (New York: Harper & Row, 1963).

Colonial through Civil War

At the conclusion of the Revolutionary War there was very little structure above the level of the parish. The Methodists, in accord with the plan worked out by John Wesley, did have a centralized circuit and conference system.[5] They were the first to set up a national organization in 1784 at the "Christmas Conference" in Baltimore.[6] The constitutions of the Presbyterian and Protestant Episcopal Churches were formulated in Philadelphia from 1785–1788 at the same time and place as the Federal Constitution. It has been maintained that there was an interplay of influences between the civil and ecclesiastical forms of government.[7] Certainly the Episcopalian practice of including lay representatives in the annual assemblies and the holding of national conventions reflects the new American spirit. The Dutch Reformed Church adopted a synodal form of government in 1792. The Lutherans began to organize synods in the different states; then in 1820 four states formed a General Synod.

New England Congregationalism resisted the centralizing and nationalizing trends. In Massachusetts, especially, there was a strong commitment to the independence of each congregation. Nathaniel Emmons in opposing the formation of a state association argued in 1803: "Association leads to Consociation; Consociation leads to Presbyterianism; Presbyterianism leads to Episcopacy; Episcopacy leads to Roman Catholicism; and Roman Catholicism is an ultimate fact."[8] Despite these objections state associations were indeed formed, but the Congregationalists did not adopt a national organization until 1852.

The migration westward over the Alleghenies aroused fears on the part of Eastern Protestants that the hazardous conditions of frontier society would lead to the loss of religious values. Samuel J. Mills, a Congregationalist minister who ardently promoted the foreign missions, wrote that on a visit to the capital of the Illinois Territory in 1814 he found only five bibles in one hundred families.[9] Similar reports stimulated wealthy laymen to found national agencies in order to counteract the evil. The American Bible Society and the American Education Society were established in 1815, soon

[5]Winthrop S. Hudson, *American Protestantism* (Chicago: University of Chicago Press, 1961), p. 58.

[6]William Warren Sweet, *The Story of Religion in America* (New York: Harper and Brothers, 1950), p. 193.

[7]Ibid., p. 200.

[8]Ibid., p. 204.

[9]Ibid., p. 253.

followed by the American Tract Society (1823), the American Sunday School Union (1826), the American Home Mission Society (1826) and the American anti-Slavery Society (1833). By 1827 there were fourteen national societies only four of which were under denominational auspices.

> The managers of the societies stressed the need for "systematic" operations: effective central staffs numbering as many as ten; national advertising and promotion through magazines; voluminous annual reports; anniversary meetings; an energetic group of field agents to speak at every sort of ecclesiastical assembly and to organize local auxiliaries. Above all, they had secure financial foundations based upon nation-wide sales of uniformly-priced and packaged merchandise, upon regular financial drives, and upon the Dudley method of collection that organized responsibility through neighborhood teams.[10]

Structurally independent of the churches, the agencies achieved immediate success because they needed no formal approval and thus avoided sectarian differences.[11]

There was, however, considerable opposition to these agencies on the part of the Baptists and the followers of Alexander Campbell, the Disciples of Christ, the first large indigenous denomination to arise on this continent

---

[10]Primer, p. 20.

[11]Gibson Winter of the Chicago Divinity School identifies the use of special agencies to carry out limited mandates as a common feature of all American denominations. "Agencies here mean the task forces, voluntary associations, boards, and committees developed to cope with emerging problems. The proliferation of agencies posed a serious problem of unity of command within the religious organizations, for agency bureaucracy grew up before a corresponding ideology or ecclesiology was developed for their control.

"Several consequences followed from these ambiguities in ecclesiological formulation:

"1. The problem of church unity of command was aggravated by differing perspectives on the validity of given forms of organization, particularly when mergers brought together conflicting traditions of organization.

"2. The goals of an organized activity could easily become divorced from the organization's original theological task because there was no clear articulation of the relationship between that task and the administrative form utilized to achieve it.

"3. The parent religious organization was often denied effective participation in the decision making of an agency as a result of the church's failure to become organizationally sophisticated.

"Such problems form underlying themes in the history of religious institutions; as problems they become much more pressing in a period of organizational revolution." In *The Emergent American Society: Large-Scale Organizations*, ed. W. Lloyd Warner et al. (New Haven: Yale U. Press, 1967), 1:409–410. An updated and revised version of Winter's study was published separately in *Religious Identity* (New York: Macmillan Co., 1968).

early in the 1830's.[12] Not only did they resent the charge of irreligion in the West, but also the threat to local autonomy through the centralization of authority. Societies with their officers and paid secretaries seemed to be a violation of Baptist principle without Scriptural warrant. Undoubtedly jealousy of the better educated missionaries also fanned the hostility. Campbell wrote that God did not send Jonah to Nineveh through a missionary society, nor did he send him "to a seminary of learning to prepare him to preach to these Gentiles," "neither did he look back to a society formed to raise money for his support."[13]

Gradually, with greater social stability and the reassertion of sectarianism, the effectiveness of the independent agencies declined. Concurrently the various denominations were establishing their own agencies. The denominational organizations had an advantage in that they could tap the resources of the parishes directly. Accordingly, the Protestant Episcopal Church set up a Board of Missions which provided for expansion into the new territories. Methodists were better prepared for frontier ministry. Preachers were assigned to wide circuits rather than to a single church. Circuit riders travelled from village to village and from house to house. Soon evangelism was carried on chiefly through camp meetings and only in time were Methodist churches constructed.[14] A missionary society provided salaries and supplies for these evangelists. Baptist preachers who came from the people and were self-supporting needed little outside help. Baptist societies had only to support foreign missions and promote denominational publications. The Christian Church or Disciples of Christ after a series of meetings formed in 1849 the American Christian Missionary Society which was strictly voluntary and exercised no power over the local churches. Its non-Scriptural status, however, doomed it to ineffectiveness.

By the time of the Civil War, then, the non-sectarian agencies had fallen under denominational control, usually supervised by a national convention.[15] Appointed boards composed of a specified proportion of clerical

---

[12]Gary P. Burkart, "Patterns of Protestant Organization," *American Denominational Organization: a Sociological View*, ed. Ross P. Scherer (Pasadena, CA: Wm. Carey Library, 1980), p. 53.

[13]Sweet, p. 257.

[14]Primer, p. 29.

[15]"Diaries of colonial clergymen revealed that man had almost no churchly duties apart from the Sabbath sermon. The rise of the 'activity church' meant that the minister ran an ever more complex organization. As the interdenominational agencies were increasingly crowded out by denomination directorates around 1837, pressures were placed on local churches to be productive in the competitive society. . . . The success motif prevailed." Martin E. Marty,

and lay members were entrusted with direct responsibility for the operation. Since the entire board would meet only once a year, certain members of the board were chosen as managers for a more regular oversight. The day-to-day administration fell to secretaries, ordained clergymen, who were expected to promote the work of the agency, recruit missionaries and raise funds. The goals were as clear as the organization was simple, to spread the kingdom of God.[16]

Progressive Reformers

Differences among the denominations in size, geographic distribution, social and economic status, as well as polity would affect organizational changes after 1876. The Protestant Episcopal Church was concentrated in the industrial Northeast with a middle and upper class constituency; its ministers were well educated and professionally trained. The Methodists, though strong in the North and West, were centered mainly in New York, Pennsylvania and the Ohio valley; they appealed largely to a middle class, increasingly urbanized and educated. The Disciples of Christ and the Baptists with a membership of farmers and share croppers were found in the Old Northwest and the border states of Kentucky, Tennessee and Missouri; they remained skeptical of an educated preacher. "The Disciples did not have formal ministerial training (never theological education) until the 1890's."[17]

The great changes which took place in American society after the Civil War and Reconstruction were bound to affect the churches. The population was shifting from farm to city. Whereas in 1850 only one in eight lived in an urban area (i.e., over 8,000), by 1880 the number had risen to one in four. Factory and industrial output was soon treble that of the farms.[18] The completion of the transcontinental railroads and the improvement in communications, especially through the telegraph, enabled businesses to operate on a national level. Consolidation in politics witnessed the growing power of the federal government at the expense of the states. The most significant economic, political and professional organizations grew enormously in size and complexity. Until the Civil War, for example, the railroads were short lines run by numerous independent companies.

Righteous Empire: The Protestant Experience in America (New York: Dial Press, 1970), p. 74.
   [16]Primer, pp. 35–37.
   [17]Ibid., pp. 37–39.
   [18]Ibid., p. 43. Also see Marty, pp. 156–157.

Gradually they were merged into a few powerful corporations. Similarly fifty telegraph companies were soon coalesced to two.[19] "Bureaucratization was as much a process as a result, and as organizations sought to control their internal and external environments, they continually influenced other institutions and the lives of millions of Americans."[20]

As the United States entered its second century the steady growth of religious membership continued. The proportion of the population on church rolls rose from 6% in 1776, to 15.5% in 1850, and 35.7% by the turn of the century. Protestants numbered about nine million and Catholics six million in a population of fifty million.[21] In many instances church agencies grew at a faster rate than the denominations. New agencies proliferated: for work among black Americans; for the care of retired clergymen; for coordinating the work of hospitals, rest homes and orphanages; and for a broad range of social services.[22]

No longer could a few wealthy benefactors be relied upon to finance these enterprises. Appeals to the local churches became increasingly necessary, with the result that some parishes were overburdened while others offered no help at all. "By the 1890's some four to eight national organizations in each Church expected local pastors to spend at least one Sunday annually promoting their work. In addition there were various state, diocesan and local offerings to be taken." *The Christian Standard*, a publication of the Disciples of Christ, editorialized that the failure of three-fourths of the congregations to contribute was "a fact so humiliating that we could wish to hide it from knowledge if it were not that it should provide a spur to greater exertions." The parishes in turn criticized the agencies for the excessive cost of administration, sometimes as high as one-half their income. "Increases in the size of the central staff had to be justified by both the expanding work and the 'exceptionally small' expense of administration."[23]

Efforts were made to alleviate the distress by instituting an "omnibus" collection, one annual offering divided among the several organizations. A generally successful method was to assign a quota to each congregation.

---

[19]Sweet, *The Story of Religion*, pp. 347–348.

[20]Primer, p. 2.

[21]Marty, p. 169. For an analysis of church membership from 1870 to 1950 see Gibson Winter, *The Suburban Captivity of the Churches* (Garden City, NY: Doubleday, 1960). Also see Edwin S. Gaustad, "America's Institutions of Faith: a Statistical Postscript," *Religion in America*, ed. William G. McLoughlin and Robert N. Bellah (Boston: Houghton Mifflin, 1968), pp. 111–133. In 1970, 62.4% of the population identified with a religious body. In 1982 the number had declined to 59.9%.

[22]Primer, pp. 44–45.

[23]Ibid., pp. 47–48.

Another device was the special appeal for a specific project such as a mission school or hospital. Individual missionaries solicited the parishes either by mail or on personal fund-raising tours. Charismatic personalities were able to attract contributions regardless of any overall evaluation of their appeal. The Board of Managers of the Domestic and Foreign Missionary Society of the Protestant Episcopal Church reported in 1901: ''it often happens that work of lesser importance, represented by effective speakers, secures a much larger response than can be awakened by speakers of less preeminent gifts.''[24]

Limited resources stirred up rivalry among the agencies, but competition was not limited to finances. There were jurisdictional disputes concerning overlapping competencies. The Methodist Board of Missions, for example, fought with the Methodist Sunday School Board over the organization of religious education in the missions. There was even friction over the time allotted the agencies at the national conventions.[25]

By the turn of the century executives of the agencies began to realize the serious problems at hand. The enterprises had grown so large that their administration was wholly inefficient. Though the staffs had increased, no move had been made toward departmentalization or specialization, let alone coordination among denominational boards. Unlike industrialists, religious leaders had not yet perceived the advantage of a centralized bureaucracy.

> After 1910, however, these conditions changed. The boards sought to resolve the problem of chaotic finances, inefficient administrations, and conflicting authorities in order to facilitate the accomplishment of their traditional goals. This process of change, however, involved more than a history of adjustment to structural dilemmas. A more positive rationale for change began to influence the leaders in the Churches; they were touched by the Progressive fascination with organization, efficiency and system. As a result, the agencies of the Churches became central figures in the Church's adjustment to the twentieth century. They became in effect symbols of Protestant modernity.[26]

The progressive spirit sought to bring about order and harmony in society through the application of scientific methods.[27] Frederick W. Taylor's *The*

---

[24]Ibid., p. 51.

[25]Ibid., p. 54.

[26]Ibid., p. 57.

[27]For a treatment of progressivism see John M. Blum, *The Republican Roosevelt* (New York: Atheneum, 1971).

Principles of Scientific Management in 1911 typifies the systematic approach to problem solving. The facts had to be assembled and analyzed, then a rational plan devised for coping with the situation. The use of experts, professionally qualified specialists, was considered essential for a well-functioning organization.

The churches quickly moved to apply the new methods. Though the ways of business may seem foreign to religion, "Organization and administration," Bishop William Huntington of the Episcopal Board wrote, are to "the fishers of men what their nets were to the plain fisherfolk who plied their craft upon the waters of Galilee."[28] All denominations recognized the need for system and method to promote efficiency. Organization in the field of religion refers primarily "to the coordination of activities, the introduction of rational systems of accounting, the use of functionally specialized staffs, the application of objective criteria to gauge performance, and the designation of specific goals to be served by functional units within the enterprise."[29]

The newly-discovered organizational principles were applied first in the area of fund raising. Elaborate schemes were developed to assure a "systematic finance." The goal was to have a regular weekly giving in accordance with a definite pledge. The Every-Member Canvass had well-coached teams approach individual parishioners with a suggested quota. The duplex envelope, among other stewardship techniques, had one pocket for local expenses, the other for national needs. Reports were published grading churches on their "benevolences." A minister's status in the denomination depended upon his ability to raise funds, thus favoring the salesman over the academic. Churches were given the "privilege" of supporting missionaries for a specified sum. Educational programs were designed to interest parishes in the work of the central church. Agencies established publicity departments to promote their work, as did the Baptist Home Mission Board in 1910. Efforts were made to set up endowments through annuities and bequests. Studies were undertaken to determine a pattern of contributing. It was found that small churches, that is, those with less than fifty members, even though more generous on a per capita basis gave less to the missions because of local needs. Care, therefore, had to be taken to avoid overbuilding in view of the denominational budget. "In effect, denominational executives had created for their local churches a demographic profile that would produce maximum national support—

[28]Bishop William R. Huntington, "Things Old and New," *The Churchman* 78 (September 24, 1898) 653, cited by Primer, p. 70.

[29]Winter, in *The Emergent American Society*, p. 411.

instead of maximum effectiveness in terms of the direct relationship between the individual and the church.''[30]

The terminology of the marketplace crept into the vocabulary of denominational leaders: the church was conceived as a "great corporation" with a commodity to sell. A successful advertising executive, Bruce Barton, published in 1925 *The Man Nobody Knows*, portraying Jesus as a real business go-getter. "Know you not that I must be about my Father's business" (Lk 2:49) established the orientation of his career. Far from being a weakling, Jesus was "dynamic and inspiring, a thinker, doer, leader, outdoorsman, mixer, a man. He founded modern business by taking twelve ordinary men and building a corporation. Jesus was like David Lloyd George, Henry Ford, and J. Pierpont Morgan! Wrote Barton: Jesus' motto might well have been, 'Never explain; never retract; never apologize; get it done and let them howl!' ''[31]

One enterprising New York City pastor coaxed on a billboard "Come to church—Public Worship Increases Your Efficiency.''[32]

The dean of the School of Religious Education at Southern Seminary, Gaines S. Dobbins, offered a rationale for the application of the business model in *The Efficient Church* published in 1923. He continued to advocate the use of business techniques in other writings such as *The Church Book* and *Building Better Churches*, "always updating them as the business model changed.''[33] No wonder that religious purposes appeared tarnished and people began to look upon the church as a commercial institution. Henry Steele Commager in his classical work *The American Mind: an Interpretation of American Thought and Character in the 1880's*, called attention to the church's changing role in American culture: it has "largely forfeited its moral function and assumed, instead, a secular one— that of serving as a social organization.''[34]

Still, "systematic finance" put the central church agencies on a firmer footing.

> Thanks to their financial success, agencies and boards were becoming the principal sources of power in twentieth-century

[30]Primer, p. 116.

[31]Bruce Barton, *The Man Nobody Knows: a Discovery of Jesus* (Indianapolis: The Bobbs Merrill Co., 1925). Citation is from Clyde L. Manschreck, *A History of Christianity* (Englewood Cliffs, NJ: Prentice-Hall, 2nd ed. 1984), p. 2.

[32]Primer, pp. 116–117.

[33]E. Glenn Hinson, "The Baptist Experience in America," *Review and Expositor: a Baptist Theological Journal* 79 (1982) 227.

[34]Henry Steele Commanger, *The American Mind: an Interpretation of American Thought and Character in the 1880's* (New Haven: Yale U. Press, 1950), p. 426.

American Protestantism. The older pastoral structure still remained an important nexus of power at the local level, but even it was increasingly influenced by the national agencies. The two structures coexisted as best they could, with local institutions becoming more slaves than masters of the boards they had originally established.[35]

Financial growth stimulated and was itself enhanced by administrative developments. After 1900 the agencies began to departmentalize their operations, at first on an ad hoc arrangement. The Boards of Missions of the Methodist Episcopal Church, for example, reached a point in 1919 where more than a dozen departments were reporting to the corresponding secretaries. The Board was then streamlined into three divisions: Home Missions; Foreign Missions; and Treasury.[36] In the reorganization necessitated by growth, professional management consultants and efficiency experts were hired. Office forms, procurement and accounting procedures were introduced. Employee newsletters and inter-office publications promoted communication. Staff meetings or conferences were held to exchange ideas and assure coordination. Monthly reports in standardized format from each department as well as statistical data were exchanged. Five-year budgets were projected. By 1920 there could be no doubt that religion had adopted the methods of business.

Similar techniques were recommended for use on every level. Exact record-keeping was seen as a means for measuring effectiveness.

For the Sunday School, for example, an 8-point record-system was developed, checking key items emphasized: being present, bringing Bibles, reading assigned lessons, giving to the Church systematically, staying for worship, and so on . . . . For the overall organization of the Church an emphasis was placed on recording data about attendance, participation, contributions, decisions, and other matters. The net result was . . . an improvement in all these categories. Keeping records primed the pump, as it were, and got many church programs flowing in a steady stream.[37]

In a recent ecumenical dialogue a professor of church history at the Southern Baptist Theological Seminary in Louisville, Ky. described how the larger urban churches typically operate on the business model.

[35]Primer, p. 120.
[36]Ibid., p. 130.
[37]Hinson, p. 227.

The members form a corporation. They elect a Board (of deacons) and entrust them with the direction of the corporation. The Board seeks an executive (the pastor). They offer him $30,000 a year plus a housing allowance, car allowance, book allowance, retirement, and various other benefits. If other corporations (churches) compete, the Board may raise salary and/or benefits to ensure that they keep a good executive. The Board puts pressure on the executive to produce documentable results—X-baptisms, Y-additions by letter [i.e. transfer], Z-contributions. If the latter fails to meet expectations they put pressure on him. If he cannot improve, they bring the matter to the attention of the stockholders, and he may get fired or eased out in some way. Usually some effort is made to reduce the amount of embarrassment, often by offering continued salary for a time. To ensure success, the executive puts on a major advertising campaign. He starts a busing program to increase attendance, sending buses in a 50-mile radius around the church. He gives incentives to bus drivers for securing the most riders. The bus drivers give candy bars and balloons to the kiddies and place 5-dollar bills under certain seats. The executive advertises on radio and TV. He promises money-back satisfaction: "Jesus will meet every need." Thus flourishes the corporation.[38]

The professor acknowledged that though the use of this model raises serious questions, it has produced results. The Southern Baptists are now the largest Protestant denomination in this country and are said to be the fastest growing religious group. In 1900 they numbered 1.6 million; by 1950 they were 7 million and by 1981 had doubled to 14 million.[39]

Contemporary Development

As with the agencies, so with the governance of the whole church. Organizational growth in the Protestant denominations followed three general trends: "(1) elaboration of administrative staff; (2) centralized control of fund-raising and budgeting; (3) functional specialization through agencies and boards."[40] The differences in polity—congregational, presbyterian or episcopal—were inconsequential; all churches developed along pragmatic lines. "[W]hatever the ecclesiological base, the various denom-

[38]Ibid., pp. 227–228.
[39]Frank S. Mead, *Handbook of Denominations in the United States* (Nashville: Abingdon Press, 7th ed. 1980), p. 41.
[40]Winter, *The Emergent American Society*, p. 431.

inations have followed a roughly comparable pattern of large-scale bureaucratic organization.''[41] It is, in fact, ironical, that the leadership in the American Baptist Convention oftentimes exerts power ''greater than the official ecclesiastical authority of the Episcopalian or Methodist bishop, or the Presbyterian moderator.''[42] Since congregationally structured denominations have extremely loose definitions of power, their executive staffs have ''the freedom to initiate new programs, while executive staffs in episcopal and presbyterian denominations are restricted by the closer constitutional definitions of positional powers. On the other hand, the singular ideological emphasis on local church autonomy and correspondingly pervasive deficiencies of definitions regarding supralocal church structures in congregational denominations allow organization interests to take their 'natural' course—centralization.''[43]

Even denominations with an ideological opposition to ''ecclesiasticism,'' such as the Disciples of Christ, were forced to a gradual modification of a position that ''recognized no structures between God and man to one that now views the constituent parts of the denomination (at whatever level) as authoritative parts of the whole church.'' The mission of the church was correspondingly expanded. ''While the early Disciples were one of the strongest conversionist, evangelical groups on the American frontier, they have today developed a great interest in ecumenism and social action. Disciples are today involved in numerous programs not only of a social 'welfare' but also of a social 'reform' nature.'' Some Disciples, to be sure, resisted any bureaucratization. The introduction of the convention and autonomous agency led ultimately to the schism of the Churches of Christ in 1906. The increasing centralization and social action caused a second major split in the 1950's.[44]

The American Baptists, though committed to congregational independence, formed associations of local congregations for purposes of ''guidance and mutual edification'' and eventually a national convention. The

---

[41]Ibid., p. 434.

[42]Paul M. Harrison, *Authority and Power in the Free Church Tradition: a Social Case Study of the American Baptist Convention* (Princeton, NJ: Princeton University Press, 1959), p. 92. All subsequent authors in the field refer to Harrison's work as monumental.

[43]Takayama, p. 330. See John Niles Bartholomew, ''A Sociological View of Authority in Religious Organizations,'' *Review of Religious Research* 23 (1981–1982) 118–132; James G. Hougland and James R. Wood, ''Determinants of Organizational Control in Local Churches,'' *Journal for the Scientific Study of Religion* 18 (1979) 132–145; Randolph L. Cantrell, James F. Krile, George A. Donohue, ''Parish Autonomy: Measuring Denominational Differences,'' *Journal for the Scientific Study of Religion* 22 (1983) 276–285.

[44]Burkart, p. 55.

agencies created to carry on denominational life initially carried on an autonomous existence but from 1910–1950 fell under the close supervision of the convention which approved budgets and sought coordination. Finally in 1973 the American Baptist Convention renamed the agencies as "divisions" of the convention structure. Vertical structural integration was also achieved with the national, state and local conventions. The development of a national structure meant abandonment of the old local autonomy and the fierce opposition to any interference between the individual and his God. The bureaucratization "has placed strain upon their authority principle, and today American Baptists are compelled to recognize the authority of the national convention. The former legitimizing principle has been modified to recognize the authority of the church as a whole." Again, the adoption of greater organization and social involvement produced a number of schisms.[45]

According to Lutheran theology the organizational form of the church is an adiaphoron, that is, a matter of indifference, neither prescribed nor forbidden in Scripture. Hence church structures here in America, freed from European nationalism, "could develop largely out of expediency, not from ideological dictates." On the premise that "Christ committed the ministry of the means of grace to the congregations collectively, Lutheran bodies generally accept the belief in their own collective authority and power to dispense such grace. Thus the *local congregation* is viewed as *only one manifestation* of the larger church."[46]

It is difficult to speak in general terms about the Lutherans in this country, since they stemmed from different language and cultural groups and arrived at different times. Prior to 1820 there were several Lutheran synods or regional units. After a series of mergers over the next century, the American Lutheran Church was formed in 1960 and the Lutheran Church in America in 1962. They differ "primarily in the extent of vertical integration. The ALC conceives of its constituent synods ('districts') as administrative branches, whereas the LCA allows these synods more autonomy." The two churches have agreed to unite by 1986, but as of this writing the Commission for a New Lutheran Church had not yet accepted a design; the degree of centralization was still an issue.[47]

[45]Ibid., pp. 57–58.

[46]Ibid., p. 63. See Jaroslav Pelikan, *Obedient Rebels: Catholic Substance and Protestant Principle in Luther's Reformation* (New York: Harper and Row, 1964); idem, *Spirit Versus Structure* (New York: Harper and Row, 1968).

[47]Arland J. Hultgren, "Merger Watch: Toward a New Church Design," *Dialog* 23 (1984) 114–117.

The Episcopal Church also moved to centralize its operations in the interest of efficiency. A Committee on Missionary Organization and Administration sought to unify the three major boards of the church: missions, religious education, and social service. As early as 1913 it was proposed to bring all general administration of the church under the presiding bishop and a council of advisors. This body would act as the "permanent executive of the General Convention between its sessions" and present plans and budgets to the convention. Not until 1919, however, were the boards actually united under the presiding bishop and a council, soon known as the National Council. The entire church was soon restructured along analogous lines: the bishop and executive council at the diocesan level, and the rector and council at the parish level.[48]

Patterns of Governance Structures

The mainline denominations generally have a three-level administration. The national directorate in addition to establishing theological or philosophical policy, develops program resource material, especially curricula for use in the congregations. Supported by the parishes, it also sponsors home and foreign mission programs. "The denomination ensures that clergy, staff, and laity of its congregations have opportunities for training, provides informational convocations, and maintains internal communications. It oversees seminaries, sustains publishing ventures, and supports experimental mission projects. This level sets the tone for the congregations throughout the land."[49]

The regional or judicatory level, which resembles a Catholic diocese, is an "intermediary between national denominational office and local congregations." Its function is to inform the national office of local needs and refer back the programs formulated. It administers such auxiliary services as colleges, seminaries, homes for the aged, and similar institutions. "This level is charged with ministerial recruitment and certification, as well as raising the money for the pension plans (in certain denominations) under which clergy may retire."[50] It also assists the congregations with subsidies, personnel and other resources in times of need. The regional office is organized around program areas and operates within established general goals.

[48]Primer, p. 141.

[49]Douglas W. Johnson, "Program Dissensus between Denomination Grass Roots and Leadership and Its Consequences," in *American Denominational Organization: a Sociological View*, p. 331.

[50]Ibid., p. 332.

The congregational level serves the laity through the sacraments and religious instruction, as well as stimulates interest in the missions. It supports the other two levels and implements the programs they devise. If, however, the congregations perceive that their needs are not being met, they may withhold their contributions. "The denomination as a system is closely interrelated, but it is by no means hierarchical. It is based on the *authority of persuasion* that comes as a result of meeting program needs."[51]

Congregational Polity

At all levels in the Protestant churches the laity have a decisive voice. Their authority is most obvious in a congregational polity which recognizes no jurisdiction beyond the local assembly. The Baptists even refrain from identifying the denominational body as a "church" but speak only of Shiloh Baptist Church or the First Baptist Church of such-and-such a place. A newly baptized person does not become a member of the denomination but of a particular congregation.[52] In 1963 the Southern Baptist Convention approved a "Statement of the Baptist Faith and Message" which describes the congregation as "operating through democratic processes." It is maintained, based on the sixth chapter of the Acts of the Apostles, that the Lord's will is discovered more readily when responsibility is placed in the entire community rather than in the hands of a few. This conviction is held so firmly that, except in a very few instances where congregations have specified a voting age, even children are entitled to vote. "This does not mean, of course, that every decision in and for the church must be settled by vote of the congregation. Responsibility naturally and necessarily is delegated, to the minister, to church staff, to committees, or to deacons. It does mean, however, that the entire congregation claims the responsibility for delegating powers, and that any matter could, in practice, be called up specifically for congregational vote."[53]

The Baptist statement recognizes that its "Scriptural officers" are pastors and deacons (Phil. 1:1). The distinction between laity and clergy is inappropriate in the Baptist understanding of ministry. The members of a congregation vote on a candidate for pastor who will lead in public

[51]Ibid., p. 333. Also see Harlan P. Douglass and Edmund de S. Brunner, *The Protestant Church as a Social Institution* (New York: Russell and Russell, 1935, reissued 1972), esp. Chap. V, "Church Organization and Life," pp. 82–103.

[52]John E. Steely, "Christ and Ministry in Baptist Perspective," *One in Christ* 127 (1981) 238.

[53]Ibid., p. 239.

worship, preach, and shepherd the flock. Deacons are chosen, usually for a specified term, to perform a variety of services, especially parish visitations. In some cases they serve as an executive board, in others as an advisory council to the pastor.[54]

Since the Church connotes mission, Baptists have found it necessary to establish structures that extend beyond the local congregation. Churches are joined in associations, local, state and national. The representative principle holds throughout. ''Messengers'' are sent to participate in conventions which receive reports and make recommendations but which have no authority to enforce decisions.[55]

Presbyterian Polity

The Presbyterian model of church government provides for equal participation of clergy and laity. The 1968 *Book of Order of the United Presbyterian Church in the U.S.A.* provides ''Ruling elders, the immediate representatives of the people, are chosen by them, that, in association with the pastors or ministers, they may exercise government and discipline, and take the oversight of the spiritual interests of the particular church, and also of the Church generally, when called thereunto'' (39.04).[56] It was an American innovation due to the rapid expansion of lay activity in the nineteenth century that they were ordained. One of the visible differences distinguishing the sectional churches was the role of the ruling elders in the ordination of ministers, the North rejecting and the South approving.[57] The reunited Presbyterian Church (U.S.A.) approved in 1983 the statement that ''ordained officers differ from other members in function only.''[58] Henceforth there are two kinds of presbyters: ministers of the Word and elders. (The proposal to change the title of minister to ''continuing members of presbytery'' was not accepted.[59])

All members of a local congregation in good and regular standing are entitled to vote in the election of ruling elders, who serve for a three-year

[54]Ibid., p. 242.

[55]Ibid., p. 241.

[56]*The Constitution of the Untied Presbyterian Church in the U.S.A.: Furt II Book of Order* (Philadelphia: Office of the General Assembly of the United Presbyterian Church in the U.S.A., 1968).

[57]Lefferts A. Loetscher, *A Brief History of the Presbyterians*, With a New Chapter by George Laird Hunt, 4th ed. (Philadelphia: Westminster Press, 1983), p. 107.

[58]Ibid., p. 195.

[59]Ibid., p. 168.

term which may be renewed once. The congregation also votes on the call of a pastor or associate pastor (50.01). The pastor or co-pastors of a parish church together with the elected elders in active service constitute the session. Administrative authority is vested in the session and not in the whole congregation.

The churches of a given area, at least twelve in number, are joined in a presbytery. A presbytery consists of all the ministers and at least one ruling elder from each church. "Every congregation . . . has a right to be represented by ruling elders in number equal to the total number of its installed pastors, associate pastors and assistant pastors" (42.03). The presbytery is directly responsible for the admission, training and ordination of ministerial candidates. It confirms a "call" to a specific pastorate. In general, the presbytery oversees the discipline of its constituent congregations. If the session of one of the congregations is "unable or unwilling to manage wisely the affairs of its church, the presbyters may appoint a commission composed of ministers and ruling elders, with the full power of a session" (41.15). Ruling elders "sit and vote with the same authority as do ministers of the Word" (39.02). They may also be elected to any office, even to that of stated clerk, the chief administrator of the presbytery. Among its responsibilities, "every presbytery is to establish its own procedures for collaborating and counselling with its pastors in each marriage involving divorced persons" (42.08).

Just as a presbytery consists of the ministers and ruling elders within a district, so neighboring presbyteries, at least three in number, constitute a synod which is to meet annually (43.01). The synod serves as a court of appeal from decisions of the presbytery. It acts as intermediary between the general assembly and the presbyteries. The general assembly, the highest representative body and judicial authority in matters of doctrine and discipline, is composed of equal numbers of ministerial and elder commissioners. They are elected by the presbyteries in proportion to church membership.[60]

Episcopal Polity

The Episcopal Church, though hierarchical in constitution, accords the laity a significant share in government. The parish is organized with a rector, wardens and vestrymen who are elected to office. The vestry members are the trustees of the religious corporation. They are the "agents and legal

---

[60]Robert McAfee Brown, *The Presbyterians* (Glen Rock, NJ: Paulist Press, 1966), p. 9.

representatives of the Parish in property matters and in relations of the parish to the clergy."[61] The national canons do not determine the number, qualifications, specific duties or mode of election of the vestrymen. It is left to the dioceses to draw up specific regulations. The vestry nominates the rector of a parish, while the bishop gives his "license and authority to perform the office of a priest" in a parish of his diocese. It seems, however, that the bishop has little power beyond that of persuasion to block the call of a person whom he disapproves.[62] Since by common law of the church the pastoral relation is permanent, the vestry may not terminate it unilaterally or force a rector's resignation by reducing his salary or denying him access to the property. The rector in turn is not to resign arbitrarily. In case of serious differences between the rector and the vestry the bishop with the advice of the standing committee renders judgment.[63]

Each diocese has its convention which acts as a legislative body. All clergy of the diocese belong as voting members. Parishes and missions are represented by lay delegates; in some dioceses representation is in proportion to the membership of the various parishes. Important matters may require a "vote by orders"; that is, the clergy and laity vote separately with the concurrence of both necessary for a measure to pass. The convention elects the diocesan bishop who must ultimately be approved by a majority of bishops having jurisdiction in the United States.[64]

The diocesan convention selects clerical and lay delegates to the General Convention which meets every three years or on call. The convention is bicameral, as is the United States Congress, consisting of a House of Bishops and a House of Deputies. The president and vice president of the House of Deputies are elected by membership of that body and must be of different orders (one clerical, the other lay). Each house can initiate legislation but both must approve before it is adopted.[65]

CONCLUSIONS

The tension in the Church of being in the world but not of the world leads to what has been called by Robert Lee of Union Theological Seminary the "organizational dilemma":

[61]Daniel B. Stevick, *Canon Law: a Handbook* (New York: Seabury Press, 1965), p. 143.
[62]Ibid., p. 193.
[63]Ibid., p. 191.
[64]Ibid., pp. 201–203, 185.
[65]Ibid., p. 125–128.

on the one hand, if the church is to take seriously its obligation as
a missionary and witnessing movement, it must maintain some
semblance of continuity, stability, and persistence; it must develop appropriate organizational and institutional forms. Yet, on
the other hand, the very institutional embodiments necessary for
the survival of the church may threaten, obscure, distort, or
deflect from the purposes for which the institution was originally
founded. Thus it is hardly sufficient to say that the task of the
church is to be obedient or to be faithful if obedience and
faithfulness are detached from the question of institutional self-
maintenance.[66]

The Church necessarily exists "in a particular social context and
interacts with its surrounding culture." The danger is that the "goals
which the organization was created to achieve tend to be displaced by the
goal of organizational self-perpetuation."[67] "The search for that theoretical point which will allow the church to remain true to its purposes and yet
operate through viable institutional forms that will preserve its gains and
extend its influence must be an ongoing, neverending quest. Although
there can be no simple resolution of the dilemma, it may become easily
obscured, or perhaps, misunderstood, so that equally truncated views are
adopted—views which interpret the church only as an organization or as a
spiritual entity devoid of organization."[68]

One sociological study of such denominations as the Disciples of Christ,
the Assemblies of God, the Lutheran Church in America, and the United
Methodist Church concludes:

Our case histories would tend to warrant the original, theoretical
assumption that religious ideology (purpose) and religious organization (praxis) stand *in a dialectical relation* to one another.
Ideology functions to create an image for the denomination to
develop within, but religious ideologies are nurtured, changed, or
ignored in light of environmental and organizational influences.
Thus, we see the wisdom of much religious thought and the
insight of Max Weber that religion and the world stand in a

[66]Robert Lee, "The Organizational Dilemma in American Protestantism," *Ethics and
Bigness, Scientific, Academic, Religious, Political, and Military*, ed. Harlan Cleveland and
Harold D. Lasswell (New York: Conference on Science, Philosophy and Religion in Their
Relation to the Democratic Way of Life, Inc., 1962), pp. 187–188.
[67]Harrison, p. 136.
[68]Lee, p. 192.

relationship of *tension* one with another. If religion remains at the ideological level alone, it is ineffective in reaching its purpose; on the other hand, if religion becomes too involved in the world, it may lose its purpose or meaning for existence.[69]

Our survey has shown how even the most anti-institutional charismatics of Protestantism were forced to accept greater or lesser organizational forms in order to survive and expand. It is not surprising that for their organizational model Protestants turned to the thriving world of business with consequences both beneficial and deleterious. Phenomenal growth was achieved sometimes at the expense of the spiritual image.

Abhoring crass commercialism, Catholics can well learn from the Protestant experience. Up until recently our growth has been achieved largely through a favorable birth rate and immigration. We have not had to be aggressively evangelistic. Today, however, it is estimated that there are at least 15 million inactive, baptized Catholics; 26% of all baptized Catholics over the age of 18 do not practice their faith.[70] Almost 40% of young Catholics between the ages of 15 and 29 leave the Church for a period of two years or more.[71] With the decline of our parochial school system we cannot face the future with equanimity. Protestants have much to teach us about the techniques of attracting people to their churches. Take such an elementary tool as advertising. Almost invariably their churches have a tasteful sign outside indicating the hours of service, and notices of their activities appear in the local papers. By contrast our parishes make little effort to communicate with the immediate neighborhood. Diocesan offices of evangelization could well concentrate on simple techniques for making the Catholic presence known and accessible as they strive to implement the mission thrust of the Church.

With the retrenchment of Catholic schools it is imperative that we find more effective ways of holding on to our youth. According to the conservative figures of *The Official Catholic Directory* there were 1.4 million less public and parochial students under instruction in 1985 than there were in 1975. All too often our C.C.D. and C.Y.O. programs are haphazard and ineffective. Protestants who rely almost exclusively on the

[69]Burkart, p. 68.

[70]Alvin Illig, *Another Look: A National Ministry for the Inactive Catholic* (Washington, DC: Paulist Fathers' National Catholic Evangelization Association, 1983), p. 1, citing the Gallup Study of the Unchurched American.

[71]Dean R. Hoge, *Converts, Dropouts, Returnees: a Study of Religious Change among Catholics* (New York: Pilgrim Press, 1981), p. 10.

Sunday School for imparting religious instruction have a long tradition upon which we can draw. From the early 19th century they have accorded it a top priority while our dioceses for the most part have not exerted strong leadership in the field.

Protestants also have a history of working with structures which are rather new to us. Almost every congregation has the equivalent of a parish council with real authority. In the course of two centuries the various denominations have developed procedures for the nomination and election of officers, the transaction of business, and continuity of operation. Business affairs in particular have been carefully regulated, a resource for us as we set up the financial council mandated by canon 537 of the 1983 code. District and regional representative assemblies have been characteristic of Protestantism from the beginning. We may well study their development and profit from their wisdom as we organize our diocesan pastoral councils in accord with canons 511–514.[72]

Diocesan pastoral councils do bring representatives of parishes together, but more often than not embrace a broad geographic area. Some Protestant denominations have an intermediary structure at the district level, comparable to our deaneries which help bring congregations together on a more intimate or familiar pattern. "It is evident that, at the level of experience, most people live out their faith as members of the body of Christ in their parish. On a week-to-week, year-to-year basis, the parish inevitably dominates their consciousness of the church as a tangible reality."[73] Since, however, the local parish is not "complete in itself as a model of the church," there must be specific ways in which its relation to the other parishes finds expression. "It is dangerous to take the local congregation as the norm for the local church. A parish in a given area, allowing for obvious exceptions, can quite easily reflect a rather homogeneous gathering of people, a group drawn principally from one ethnic or social group."[74] Ways must be found to lift the vision of a parish beyond its parochial boundaries. The 1983 code in canons 553–555 does provide a structure in which neighboring parishes within the diocese are grouped together, the vicariate forane or deanery. While these canons are concerned almost exclusively with the supervision and care of the clergy, there is no

---

[72]Oakland, California became the 57th out of 172 US dioceses to institute a diocesan pastoral council as reported in *Crux* November 5, 1984.

[73]Louis Weil, "Anglican Understanding of the Local Church (with special reference to the Book of Common Prayer 1979)," *Anglican Theological Review* 64 (1982) 197.

[74]Ibid., p. 199.

reason why the deanery could not facilitate contacts and relationships among the parishes as is done in other churches.

Other procedures set up by certain denominations may be of interest to us in the face of common contemporary problems. The Presbyterians, for instance, provide for pastoral collaboration and counsel in each marriage involving divorced persons.[75] In view of the large number of annulments today it may be that for the good of the individuals concerned as well as of the community, we should institute some review of prospective remarriages. Again, the Presbyterians have made provision for a series of administrative appeals. Though, for us, appelate recourse under canons 1732–1739 is rather restricted, hope has not been abandoned that the value of the American experience will eventually be recognized.

Above all, Protestants have much to teach us about lay participation in the government of the Church. Because of our theological commitment to the hierarchical principle we cannot simply borrow wholesale from non-Catholic churches but we have no alternative to getting the laity more involved. For all too long Catholics have been content with a clerical monopoly on leadership. Now a variety of circumstances have made it impossible for the ordained ministry to fulfill all the responsibilities traditionally assigned them. The practice of centuries, however, is not easily reversed. Except for fund raising our people have been generally lethargic in contributing to the work of the Church.

Protestants, on the other hand, have been amazingly successful in stimulating the laity and giving them a meaningful role in ecclesial affairs. In many instances it seems that congregations have more of a stake in the successful operation of the church than do the professionals. Clergy come and go but the people often have roots in a parish or an area that go back for generations. We Catholics need to find structures that will energize and give legitimate expression to this attachment.

The 1982 Lima statement of the World Council of Church's Faith and Order Commission (in which the Catholic Church is an active participant) on "Baptism, Eucharist and Ministry" offers three considerations for the exercise of the ordained ministry in the Church. It should be exercised in a personal, collegial, and communal way.

> It should be *personal* because the presence of Christ among his people can most effectively be pointed to by the person ordained

---

[75]"Every presbytery shall establish its own procedure for collaborating and counselling with its pastors in each marriage involving divorced persons." *The Constitutions of the United Presbyterian Church in the U.S.A.*, no. 42.08.

to proclaim the Gospel and to call the community to serve the Lord in unity of life and witness. It should also be *collegial*, for there is need for a college of ordained ministers sharing in the common task of representing the concerns of the community. Finally, the intimate relationship between the ordained ministry and the community should find expression in a *communal* dimension where the exercise of the ordained ministry is rooted in the life of the community and requires the community's effective participation in the discovery of God's will and the guidance of the Spirit.[76]

The Lima statement follows through on a recommendation made by the First World Conference on Faith and Order at Lausanne in 1927, namely:

> In view of (i) the place which the episcopate, the council of presbyters and the congregation of the faithful, respectively, had in the constitution of the early Church, and (ii) the place which the episcopal, presbyteral and congregational systems of government are each today, and have been for centuries, accepted by great communions in Christendom, and (iii) the fact that episcopal, presbyteral and congregational systems are each believed by many to be essential to the good order of the Church, we therefore recognize that these several elements must all, under conditions which require further study, have an appropriate place in the order of life of a reunited Church . . . . [77]

The Vatican II *Decree on Ecumenism* counselled that "Catholics must gladly acknowledge and esteem the truly Christian endowments from our common heritage which are to be found among our separated brethren." The decree went on to say, "Nor should we forget that anything wrought by the grace of the Holy Spirit in the hearts of our separated brethren can contribute to our own edification. Whatever is truly Christian is never contrary to what genuinely belongs to the faith . . . " (no. 4). We turn, therefore, to our separated brethren not only out of pragmatic motives to improve our organizational techniques but in faithfulness to the spirit of ecumenism, to appreciate their contribution in building up the Body of Christ.

---

[76]*One in Christ* 18 (1982) 375–376.

[77]*A Documentary History of the Faith and Order Movement 1927–1963*, ed. Lukas Vischer (St. Louis: Bethany Press, 1963), p. 35, no. 39.

POWER AND AUTHORITY IN THE CHURCH

Agnes Cunningham, S.S.C.M.

"Power" and "authority" are two words which carry with them many levels of significance. Any attempt to bring them together can lead, on the one hand, to identification, ambiguity or confusion; on the other, to distinction, opposition or tension. Initially the reason for this is rooted in our experience. We are familiar with formal and informal power in every human society. We are aware of the fact that power can be absolute, corrupt or tyrannical, at one end of the scale; lame, seductive or simply ineffective, at the other. Power can be acknowledged or challenged. It can be resisted or acclaimed.

In a similar way, experience has influenced our assessment and perception of authority. We associate it with office and mandate, with duties and honors. We have found it to be competitive as well as conciliatory. It can be flaunted or betrayed. Authority can be a burden, but it can also assure status and privilege.

Further reflection on our experience teaches us that our understanding of power and authority is based, more often than not, on two presuppositions. In the first place, we confuse power with its use or abuse and authority with its exercise or manipulation. In the second place, we tend at times to resent persons whose authority legitimizes their power in our regard and to be, perhaps unreasonably, captivated by those to whom authority is ascribed because of their display of native power in art or science, sports or entertainment, scholarship or one of the professions, business or communications.

In this paper, I propose to examine the concepts of *power* and *authority* as they are found *in the Church*. I shall begin with a review of the evolution of the words themselves, as that development preceded and then became part of the Judaeo-Christian tradition. Next, I shall investigate the foundations of the use of power and the exercise of authority in the Church. Then, I shall discuss Christian power and authority as their relationship was gradually modified by the various influences which resulted from contextualization of a Church conditioned and challenged, temporally, geographically and culturally. Finally, I shall attempt to suggest theolog-

80

ical and pastoral implications which derive from this paper for diocesan governance today.

Power and Authority: Linguistic Dimensions[1]

The Indo-European roots of "power" (*poti-*, *pot-*) refer to the leader of a group. This leader can be a master or mistress, a spouse, even a despot. The range of meanings from Sanskrit to modern English touches every nuance and shade associated with the idea of a powerful person or with the quality considered in itself. Actually, to speak of power as a quality is inexact. It is defined, rather, as an ability, a capacity, a faculty, or an aptitude. It is associated directly with effective action.

In classical Greek, for example in Homer, power (*dynamis*) signified first of all bodily strength. A secondary meaning ascribed to the word referred to outward influence or authority. In the third place, power was equated with force for war. Later, under the influence of philosophic thought, *dynamis* was understood as the power of a natural faculty or capacity which might be put to good or evil purposes. In time, "power" was applied to every domain: speech, *flora*, money, medicine, mathematics. What remained constant was the perception that any such *power* was a *natural* capacity or faculty, proper to the person exercising it.

A similar development applies to authority, although this word has its own history. "Authority" seems to have come into the English language from Latin, through French. The Indo-European root underlying it, however, conveys the notion of fostering growth (*aug-*). It is further related to favorable omens, harvesting, and in one extension, sale to the highest bidder! We have come to know the word, linguistically, as "the right and power to command, enforce laws, exact obedience, determine or judge." It also signifies a person or group invested with such power.

Proper to the meaning of *authority* is the notion of the actual possession or use of a "power" to be exercised on the basis of a moral or legal right. There is, furthermore, a specified domain within which such authority is exercised. The person in authority always knows to whom or to what principle appeal is to be made in support of the authoritative word spoken and in defense of an authoritative action taken. Authority belongs to one who is master, to one who holds dominion.

---

[1] The following references will be helpful to anyone choosing to pursue this linguistic discussion: Vigouroux, *Dictionnaire de la Bible*, Vols. 1–5 (1895–1912); Liddell and Scott *Greek-English Lexicon*.

How do these concepts relate to the Scriptural understanding of power and authority? Actually, if we examine the Old Testament, we find that the translators of the Septuagint employed *dynamis* to express at least twenty-six separate Hebrew words and phrases. Thus, *dynamis* signifies the powers of nature,[2] human labor and industry.[3] It can mean human free will, as in Genesis 1:26, or political and military power. In its spiritual connotations, power in the Old Testament refers particularly to God, although it is also applied to the spirit world: good or evil spirits, dragons, or even Satan. On the whole, however, power throughout the Old Testament is an affirmation of divine power manifested in creation and in historical events.

The Hebrew language contains no word that expresses the abstract notion of authority. In this case, as with *power*, the translators of the Septuagint settled on one word, *exousia*, to convey the ideas expressed in a number of Hebrew words. Nonetheless, throughout the Old Testament the authoritative manifestation of divine power is affirmed in creation and in historical events. Although authority in the Old Testament appears as multiform, it is taken for granted that "all authority comes from God." It is, therefore, to be subordinated to the divine will. It is never absolute. The people of God are entrusted with the authority that belongs to God's agents. They exercise the authority of messengers mandated with a mission.

When we turn to the New Testament, we note a striking absence of the vocabulary which means power or authority in classical Greek. *Dynamis* and *exousia* seem to be the words through which we can arrive at the way in which Jesus and the Apostles understood power and authority. This understanding carries some dimensions of the Old Testament connotations of these words. Thus, the notions of power expressed in the Vulgate translation of the Old Testament[4] are reflected in the New Testament as well.[5] Also, "power" in the New Testament refers commonly to the realm of angels or demons.[6]

However, in the New Testament, we find meanings that are attached directly to the person of Jesus Christ. Thus, there is "power" manifested in the miracles of the Lord.[7] Jesus communicates to Peter the "power of

---

[2] Cf. Exodus 20:5–6.

[3] Cf. Kings 5:13–18; 9;15–22.

[4] Cf. Deut. 4:43 (*in virtute sua*); II Sam. 22:33 (*potentia*); Ps. 65(66):7 (*in virtute sua*).

[5] Cf. Mt. 9:6 (*potestatem*); Mt. 28:18 (*potestas*); Phil. 3:10 (*virtutem*).

[6] Cf. Eph. 1:21; 3:10; 6:12; Col. 1:16; 2:10, 15; I Peter 3:22.

[7] Cf. Mt. 7:22; Lk. 10:13; Mk. 14:62.

the keys'' and to all the apostles the "power to bind and to loose." Jesus also gives his followers his own authority to forgive sins,[8] to cure diseases,[9] to expel demons,[10] and to proclaim the coming of the Kingdom.[11] This sharing of authority is possible because of the new disclosure of authority in the unique experience of the Lord, as he forgave sins, expelled demons, and won for God dominion over Satan and his authority over the earth.[12] Any exploration of or reflection on power and authority in the Church must begin with Jesus Christ. It is in him—his person, his life, his mission and ministry—that the foundations of the use of power and the exercise of authority in the Church are to be discerned.

Power and Authority in the Church: Foundations

A number of unique realities led to the fashioning in Christian antiquity of "the abiding presuppositions of the whole succeeding development of office in the Church and of its spiritual authority."[13] First among these unique realities is the person of Jesus Christ. In Jesus, power (*dynamis*) and authority (*exousia*) are united in a once-for-all, never to be repeated manner. Commission and office are found together in his person. He himself, and his decisions provide the support, the argument—we might say the rationale—for the words with which he preached and taught "as one having authority"[14] and for the miracles and "deeds of power"[15] he performed. He had no need to invoke validation of his authority or to explain the source of his power.[16] The mystery of the person of Jesus becomes the foundation for the discontinuity that necessarily exists between him and every Christian leader who comes after him. This same mystery, however, assures the continuity that binds the leadership exercised in subsequent stages of the community's life to the Lordship of Christ.

In tracing the development of power and authority in the Church, from Jesus and the Apostles to later understandings of church order and

---

[8] Cf. Mt. 16:19; 18:10; Jn. 10:23.

[9] Cf. Lk. 9:1.

[10] Cf. Mk. 6:7.

[11] Cf. Mt. 10:7–8.

[12] Cf. Mt. 28:18; Lk. 4:1–13 (esp. v.6); Jn. 1:12, 10, 18; 17:2; 19:10–11; 1 Jn. 5:19.

[13] Hans von Campenhausen, *Ecclesiastical Authority and Spiritual Power in the Church of the First Three Centuries*, trans. J.A. Baker (London: Adam & Charles Black, 1969).

[14] Mk. 1:22.

[15] Cf. Mk. 5:30; 6:56.

[16] Cf. Mk. 11:33; 2:9–11.

ecclesiastical office, it is important to take into account the claim of von Campenhausen: there seem to have been no significant changes in understanding the doctrine of office and the meaning of ecclesiastical authority between the end of the third century and the age of Scholasticism.[17] Whether or not this thesis can be verified is a question that lies beyond the scope and focus of this paper. Nonetheless, the importance of examining the foundations of power and authority in light of the experience of biblical and early patristic evidences cannot be underestimated. The first three centuries of the Christian era are marked by a combination of factors that are not to be found in quite the same way in any succeeding era of church history: great diversity in the area of ecclesial office, the clear but gradual emergence of a pattern of ecclesiastical organization, the eventual acceptance of a prevailing mode of church governance. This evolution involved succeeding generations of ministers in the Christian community and the impact of both internal and external influences on modes of church governance.

It is not possible to repeat here the complexities attached to the signification of the word "apostle" as that discussion has been elaborated by Scripture scholars.[18] Several affirmations, however, can be made regarding the power and authority exercised in the Apostolic Age and the role in that exercise of those who were called "apostles." In the first place, the apostles were vested with the power and dignity of the Lord. Second, their authority rested on a direct call by the risen Lord who commissioned them to go into the whole world to teach, to baptize, and to make disciples of all nations. Third, the teaching and the signs of Christ were continued in the word and the work of the apostles. They "are clothed with power from on high" to do the works that Jesus did.[19] Finally they, too, represent a unique, once-for-all leadership in the Church. Their rank and authority are restricted to the apostolic generation. It cannot be continued or renewed after that age has come to an end.

A paradox of discontinuity and continuity marked the power and authority which Jesus possessed in his own person and that which the apostles received in his name. The experience of Jesus occurred in a once-for-all given moment in human history. At the same time, the Lord chose to share his authority with the apostles, so that they might continue

---

[17] von Campenhausen, p. 293.

[18] This question has been thoroughly discussed by leading Scripture scholars in recent years. Cf., e.g., *Peter in the New Testament*, ed. Raymond E. Brown, Karl P. Donfield, John Reumann (Minneapolis: Augsburg Publishing House; New York: Paulist Press, 1973).

[19] Lk. 24:49; cf. also Jn. 14:12.

to exercise the works of power which characterized his mission. At this point it is important to recall the fact that all the apostles were gifted in this way by the Lord. The integrity of each apostolic tradition was affirmed by both Polycarp of Smyrna and Irenaeus of Lyons against the claims of Victor I and Anicetus.[20] The primacy accorded to the church of Rome was not, initially, unrelated to the fact that *two* apostles had founded that church and had both been martyred in that city.

Indeed, as we consider the whole company of the apostles, two individuals stand apart by reason of the specific nature of their role. To Peter and later to Paul, the risen Lord gave a particular mandate and the power to carry out this charge. Peter emerges as an outstanding, decisive figure in primitive Christianity, although he has left us no indications of the way in which he understood his authority. Paul, on the contrary, tells us openly that both his call to apostleship and his authority come directly from Christ and "not from men nor through man" (Gal. 1:1). Therefore, he insists, his authority is independent of and beyond human control. Paul's efforts to win the recognition and support of the saints in Jerusalem (cf. Acts 9:26–27) and equal status with them derived from his conviction that he, too, was an apostle—as fully as Cephas, James, or the others (II Cor. 12:11–12).

The pattern of continuity-discontinuity in the transmission of authority and power from Jesus to the apostles can be found again as the apostles prepared or chose leaders to succeed them in the governance of the early Christian communities. At this point we become aware of the diversity and hierarchy of ministries that existed in the Church (cf. I Cor. 12; Romans 12; Eph. 4:7–11). The earliest ministers seem to have been the *presbyteroi*, a term which originally meant one who was superior by reason of age: an elder. The "elder" was older, hence by implication, presumably wiser. The council of elders (*presbyterion*) fulfilled an important role in the community. Elders were known to Peter, James, and Luke; they are mentioned in Acts and Revelation. The role of the elders in the community, at times, was one of authority in the exercise of office. At other times, they were rather the fathers of the community, exerting a spiritual or moral power. They were the leaders chosen to preserve and transmit the Tradition received from Jesus through the apostles. They were the shepherds who were to tend God's flock. The need for a new authority to "preside in

---

[20] The question in each instance concerned the date of the celebration of Easter in the Quartodeciman controversy, settled finally at Nicaea in A.D. 325.

love'' as numbers increased, as heresies surfaced, as enthusiasm waned, was met by the system of elders.

The term *presbyter* also referred to that elder who was chosen or delegated to be the *overseer* of the community. In this capacity the title *presbyteros* was used interchangeably with *episkopos*. With the development of the role of the deacon and the clarification of the ministry of the bishop, the presbyter emerged as a distinct member of the tripartite hierarchy known to both Clement of Rome and Ignatius of Antioch. Treatises from Gregory of Nazianzus, John Chrysostom and Theodore of Mopsuestia helped to further an understanding of the ministry of the presbyter, whether he was ''bishop'' or not. Even though the terms were still used interchangeably by Gregory the Great, Leo the Great had earlier used the word ''presbyter'' in addressing letters to abbots.

With the increase of liturgical and catechetical needs in the Church, ministries and ministers continued to multiply: prophets and teachers; widows and virgins; confessors, martyrs, ascetics and, in time, what came to be known as the minor orders. Each one shared in the life of the Church through the exercise of an authority appropriate to a specific office. Clement of Rome described his understanding of church authority in writing to the Corinthians:

> Let us, then, brethren, do soldier's duty in downright earnest under the banner of his glorious commands. . . . Not all are prefects, or tribunes, or centurions, or lieutenants, and so on; but *each in his own rank* executes the orders of the emperor and the commanders.[21]

Congar, observing the same phenomenon, concludes that all ministries were included in the service known as *diakonia*: apostles, doctors, prophets, evangelists, teachers, pastors, bishops (supervisors), presbyters (elders, ancients), ministers, leaders, superintendents, presidents, stewards, administrators. All were forms of a service (*diakonia*) which transcended all of them together, while including each of them.[22]

As we try to discern the reasons for the diversity of ministries and of ministers in the early church, we begin to understand that both gifts and needs were the source of the multiplicity of services to be found in any one local ecclesial group and of the differences that could be discovered from

---

[21] *The First Epistle of Clement of Rome to the Corinthians* (I Clement), trans. James A. Kleist, Ancient Christian Writers, 1; 37, p. 32.

[22] Ian MacNeill, ''Attitudes to Authority in the Medieval Centuries,'' in *Problems of Authority*, ed. John M. Todd (Baltimore: Helicon Press, 1962), pp. 120–121.

one local church to another. The gifts, of course, were the charisms poured out by the Spirit upon church members. The needs fell into several categories. One of these is particularly significant for the question of authority and power: church order.

Deep divisions exist among ecclesiologists and other scholars because of the answer one or another of them might give to the question of the foundation of the Church by Jesus Christ. For a good number of them the tension lies in the relationship between charism and office in the Church. When an author draws a radical distinction between ecclesial office and the gifts of the Spirit, he will often also maintain the solely human origin of office, with no authority attributed to it for constitutive power in the life of the ecclesial community.[23] Actually, contemporary discussion among Scripture scholars seems to point to two facts: (1) there was more diversity in modes of church order, even in the New Testament, than has been previously thought; (2) there is more continuity of ecclesiastical structures and church order between the New Testament churches and later ecclesial groups.

In another context it would be profitable to study the diverse forms of church order that could be found in the Petrine, the Johannine, and the Pauline communities. It would, further, be highly instructive to compare and contrast the variety of church orders that Paul chose to determine for the churches he had brought to life through the gospel, according to each one's need. In some, charism prevailed; in others, office; in still others, a modified form with characteristics of both. The one characteristic that applied to all the churches was the diversity which prevailed in attempts to establish church order.

Power and Authority in the Church: Development

In the Pauline communities the Apostle himself set the basic parameters of the elements required so that the community might live in Christ as spiritual—that is, spirit-filled—women and men. In the face of human limitations and failings, of conflict with church structures and ecclesiastical authority, Paul continued to exhort and insist on the ideal of holiness to which all Christians are called and toward which all are enabled to strive through the gifts assured by the Spirit. Authority in the community was one of the gifts (*charismata*) given by the Spirit "for the common good" (I

---

[23] Cf. review by Hamilton Hess of von Campenhausen, *The Jurist* 30 (1970) 245. Cf. also the review by E.J. Yarnold, *New Blackfriars* 51 (1970) 157–158.

Cor. 12:7). Administration by those gifted with that ministry was complemented by other ministries exercised by all the members of the Lord's body, the Church. Obedience and love protect the office that exists because of the unity of those who are one in Christ.

Whatever one's view of the type of church order or the concept of office that existed in the churches of the New Testament, by the end of the first century of the Christian era there was a clearly developing church structure. In some instances groups of presbyters (elders) were responsible for the administration and pastoral care of a church.[24] Clement of Rome and Ignatius of Antioch both knew a tripartite hierarchy. In the case of Clement, who wrote according to the Judaic pattern, all members are involved in the life of the Church. His is a concept of shared governance:

> Special functions are assigned to the high priest; a special office
> is imposed upon the priests; and special ministrations fall to the
> Levites. The layman is bound by the rules laid down for the
> laity.[25]

For Ignatius, the bishop is to represent God the Father; the deacon exercises the ministry of Jesus Christ; the presbyters take the place of the council of the Apostles. The entire *ekklesia* is gathered in unity with the bishop around and through the Eucharist. The bishop and his people engage in reciprocal service as a Eucharistic community. The bishop emerges from the pen of Ignatius as someone who is to be reckoned with, only because he—the bishop—has to reckon with the community. He is further challenged by his own call to holiness and, above all, by God.

Throughout the subapostolic age there seems to be a constant effort to bring together what von Campenhausen calls the "pneumatic-charismatic" and the "official-sacramental" elements in church governance. Clement's insistence on the need for restoration of harmony and order in the Church at Corinth through reinstatement of the deposed leaders is presented as the consequence of the apostolic tradition and the apostles' provision for the exercise of authority in the Church. For Clement, finally, office belongs to the constitution of the Church. True spiritual power resides in such office. For Ignatius, office is subordinate to the unity of the Church. Indeed, for Ignatius, "there is nothing that can be called Church" without bishops, presbyters and deacons.[26] In Ignatius,

---

[24] Raymond E. Brown, *The Community of the Beloved Disciple* (New York/Ramsey: Paulist, 1982) p. 99.

[25] I Clement, p. 34.

[26] "Trallians," 3:1. *Letters of Ignatius of Antioch*, ACW 1, p. 76.

the pneumatic and the official are combined in his understanding of governance in the Church: spiritual power is the reality that invests and directs the exercise of authority.

The "freedom in Christ" insisted on by Paul as a fundamental principle for the exercise of authority in the churches which he founded was reflected in various ways in the development of church order in other ecclesial communities. Most frequently it was expressed in the desire and the effort to bring together the power of holiness with the authority of a recognized office in one and the same person. Thus we find the Church in *The Shepherd* of Hermas represented as a community of reconciliation. There, repentance and renewal are possible, even amid signs of contradiction between the holiness of an individual and the authority of the office he holds. Care was needed to provide leaders who would not be led astray by access to money, temporal influence, or the seduction of false teachings. Examples of presbyters who had been deposed because of failure to fulfill their responsibilities as "spiritual men" can be found in Hermas. The true shepherd is the one who could reach out to admonish and teach those who had fallen into heresy. As long as the erring called themselves Christian, there was an obligation on the part of the faithful to seek to correct their false ideas and call them back to the unity of the body of the Lord.

Two developments in the early patristic period influenced and supported the effort to maintain unity between power and authority in church governance. The first of these was the articulation of the *Apostolic Tradition*: the *tradito*, the *paradosis*. Although several early Christian writers can be credited with the development of this concept, it was really Irenaeus of Lyons, the "Father of Tradition," who contributed most fully to the understanding of Tradition as the hallmark and the touchstone of orthodoxy and orthopraxy. Irenaeus' well-known list of the bishops of Rome, which he set forth as an example of the "Tradition traditioned," became a powerful argument in favor of the choice of leaders, in every church, whose fidelity in teaching and witness allowed them to stand in the company of those who had been chosen from the beginning.

The second development had to do with the nature of *episkopē* in the Church, that is, the nature of the role of the bishop and the values that were highlighted in the various styles of leadership exercised by bishops in successive generations.

If we try to envision these values in concrete terms and specific motivating ideas, we can trace the development of ecclesiastical office along a challenging and dynamic trajectory, following a train of Christian heroes and theological intuitions.[27] From the Apostles whose authority came from the Lord and was expressed in the power of *diakonia*, we come to those men who were, at one and the same time, men of the Church, men of the Spirit, men of the Word. From the evidences we have it seems that they were all—each in his own manner—strong leaders, humble servants, devoted pastors. Styles of leadership differed from one to another of these early bishops. Each was convinced that his implementation of church order, in the exercise of an authority that was rooted in and accompanied by the power of the Spirit, was no new invention. With Irenaeus, each one could have claimed that he taught only what had come from the Apostles.[28]

Thus, Clement of Rome seems to have understood that his authority did not stand apart from that of the entire church of Rome. Ignatius of Antioch was a bishop who stood both over and at the heart of his community, looking to the deacons, above all, as his helpmates and assistants in the task of preserving the unity of the Church. Irenaeus celebrated a mode of church governance that was validated by its continuity with the "ancient and Apostolic Tradition." Cyprian of Carthage, in the midst of both doctrinal and disciplinary controversies that threatened the faith in North Africa, affirmed a doctrine of collegiality that allowed for individual autonomy and avoidance of embarrassing communion with even the bishop of Rome, according to personal bias or preference. However, it is not clear that spiritual power was required by Cyprian for the exercise of the authority which, he claimed, "resides uniquely with the bishops."[29]

As the third century drew to a close, the signs of a move toward some degree of centralization in church governance was reflected in manuals such as the *Didaché*, followed by later documents such as the *Didascalia Apostolorum*, the *Apostolic Constitutions*, and the *Apostolic Tradition* of Hippolytus.[30] However, the principle enunciated by Irenaeus still prevailed: unity of faith does not require uniformity of *praxis*. The great bishops were still men in whom spiritual power and the authority of office resided in harmony.

---

[27] Cf. Yves Congar, "The Historical Development of Authority in the Church: Points for Christian Reflection," in *Problems of Authority*, pp. 119–155.

[28] Cf. *Adversus haereses*, *passim*.

[29] Cf. von Campenhausen, pp. 265–292, 299. Cyprian's teaching is modified to some extent by his insistence on the bishop's need to be in unity with his people and with other bishops regarding true doctrine and *praxis*.

[30] John E. Lynch, "The History of Centralization: Papal Reservations," in *The Once and Future Church: A Communion of Freedom*, ed. James A. Coriden (New York: Alba House, 1971), pp. 57–109.

Another kind of authority was exercised by teachers like Tertullian, Clement of Alexandria and Origen, and the theological schools they represented. More than a century was to elapse before Nicaea would establish the metropolitanate, introduce the beginnings of the patriarchate system, and determine a uniform date for the celebration of Easter. Ecclesiastical authority could be described, on one hand, as diverse from place to place:

> In Rome the bishop is primarily the supreme cultic official of his congregation, in Syria he is its spiritual example and sacral force, in Asia Minor he is above all the ordained preacher of the apostolic teaching.[31]

On another, it represented, wherever it was exercised, an integration of several values:

> a strong insistence on authority, a very close link with the Christian community; a marked charismatic of spiritual character.[32]

The question of power and authority in the Church did not come to an end with the dawn of the fourth century. It had not developed through the early Christian ages in a vacuum, nor would it continue to do so. A number of influences, both secular and religious, came to bear on this issue as on every other faced by the Church in her history. In other words, the factor of contextualization is one that must be taken into account when considering the relationship between charism and office in the Church.

Power and Authority in the Church: Contextualization

Throughout the second century a number of questions and problems arose to challenge the young church. There were, of course, heterodox approaches to both doctrine and discipline, which called for clearer identification of those who remained faithful to the Catholic Christian tradition. It became increasingly necessary to acknowledge and deal with sins committed after baptism, even by those who remained faithful to that tradition. Tradition itself became a problem as efforts to distinguish the "true" from the "false" developed, particularly in the face of gnostic

---

[31] von Campenhausen, p. 120.
[32] Congar, p. 124.

teachers and schools. Martyrdom continued to ravage the Christian community, following the whims and persuasions of emperors and governors. The manner of responding to needs occasioned by these pressures on the diverse ecclesial communities was not universally uniform. Practices of penitence and reconciliation differed from one local church to another.[33] Appointment to office began to take on more substantial and sacramental form. The value of diverse apostolic traditions was highlighted in support of multiple practices of the one faith.

By the end of the second century another stage had been reached in the concept of church authority. From the writings of Irenaeus and Hippolytus foundational principles were to emerge for the development of church order. The spiritual power of the bishops of that era was not less a factor in this development. Even the distinction brought about by "ordination" of clerics and "appointment" of other ministers does not yet interfere with the coexistence of what von Campenhausen calls the "pneu-matic-charismatic" and the "official-sacramental" elements in church authority.[34] There were also examples of teachers, like Clement of Alexandria and Tertullian, whose authority lay in the power of their teaching and not in any formal office or position.

It is important to point out that following Irenaeus, development in church office and the concept of authority was influenced by the emer-gence of three distinct theological trends or movements: the African, the Alexandrian, and the Antiochene. Concerns among the Greeks and in the East remained primarily theological, as christological and trinitarian controversies continued. Among the Latins and in the West, the conflict was focused on the question of sin and repentance. The penitential controversies in the West contributed to an unprecedented development in the concept of office because of the relationship perceived between the power of the keys and the institution of office. Concepts of ecclesiastical office in the East developed concurrently with growth in spirituality and theological insights.

Church historians agree that the year A.D. 313 marked a decisive moment in the life of the Church. In that year, Constantine was to declare his friendship for Christianity and the woes that Bernard of Clairvaux would regret, eight centuries later, were introduced. With the Constantin-ian church, Church-State relations became a reality. The influence—or

---

[33] For example, Origen cites seven ways in which sins can be remitted in the Church (cf. *Hom. in Leviticum*, ii, 4).

[34] Cf. von Campenhausen, pp. 172–177.

interference—of the emperor introduced a new dimension into church governance and into the understanding of power and authority as these were to be exercised in a State that was now professedly Christian.

A growing tension between power and authority seems to have characterized the exercise of governance in the Church increasingly, as the concept and nature of ecclesiastical office were clarified and developed. This was due in part, certainly, to the growing identification of the *Ekklesia* with both the religious and the secular dimensions of life and the presence of two preeminent authority figures: one, royal; the other, priestly. Still, although imperial styles of governance were adopted in ecclesiastical office, the integrity of the Church was preserved through the efforts of truly great bishops who were also truly holy men.

Thus it was that in the Golden Age of the Fathers (ca. A.D. 325–ca. A.D. 430), concepts of ecclesiastical office, church order and ecclesial governance reached a new degree of clarification. This development was due to several factors. In the first place, the choice of these men for the ministry of *episkopos* was based on a previous experience of their competency as leaders and their reputation as persons of integrity. Several of them had achieved recognition in public office. Some of them were from families associated with governmental responsibility. Further, they were known to be just, concerned for the poor and the needy, men of virtue and uprightness.

In Ambrose, Augustine, John Chrysostom, the Cappadocians, Leo the Great, and Gregory the Great, we find bishops who fought to maintain the freedom of the Church from domination by the State. Ambrose is, perhaps, the most outstanding figure in this regard, setting out principles for Church-State relations that still have merit today. Leo and Gregory, both popes at a time when the Church and the Empire were being besieged at every level, knew how to assume leadership as bishops of the church of Rome along with a keen sense of the duties and rights that belonged to one who knew he was universal pastor, ''servant of the servants of God.''

A number of underlying theological intuitions contributed to the development of the concept of church authority as each of these men assumed leadership in the Church. For all of them, the idea of Church—*Ecclesia*—was primary. In their minds, this *ecclesia* was the Christian community, the *verum corpus* of the Lord, ''the assembly or unity of Christians.'' There was no division between the *episkopos* and the community. Hierarchical structure and communal exercise of all ecclesial activities were not contradictory realities. The bishop proclaimed the call to unity, symbolized unity, assured unity in the ecclesial community.

Participation of the laity in the life of the *ecclesia* was a natural consequence of understanding Church as *communio*.

As styles of governance and modes of church order developed, changes in vocabulary reflected the underlying paradigm shifts. Augustine, in referring to the specific role of presbyters and *episkopoi* as leaders or heads of Christian communities, had recourse to a military term: *praepositi Ecclesiae*. The basic concept is still that of the *Ecclesia*. However, in the present dispensation, government and direction by chosen or appointed leaders are necessary. These are the *praepositi*. The term was to last until it was replaced in the Middle Ages by *praelatus*.[35] Other concepts reflected the manner in which the Holy Spirit was understood to be present with those who carried responsibility for the exercise of authority in the Church: *Deus inspiravit, inspirare, inspiratio, revelare, revelatio*. So closely were the mystical and the juridical elements interfaced that "grades of spirituality" were considered to be linked to "grades of dignity."[36] The bishop was thought of as both a spiritual man and a kind of prince. As he was a leader of his people, so he was led by the Spirit of God. The exercise of his authority, furthermore, was a service: *ministerium*.

Much of this attitude was due to the influence of monasticism on many of the bishops of the patristic period. Nearly every great bishop-pastor-theologian from the fourth century to the end of the Age of the Fathers had known monastic life, if only temporarily. Thus, the influence on the lives of men called from the monastery to assume episcopal responsibilities fostered the union of power and authority, of charism and office, against the background of a life directed toward the formation of the "spiritual man." Later, when abuses developed in the hierarchical structure of the Church, the "spiritual authority" that prevailed in monasticism attained its own autonomy and even came to supplant, in some instances, the authority of those bishops who could no longer be called "friends of God."

It would be an error, however, to represent the spiritual authority which prevailed in monasticism as standing in opposition to an episcopal authority that was exercised hierarchically through ecclesiastical office. The ideal of the bishop as a pastor concerned with the total care of his people, exercising authority in service and humility while pursuing a life of personal holiness, remained an ideal as the Church moved into the early Middle Ages. Into that era, however, there was also carried an understanding of authority rooted in the concept of the *Ecclesia* and expressed,

---

[35] Cf. Congar, pp. 150–155.
[36] Cf. ibid., pp. 126–127.

primarily, in the power of the keys, that is in "a sacred power that was both sacramental and judicial."[37]

Developments in the understanding and exercise of ecclesiastical authority in the Middle Ages were influenced by the need to establish the autonomy of the Church as a spiritual society with its proper rights and duties, free from domination by the State. Juridical and legal elements in the concept of authority seem to take ascendancy in this period, and "Church" seems increasingly to be equated with priestly and papal authority. At this point concepts of power and authority, along with their interrelatedness, became complex and intricate. On the one hand there was a steady progression, particularly in regard to the papacy, to assume the features and style of the imperial court. On the other hand, prophetic voices calling the Church back to the Lord and the apostles were never lacking. Developments in theology never lost touch completely with the ecclesiological elements that came from the early church and the fathers.

Congar identifies St. Gregory VII and St. Thomas Becket as the "heroes" of ecclesiastical authority in the medieval period, when terms such as *Vicarius Christi, caput, Sponsa-Mater-Magistra, regere, potestas* expressed underlying concepts of church office. From there the development continues beyond Trent to a vocabulary that includes "Church" as "the hierarchy," "magisterium," the "laity," "apostolic," and representative figures such as St. Ignatius Loyola, St. Charles Borromeo, Cardinal Suhard, and the popes from Pius IX to Pius XII.[38] From that point on we find ourselves, particularly since Vatican II, in an age of rediscovery and reappropriation of ancient values and the sources from which our heritage as Christians flows. Ecclesiastical authority and church office are two realities among others which must be brought to stand in the light of what Congar calls "the permanent sources": Scripture, Tradition, the fathers, the liturgy. The desire to strengthen the bond between spiritual power and authority calls for continued searching of these sources in relation to our present status as Church.

Power and Authority in the Church: Reflection

The question of power and authority in relation to church governance is, in the last analysis, an ecclesiological question. This is to say that symbols, models, or paradigms of the nature and mission of the Church lie at the

---

[37] Ibid., p. 136.
[38] Cf. ibid., pp. 148–150.

heart of the ways in which one might think of power and authority, charism and office, their relationship and their exercise. Further, as Newman understood so well, once the central principle or heart of an idea has been identified, its full development follows, growing out of an innermost core.

The understanding of spiritual power and ecclesiastical authority has, necessarily, been influenced by changing concepts of Church as these have been the result of or the reaction to deep shifts in the life and history of humankind: sociological, philosophical, cultural, scientific, ideological. The world on the eve of the twenty-first century is not the world of the second, the fourth, the thirteenth or the eighteenth. Community configurations, self-awareness and individualism, global consciousness, the threat of the nuclear winter: these are some of the challenges that must be faced by women and men today. In such a world the Church still has a mission. The power of the risen Lord and the authority of his Word are gifts still given by the Spirit to prevail against the darkness.

For the effective exercise of such power and authority it is necessary that the Church be made new in the mystery of the dying and rising of the Lord. Governance in the Church must enable and empower the diversity of charisms that are given for the building up of the Church as the body of the Lord and for the gathering into one of the entire family of God throughout the world. In the light of new achievements in human thought and progress, the Church, too, must know how to learn from the world in which she is to be a light to the nations. From the Christian past there is a legacy and an experience that need to be rediscovered and retrieved, insofar as they can enable us to address the problems that are of *this* time in the light of simple gospel imperatives: faith in the Lord Jesus; obedience to his Word; wisdom to ask, to seek, to knock (cf. Mt. 7:7) with courage and fidelity.

Those who have studied the questions of power, authority, office and governance in the Church affirm that we are, indeed, living in an age of rediscovery of our heritage in this domain.[39] They seem to suggest that Vatican II has set us on the right road theologically. They tell us that ecclesiologically, the time is right for a move toward restoration of a concept of authority that is in full harmony with the gospel and the best of our Tradition. Other efforts are, of course, needed as well: the recognition of each individual's empowerment through baptism into the dying and rising of Jesus; the acknowledgment of each community's pattern of expressing, strengthening and denying power in every situation; the

---

[39] Cf. especially Congar, pp. 149ff.

courage to clarify the complexities of ecclesiastical governance, the relationships between the sacred and the secular in any given culture, and between spiritual power and the authority attached to church office in general. This is a weighty agenda. It reminds us of the one task that has to precede all the others: to preach Jesus Christ in a manner that leads to full recovery of the exercise of authority as God wills it for the new world in which the Lord calls us to service.

THE ROLE OF CANON LAW IN LIGHT
OF *LUMEN GENTIUM*

John M. Huels, O.S.M.

Since 1959 when Pope John XXIII called for the revision of the Code of Canon Law, the role of law in the Church has been pondered by many canonists, theologians, church officials, and others. This reflection was especially fruitful in the period of the law's revision following Vatican II until the code's promulgation in 1983. A 1966 interdisciplinary symposium of the Canon Law Society of America was entirely devoted to the role of canon law.[1] Pope Paul VI spoke with some frequency on the topic, and this in turn prompted further discussion.[2] Pope John Paul II adverted to the role of canon law in the apostolic constitution by which he promulgated the revised Code of Canon Law.[3]

This interest in the role of law in the Church points to its centrality and importance, not only in a period of the law's revision, but even now as the Church seeks to become acquainted with and to implement the new code. Now that the Church's postconciliar discipline is more readily accessible in codified form, it is necessary not to lose sight of the law's proper place in the Church lest one unwittingly regress to the legalistic mindset that prevailed from the first code in 1918 until Vatican II. The topic of the role of canon law is also foundational to a discussion of diocesan governance. Indeed, the role of law in the Church is parallel to the role of diocesan governance since both have the same broad purpose—to serve the mission of the Church in the world by ordering its visible life. Thus, by examining the role of law in the Church one can at the same time understand the fundamental aims of diocesan governance.

---

[1] *Law for Liberty*, ed. James Biechler (Baltimore: Helicon, 1967). A summary of the conclusions reached at the seminar appears in "The Role of Law in the Church," *The Jurist* 27 (1967) 163–181.

[2] Francis Morrisey, "The Spirit of Canon Law, Teachings of Pope Paul VI," *Origins* 8 (1978) 34–40.

[3] John Paul II, *Sacrae disciplinae leges*, January 25, 1983: *AAS* 75/2 (1983) vi–xiv. All translations of this document are from *Code of Canon Law, Latin-English Edition* (Washington, D.C.: 1983), pp. xi–xvi.

A THEOLOGICAL APPROACH TO THE ROLE OF LAW

The role of law in the Church has been approached chiefly in two ways. The traditional way was to view canon law in the context of a model of Church as a *societas perfecta*; the dominant contemporary approach, on the other hand, is to look to theology for the bases of canon law. The prevailing view among canonists and others before the Second Vatican Council was that the Church is a "perfect society," like the civil state, entitled to its own law and independent governance on the basis of the philosophical and natural law principle, *ubi societas ibi et ius*.[4] In this model canon law was considered the *ius publicum ecclesiasticum*, one species of the science of law in general. The role of law in the Church in this model, therefore, is much the same as the role of law in any society— to keep peace and order, serve justice, preserve institutional values, protect individual rights and freedoms, and so forth. This is a legitimate way of addressing the topic of the role of canon law, but it is incomplete because of the uniqueness of the Church which has its foundation in the very mystery of God. Thus law in the Church does not spring simply from rational principles like justice and order; it also has roots in the divine positive law and the divine natural law. Any discussion of the role of canon law which fails to take into account the theological dimension of the Church misses entirely the uniqueness of church law as opposed to other forms of law.

Already before Vatican II the inadequacy of the perfect society model was recognized by some canonists and theologians, including Wilhelm Bertrams,[5] Yves Congar,[6] and Klaus Mörsdorf.[7] They tried to resolve the problem by establishing in various ways a theological basis for canon law. However, their views on the role of law did not noticeably influence the deliberations of the council. The council did not address the issue of the

[4] See Reinhold Sebott, "De Ecclesia ut societas perfecta et de differentia inter ius civile et ius canonicum," *Periodica* 69 (1980) 107–126.

[5] Wilhelm Bertrams, "Die Eigennatur des Kirchenrechts," *Gregorianum* 27 (1946) 527–566; idem, "Grundlegung und Grenzen des kanonischen Rechtes," *Gregorianum* 29 (1948) 588–593.

[6] Cf. Yves Congar, "Ordre et jurisdiction dans l'Eglise," *Irenikon* 19 (1933) 22–31, 97–110, 401–408; "Dogme christologique et Ecclesiologie: Verité et limites d'un paraléle," in *Das Konzil von Chalkedon III*, ed. Alois Grillmeier and Heinrich Bacht (Würzburg: Echter, 1954), pp. 239–268.

[7] Klaus Mörsdorf, "Zur Grundlegung des Rechtes der Kirche," *Münchener Theologische Zeitschrift* 3 (1952) 329–348; idem, "Altkanonisches 'Sakramentsrecht'?" *Studia Gratiana*, ed. Giuseppe Forchielli and Alphonse Stickler (Bologna: Institutum Iuridicum Universitatis Studiorum, 1953), 1:483–502.

role of law in the Church, nor did it develop a "theology of law." By and large the fathers were simply unaware of what later was called the "theological crisis of the Catholic understanding of canon law."[8] The aim of the council was primarily pastoral, not theoretical, and the predominant mood seemed to suggest that problems in canon law could be readily solved by a renewal of doctrine and a reform of discipline. There was also a certain anti-juridicism in evidence at Vatican II, particularly in reaction to the earliest drafts of the Constitution on the Church. For example, Bishop de Smedt of Bruges spoke out against "triumphalism, clericalism, and juridicism," as if all three were linked.[9] However, such criticism was not directed so much at canon law itself as against the preponderance of a juridical model of the Church which has been described as "the Babylonian captivity" of ecclesiology.[10] The council fathers wished to rediscover the deeper theological riches of the Church's nature.

In reference to the role of law in the Church, there is significance in what the council did *not* say, for it did not once refer to the Church as a *societas perfecta*. Consequently, canonists after the council abandoned the former view of canon law as the *ius publicum ecclesiasticum*[11] and began in earnest to define in light of the council's teaching the theological foundations of canon law.[12] These initial developments were sanctioned and furthered by Pope Paul VI in his 1973 address to the Second International Congress of Canonists.

> After the Council, canon law cannot but be in ever closer relationship with theology and with other sacred sciences, because it, too, is a sacred science, and certainly not that "practical art," as some people would wish, the task of which would only be to clothe in juridical forumulas the theological and pastoral

---

[8] Antonio Rouco Varela, "Die katholische Rechtstheologie heute," *Archiv für katholisches Kirchenrecht* 145 (1976) 12.

[9] Gerard Philips, "History of the Constitution," in *Commentary on the Documents of Vatican II*, ed. Herbert Vorgrimler (New York: Herder & Herder, 1967), 1:108–109.

[10] See Winfrid Aymans, "Ecclesiological Implications of the New Legislation," *Studia Canonica* 17 (1983) 65.

[11] See, e.g., the critique of Antonio Rouco Varela, "Die katholische Reaktion auf das 'Kirchenrecht I' Rudolf Sohms," in *Ius Sacrum*, ed. Audomar Scheuermann and Georg May (Munich: F. Schöningh, 1969), p. 24: "Die Lehre der 'societas perfecta' lieferte im Grunde genommen eine Rechtfertigung des Kirchenrechts, die hauptsächlich aus der theoretischen Konfrontation mit dem Staat und nicht aus der Kirche selbst entsprang und deswegen theologisch unzureichen war."

[12] For a discussion of the various postconciliar efforts to construct a theology of law, see Rouco Varela, note 8 above.

conclusions pertinent to it. With the Second Vatican Council there has ended, once and for all, the time when certain canonists refused to consider the theological aspect of the disciplines studied, or the laws that they applied. . . . Your first concern will not be, therefore, to establish a juridical order modelled on civil law, but to deepen the work of the Spirit which must be expressed also in the Church's law.[13]

A significant trend among canonists after Vatican II, perhaps even the dominant one, has been to look to theology to discover the theoretical underpinnings of canon law.[14] While it may not be necessary to refer to canon law as a "theological discipline," as does Mörsdorf,[15] there is no denying the closeness between canon law and theology. All church discipline, governance, and pastoral praxis must be based on theological expressions of the Church's faith.

Theology is the heart of canon law, supplying the legal corpus with life-giving blood. Theology is concerned with the mystery of Christ in the Church, seeking to understand and articulate the inexhaustible. By its very

[13] September 17, 1973, *Communicationes* 5 (1973) 123–131; English translation in *Origins* 3 (1973–74) 263, 272. See also Morrisey, note 2 above.

[14] Not all canonists agree that this is the necessary approach. Since canon law and theology are different disciplines with distinct methodologies, some have urged a complete separation of canon law from theology (die "Enttheologisierung des Kirchenrechts" and the "Entrechtlichung der Theologie"). This would allow canon law to serve a purely pastoral aim in the Church unfettered by disputes of doctrine. Another more methodological but also non-theological contemporary approach, identified with the University of Navarra in Spain and the so-called Italian lay canonists, uses modern techniques and methods of secular legal science in the study and application of canon law. For citations and a discussion of these positions, see Rouco Varela, pp. 13–19. There is some advantage to these approaches which keep canon law and theology methodologically distinct. Some canonists would have preferred a revised code consisting only of juridic norms not interspersed with spiritual and doctrinal elements, or at least placing such non-juridic canons in a separate section. See, e.g., Jacques Leduc, "Principles of Common Law and the 1977 Schema on Institutes of Life Consecrated by Profession of the Evangelical Counsels," *Studia Canonica* 14 (1980) 405–422; Peter Huizing, "A Methodological Reflection on the Section 'Institutes of Consecrated Life' in the *Schema Codicis Iuris Canonici*," *The Jurist* 42 (1982) 180–191. Such an arrangement would cause less confusion between what is proper to law and what is proper to other disciplines. However, even had the code been exclusively juridical, there would not be any less close a connection between canon law and theology. In a fundamental sense all canon law is rooted in theology, that is, theology in the wide sense including disciplines like Scripture, dogmatics, and ethics. See, e.g., Thomas Green, "The Revision of Canon Law: Theological Implications," *Theological Studies* 40 (1979) 593–679.

[15] Klaus Mörsdorf, "Kanonisches Recht als theologische Disziplin," *Archiv für katholisches Kirchenrecht* 145 (1976) 45–58.

nature theological inquiry is without end; something more can always be discovered. Canon law is concerned with the ecclesial embodiment of the mystery, the structures and actions which regulate ecclesial relationships. Good canon law must always flow from an understanding of the nature of the Church.

In order to understand the role of law in the Christian community, it is necessary first to achieve an understanding of the Church itself and then move to a determination of how this understanding should be expressed in canonical norms. The way this task will be attempted is by looking at how the Church sees itself in the Constitution on the Church of Vatican II and reflecting on the implications of this ecclesiology for canon law. The discussion will be limited to a review of certain key images and descriptions of the Church found in *Lumen gentium*, namely, people of God, body of Christ, temple of the Holy Spirit, mystery, and *communio*. This is not meant to be an exhaustive treatment since there is also ecclesiological significance in other conciliar documents as well as in other parts of *Lumen gentium* which are not covered here, including the chapter on the hierarchy. Nevertheless, the nature of the Church is sufficiently illuminated by these key concepts to indicate some basic objectives of canon law.[16]

KEY CONCILIAR IMAGES OF THE CHURCH

People of God

One of the principal images of the Church used by Vatican II is that of the people of God.[17] The importance of this image for canon law is

---

[16] Achieving an understanding of the Church, in the present context, necessarily has a limited meaning. Avery Dulles recognized how difficult it is to provide a fully systematic ecclesiology out of the great variety of data on the Church accumulated by modern patristic, biblical, and liturgical studies, as well as by the Second Vatican Council and modern theologians. That is why Dulles opts for the provisional methodology of models. See *Models of the Church* (Garden City, NY: Image Books, 1974). For Dulles' recent thought on this subject, see "Imaging the Church for the 1980s," in *A Church to Believe In* (New York: Crossroad, 1982), pp. 1–18.

Writing on twentieth century ecclesiology, Eric Jay points out that "never before has such close attention been paid to the question of the nature of the Church. The number of books, major articles, and reports of conferences on the subject is immense." See *The Church: Its Changing Image Through Twenty Centuries* (Atlanta: John Knox, 1980), p. 295. This was first published in two volumes by SPCK, London, 1977.

[17] There are many scriptural images for the Church mentioned in n. 6 of *Lumen gentium*

reflected in its use as a title for Book II of the revised code, *De Populo Dei*. Three key themes are related to this concept which are of consequence to the role of law in the Church: election, community, and history.

Election

> God chose the Israelite race to be his own people, and he established a covenant with it. (*LG*, 9)

The Church is God's holy people not of itself but because of God's call. The divine election of the Church is already foreshadowed in the Old Testament in the call of Abraham and the establishment of the covenant on Sinai. Vatican II frequently referred to the Church as the ''new people of God'' to indicate the new period in salvation history in which God's people has entered through the new covenant effected by the saving action of Jesus Christ in the power of the Holy Spirit (*LG*, 9–10). It was the divine call of Christ which assembled this new people of God: ''Christ instituted this new covenant, namely the new covenant in his blood (cf. 1 Cor 11:25); he called a race made up of Jews and Gentiles which would be one, not according to the flesh, but in the Spirit, and this race would be the new people of God'' (*LG*, 9). Since the origin of the Church is in divine election and since the Church exists by the Spirit, the Church is not only a conventional society but also has a transcendent element.[18]

A consequence of the divine election of the Church for the role of canon law is that canon law must always faithfully reflect the theological as well as the sociological element of the Church. Since the Church is God's chosen people, and since law is part of the life of this people, all canonical norms must in some way reveal the goodness of the divine author of the

---

(*LG*), but only the principal ones are being considered here. The structure of this section and of the next two (on the body of Christ and temple of the Holy Spirit) are chiefly inspired by Winfrid Aymans, ''Die Kirche—Das Recht im Mysterium Kirche,'' in *Handbuch des katholischen Kirchenrechts* (Regensburg: F. Pustet, 1983), pp. 3–11; and idem, '''Volk Gottes' und 'Leib Christi' in der Communio Struktur der Kirche: Ein kanonisticher Beitrag zur Ekklesiologie,'' *Trierer Theologische Zeitschrift* 81 (1972) 321–334. All translations of Vatican II documents are taken from or based on *Vatican Council II: The Conciliar and Postconciliar Documents*, ed. Austin Flannery (Northport, NY: Costello, 1975).

[18] The conclusion drawn from this by some canonists is that the essential core of church law can only be of divine origin, i.e., *ius divinum* is at the heart of *ius canonicum*. See Aymans, ''Die Kirche—Das Recht,'' pp. 4–5; Mörsdorf, ''Kanonisches Recht als theologische Disziplin,''*passim*, esp. p. 56. Although this is true in a broad, theological sense, one cannot say that *ius divinum* is behind each and every church law. Many canons of the code, for example, have no doctrinal basis whatsoever but are purely legal principles or norms of action.

Church. This means that harmful laws, divisive laws, needlessly discriminatory laws cannot truly be said to be church laws, because bad laws are not Christ-like; they are not a *lumen gentium*.[19]

Community

> God willed to make his people holy and save them, not as individuals without any bond or link between them, but rather to make them into a people who might acknowledge him and serve him in holiness. (*LG*, 9)

In his saving work God did not choose isolated individuals, but a community. All persons are called into the new people of God and they become full members of this community by the sacrament of baptism (c. 204, §1). Like Israel, the believer's association with God in history is as community. Hence, an individualistic approach to religion is alien to the essence of the Church. Those who like Rudolf Sohm have held that law is antithetical to the nature of the Church have a one-sided, radically spiritualistic conception of the Church as if it had a purely charismatic structure.[20] The Church has a theological element, but it is also a fully human institution; like any human community it needs a legal system of one kind or other. It needs law for coherence, order, and effectiveness.

While church law must serve the needs of the community and preserve institutional values, it also cannot neglect the individual. All members of the Church enjoy a radical equality and dignity in virtue of their baptism

---

[19] Two additional conclusions are suggested by the divine election of the Church. (1) Insofar as any church law is more or less directly the product of *ius divinum*, it must faithfully reflect the contemporary Church's understanding of the underlying doctrinal content, and not be based on an interpretation of the doctrine which is fixated in one particular period of history. As will be seen below, the Church is a pilgrim people moving through history, and the Church's theology and law must be on the move as well. (2) Canon law should not be based as a rule on theological opinions lest it confuse what is truly *ius divinum* with disputed theological issues, thereby "canonizing" one school of thought. An example that comes to mind readily is c. 1055, §2: there cannot be any valid matrimonial contract among the baptized which is not by that very fact a sacrament. The contention that all valid marriages among the baptized are sacramental is disputed by many Catholic bishops, theologians, and canonists. See James Schmeiser, "Welcomed Civil Marriage in the 1980 Synod of Bishops," *Studia Canonica* 17 (1983) 185–196; idem, "Welcomed Civil Marriage—Canonical Statements," *Studia Canonica* 14 (1980) 49–87; idem and Jan Larson, "Faith and the Right to Marry," *Liturgy* 4 (Spring, 1984) 51–55.

[20] According to Sohm, "Das Wesen des Kirchenrechts steht im Widerspruch zum Wesen der Kirche." See *Kirchenrecht* (Berlin: Von Duncker and Humblot, 2nd ed. 1923) 1:x and 1; Eugenio Corecco, "Theologie des Kirchenrechts," in *Handbuch des katholischen Kirchenrechts*, p. 17.

(*LG*, 32;c.208). The Church is the one people of God, one community of equals who profess one Lord, one faith, one baptism (Eph. 4:5). Because all are equal in dignity, canon law must protect individual rights and liberties and serve the life, ministries, and mission of the Church in which all members of God's people have a part.

History

> God gradually instructed this people—in its history manifesting both himself and the decree of his will—and made it holy unto himself. (*LG*, 9)

The people of God image reveals the continuity of God's covenantal relationship with his people in history. Just as Israel's salvation is worked out as a people in history, so also the Church is the pilgrim people of God which exists in history between the two comings of Christ.[21] The Church anticipates the final age, for it "is endowed already with a sanctity that is real though imperfect" (*LG*, 48). However, until this promised and hoped for restoration of all things in Christ is achieved, "the pilgrim Church, its sacraments and institutions, which belong to this present age, carries the mark of this world which will pass" (*LG*, 48). Hence the Church is imperfect, living in history the tension between the kingdom which is now but not yet.

Though incomplete and imperfect, the Church has a mission "of proclaiming and establishing the kingdom of Christ and of God" (*LG*, 5). Indeed, the Church *is* mission by its very nature since "it has its origins in the mission of the Son and the Holy Spirit."[22] The Church as *missio* is by nature "dynamic, related to the world functionally, and under an imperative to play a role in human history."[23] The Church embodies the mission of Christ and the Spirit throughout history to proclaim to the world the kingdom of God and to establish the kingdom in the world.

A consequence of the pilgrim and *missio* nature of the Church is that canon law, too, must be "on the move" in service of the Church's mission to the world in history. Church law can never be a static entity but must

---

[21] *LG*, chapter VII.

[22] Vatican II, Decree on the Church's Missionary Activity, *Ad gentes divinitus*, n. 2.

[23] Roger Haight, "The 'Established' Church as Mission: The Relation of the Church to the Modern World," *The Jurist* 39 (1979) 11; idem, "Mission: The Symbol for Understanding the Church Today," *Theological Studies* 37 (1976) 631–632. For additional studies from various perspectives on the Church as *missio*, see the product of the CLSA Permanent Seminar in *The Jurist* 39 (1979), also published as *The Church as Mission*, Permanent Seminar Studies, 2 (Washington: CLSA, 1984).

continually be reformed and updated to keep pace with changing needs and conditions. It must be open, flexible, adaptable to changing circumstances, and tentative in nature.[24] Thus, a role of law in the Church is to provide current and helpful structures to further the mission of God's people and to obviate whatever might hinder that mission.

Body of Christ

> Really sharing in the body of the Lord in the breaking of the Eucharistic bread, we are taken up into communion with him and with one another. (*LG*, 7)

Vatican II frequently employed the Pauline image of the Church as the body of Christ, a concept which has enjoyed a more constant tradition in the history of the Church than that of people of God. The use of the body of Christ image for the Church is not only justifiable but is also necessary. Through the saving actions of Christ the history of God's relations with his people found a new expression: the people of God constitutes the body of Christ.[25] Christ is the head; the Church is the body: "as all the members of the human body, though they are many, form one body, so also are the faithful in Christ" (*LG*, 7).[26] For Paul, the Church as body of Christ is intimately connected with the Eucharistic body of Christ (1 Cor 10:16–17), and this association is developed more extensively by patristic authors, including Augustine.[27] The Church is the body of Christ constituted by the sacramental body of Christ. For both Paul and the fathers, the connection between the Eucharistic and ecclesial body of Christ expresses above all the unity of the Church. At Eucharist the ecclesial body of Christ gathers around the Lord's table to share the one bread and the one cup. The Eucharist is the principal sign and source of church unity; it signifies and builds up the one body of Christ.[28]

---

[24] Richard McBrien, "A Theologian Looks at the Role of Law in the Church Today," *CLSA Proceedings* 43 (1981) 22.

[25] Yves Congar, "The Church: The People of God," in *The Church and Mankind*, Concilium, 1 (Glen Rock, NJ: Paulist, 1965), pp. 30–31; Rudolf Schnackenburg and Jacques Dupont, "The Church as the People of God," in ibid., p. 118.

[26] Cf. 1 Cor. 12:12.

[27] See Henri de Lubac, *Corpus Mysticum* (Paris: Aubier, 1949), p. 24. For Augustine, see esp. sermon 272, *PL* 38:1246–1247; English trans. in *The Mass: Ancient Liturgies and Patristic Texts*, ed. André Hamman (New York: Alba House, 1967), p. 204.

[28] See Joseph Powers, *Eucharistic Theology* (New York: Herder & Herder, 1967), p. 15; Jean-Marc Dufort, *Le symbolisme Eucharistique aux origines de l'Église* (Brussels: Desclée de Brouwer, 1969), p. 142.

The importance for canon law of this theological image of the body of Christ is evident. Since unity is a necessary constituent and end of the Church's nature and worship, canon law must be about the task of preserving and fostering this unity. This means not only that church law is to serve the harmonious interrelationships of the Catholic faithful, but also that it must as far as possible further the cause of unity among all baptized members of Christ's body.

Temple of the Holy Spirit

> The state of the people of God is that of the dignity and freedom of the children of God, in whose hearts the Holy Spirit dwells as in a temple. Its law is the new commandment to love as Christ loved us. (*LG*, 9)

Another image of the Church used by Vatican II is that of temple of the Holy Spirit. The Church is the body of Christ in a mysterious way because the Holy Spirit has fashioned it into an edifice whose cornerstone is Christ the Lord (*LG*, 6). The incarnational and the pneumatic aspects of the Church are inseparable. It is through the working of the Holy Spirit that the saving deeds of Christ are able to touch men and women in all times and places. It is by the power of the Holy Spirit that the members of the body of Christ are able to celebrate the memorial of the Lord in word and sacrament and are united to Christ their head and to each other. It is "by communicating his Spirit that Christ mystically constitutes as his body those brothers and sisters of his who are called together from every nation" (*LG*, 7). It is through the gift of the Spirit that individual members of the Church are endowed with various charisms that are "fitting and useful for the needs of the Church" (*LG*, 12).

The locus of this activity of the Spirit is the Church. There cannot be any essential contradiction between a Church of law and a Church of the Spirit because church law is a law of the Spirit. Since the Spirit's presence infuses the whole Church in all its aspects and activities, it cannot be true to say that the Spirit is divorced from church law. The Church is a sacramental community consisting of both the visible institution and the invisible presence of the Spirit. It is the same Spirit who establishes the Church as institution and who empowers it with the divine presence. According to Vatican II, "the social structure of the Church serves the Spirit of Christ who vivifies it in the building up of the body" (*LG*, 8).

Canon law is part of the Church's visible, social dimension, and therefore it must manifest and serve the life of the Spirit in order to build up the body of Christ. If canon law is truly to serve the Church, the temple of the Holy Spirit, a principal role for law must be, in the words of Paul VI, to "express the life of the Spirit, and reveal the image of Christ."[29] Or, according to John Paul II, the purpose of canon law is to create such an order in the ecclesial society that, "while assigning the primacy to love, grace and charisms, it at the same time renders their organic development easier in the life of both the ecclesial society and the individual persons who belong to it."[30] Canon law must be rooted "in the new commandment to love" (*LG*, 9). It therefore must provide appropriate means for the expression of the spiritual and charismatic dimension of the Church, not stifling individual and community charisms, but allowing them to blossom, grow, and bear abundant fruit.[31]

The Church as Mystery

> The Church, that is the kingdom of Christ already present in mystery, grows visibly through the power of God in the world. (*LG*, 3)

As the title of Chapter I of the Constitution on the Church reveals, the Church is "mystery." It consists of both the visible, social institution and the invisible presence of the Holy Spirit. However, these two elements "are not to be thought of as two realities. On the contrary, they form one complex reality" (*LG*, 8). Because the Church is mystery, because it is sacrament,[32] its visible activity is a sign of God's efficacy in the world. The Holy Spirit is mysteriously present in the Church's institutional life and activities—word and sacrament, apostolic succession, acts of justice and charity, and even canon law! This is not to say that all elements and activities of the Church are equal in importance. Certainly the proclamation of the word and the celebration of the sacraments are the primary means by which the Church makes known the presence of God in the world.[33] However, no activity of the Church is untouched by the Spirit. All

---

[29] Paul VI, address to Roman Rota, February 8, 1973: *The Pope Speaks* 18 (1973) 77.

[30] *Sacrae disciplinae leges*, p. xiv.

[31] See Hans Küng, "The Charismatic Structure of the Church," in *The Church and Ecumenism*, Concilium, 4 (New York: Paulist, 1965), pp. 41–61.

[32] *LG*, 1, 8, 9, 48.

[33] *LG*, 7; Vatican II, Constitution on the Sacred Liturgy, *Sacrosanctum Concilium*, 2. See Klaus Mörsdorf, "Wort und Sakrament als Bauelemente der Kirchenverfassung," *Archiv für katholisches Kirchenrecht* 134 (1965) 72–79; Michael Himes, "The Current State of Sacramental Theology as a Background to the New Code," *CLSA Proceedings* 42 (1980) 67–69.

aspects of the Church's visible life—be they functions of teaching, governing, or sanctifying—participate in the sacramental, mysterious nature of the Church, including canon law. Therefore canon law, while belonging to the social, visible side of the Church, also shares in the spiritual side because the Church itself cannot be neatly divided between the visible and the invisible.[34]

The Church has its foundation in the mystery of God, but it is also human and fallible. The social and theological dimensions truly form one complex reality, but the two elements remain distinct. Thus there will always be some tension between Spirit and law. Despite all efforts at reform and renewal, the Church will never be perfect. Because of its humanness and sinfulness, the Church can never perfectly manifest God's presence. This may seem obvious, but it needs to be expressed as a reminder of the proper role of law in the Church. Canon law cannot resolve all tensions and problems among God's people. It is human and imperfect, and therefore its role in the Church will always be a limited one. This fact should not discourage efforts at reform and renewal, and certainly it should not excuse bad or obsolete laws, but it serves to temper overly optimistic expectations of what canon law really can accomplish and thereby places the role of law in the Church in proper perspective.

The Church as Communio

Before Vatican II the term *communio* was used in both the code and in common ecclesiastical parlance almost exclusively to refer to Eucharistic Communion, but the council employed it frequently in its ecclesial sense

---

[34] From this observation some canonists conclude that canon law should be considered a faith science—an *ordination fidei* (Corecco), a "theological discipline" (Mörsdorf), which treats a reality which is "an object of faith" (Sobanski). This view seemingly elevates canon law to the same plane as other visible aspects of the Church which are more essential to its nature and more permanent than canon law. There is a psychological danger in such canonical maximalism because if canon law is uncritically called a "sacred science," if the laws are referred to as "sacred canons," church law can assume for some a role greater than it should have. Such an overly reverent attitude toward canon law in turn may lead to rigidity in interpretation and jurisprudence and the stifling of canonical development. Certainly that is not the intention of the canonists cited here, yet there is a danger in an uncritical acceptance of their approach which so closely associates canon law and theology.

See Corecco, pp. 23–24; Mörsdorf, "Kanonisches Recht als theologische Disziplin"; Remigiusz Sobanski, "Modell des Kirche-Mysteriums als Grundlage der Theorie des Kirchenrechts," *Archiv für katholisches Kirchenrecht* 145 (1976) 40–41. See also Antonio Rouco Varela, "Grundfragen einer katholischen Theologie des Kirchenrechts," ibid. 148 (1979) 341–352.

to refer to the church communion. Since then it has become a standard ecclesiological and canonical concept and the subject of much research and reflection, doubtless due to its theological richness and resultant pastoral possibilities.[35] The ecclesial sense of the term can be viewed principally in two ways: the Church as the *communio fidelium* and as a *communio ecclesiarum*.[36]

Communion of the Faithful

> Really sharing in the body of the Lord in the breaking of the Eucharistic bread, we are taken up into communion with him and with one another. (*LG*, 7)

In its basic meaning the term *communio* fittingly describes the reality of the Church as the socio-historical presence of God among his people.[37] The Church is "a communion of life, love, and faith" (*LG*, 9), a communion of divine life with humanity lived in faith and expressed in community.[38] St. Paul elaborated this *communio*, or *koinonia*, theme to explain the profound reality of humanity's sharing in the life of God.[39] For Paul, *koinonia* designates the two constitutive relations comprising the essence of Church: communion with God and the communion of believers with each other.[40] The concept of *communio* points to the Church both as the visibly erected community and as the spiritual community, the temple of the Holy Spirit. In this respect it expresses well the sacramental nature of the Church as a mystery. It is also related to the image of the Church as Body of Christ. Just as the Body of Christ refers both to the Eucharistic and the ecclesial body, so also *communio* embraces both Eucharistic and

---

[35] An early CLSA Permanent Seminar was devoted exclusively to an interdisciplinary examination of the meaning and implications of *communio*. See the essays in *The Jurist* 36 (1976) 1–245, reprinted in *The Church as Communion*, Permanent Seminar Studies, 1 (Washington: CLSA, 1984).

[36] Winfrid Aymans points to a third way that the council used *communio* in reference to the Church, that of *communio hierarchica*. This term was used by the council chiefly in the sense of a structural principle for the college of bishops and the sacerdotal presbyterium. Only one time was the term used to describe the whole Church as a hierarchical community. See Aymans, "Ecclesiological Implications," pp. 84–88.

[37] Robert Kress, "The Church as *Communio*: Trinity and Incarnation as the Foundations of Ecclesiology," *The Jurist* 36 (1976) 129.

[38] See James Provost, "The Church as Communion: Introduction," ibid., p. 1.

[39] Michael Fahey, "Ecclesial Community as Communion," ibid., p. 6.

[40] John Lynch, "The Limits of *Communio* in the Pre-Constantinian Church," ibid., p. 160.

ecclesial communion.[41] The Eucharistic celebration is the heart of the Church's life, the source and sign of its unity, the point of convergence for all its activity. Thus Eucharistic communion and ecclesial communion are closely interrelated. As Karl Rahner put it: "It is not only true to say that the Eucharist is because the Church is, but it is also true, correctly understood, to say that the Church is because the Eucharist is."[42]

The Constitution on the Church of Vatican II places the chapter on the people of God before the chapters on the hierarchy and the laity. By its very structure the constitution demonstrates that the Church is a *communio fidelium* in which all members have a basic equality in faith before any hierarchical distinctions are made.[43] Moreover, the constitution states that all Christians in any state or walk of life are called to holiness, to the fullness of Christian life and the perfection of love (*LG*, 39–42). The Church is a community in which all possess the sacramental mission to live and proclaim the gospel, and all have a function in the service of the whole.[44] It is a community of God's people with a mission to embody and hand on the good news, a community of vital liturgy and faith, a community with interpersonal relations based on charity and service.[45] The notion of the Church as *communio* is also related to other models and aspects of the Church, including the charismatic structure of the Church, the missionary and ecumenical thrust of the Church, and the collegial dimension of the community; and it embraces themes such as lay participation, coresponsibility, and shared decision-making.[46]

There are obviously many implications of the *communio* concept for the role of canon law, some of which have already been seen in connection with the preceding discussion, especially that on the people of God. One general conclusion is that canon law should establish a church order that makes the community itself the priority, not office-holders. Canon law should provide structures which promote the sense of Church as a community of faith, hope, and love, and not only those which build up the

---

[41] Aymans, "Die Kirche—Das Recht," pp. 10–11.

[42] Karl Rahner, "Theology of the Parish," in *The Parish*, ed. Hugo Rahner (Westminster: Newman, 1958), pp. 28–30.

[43] Aymans, "Ecclesiological Implications," pp. 82–84.

[44] See Peter Huizing, "Canon Law," in *Readings, Cases, Materials in Canon Law*, ed. Jordan Hite, Gennaro Sesto, Daniel Ward (Collegeville: Liturgical Press, 1980), p. 64.

[45] Tomás Bissonnette, "Communidades Ecclesiales de Base: Some Contemporary Attempts to Build Ecclesial Koinonia," *The Jurist* 36 (1976) 45.

[46] Fahey, pp. 5–6.

institution as such.[47] It should facilitate the redemptive presence and activity of God in the community of faith and equip the community for more effective service in the world.[48] A kind of pattern for such an ecclesial order can be seen in the Eucharistic celebration in which the universal and ministerial priesthood each has its respective roles and functions yet all members of the assembly remain in dialogue and union with each other (cc. 837, §1; 899, §2). Such a structure would preserve the social and institutional nature of the Church without imposing unnecessary canonical distinctions between clergy and laity which impede the growth of the intimate relationship of being-Church that *communio* implies.

Communion of Churches

> The Church of Christ is really present in all legitimately organized groups of the faithful, . . . in each altar community under the sacred ministry of the bishop. (*LG*, 26)

The concept of *communio fidelium* refers to the relationship of the members of the Church with God and with each other at any level of the Church, but especially at the local level characterized by the community gathered in table fellowship at Eucharist. The *communio ecclesiarum* is closely related to the *communio fidelium*, but it more precisely defines the relationship of unity among particular churches—their commonness of faith, mutual recognition, and reciprocity of membership.[49] Like *communio fidelium*, *communio ecclesiarum* also takes its inspiration from that "communion" in the body and blood of Christ which is shared at the table of the Lord.

In a volume of essays that was the product of a CLSA symposium held just before the Synod of Bishops in 1969, James Coriden wrote that the concept of *communio ecclesiarum*—a "communion of freedom"—can be

---

[47] See James Provost, "Structuring the Church as *Communio*," *The Jurist* 36 (1976) 191–245, for an analysis of how this might look.

[48] McBrien, p. 20.

[49] Particular churches are juridically defined as dioceses and their equivalents listed in c. 368. However, Ladislas Orsy suggests a broader understanding of particular church would better correspond to history and present day life. In Orsy's view, a particular church is one "that has its own specific charism, its own mind and its own heart within the universal Church." Particular churches with their own language, liturgy, discipline, and customs rarely developed in one city or diocese alone, but usually in larger territories that represented a national cultural identity. Sometimes even a whole continent acts as a particular church, such as South America. According to Orsy, the rather romantic view of particular church as the community gathered around the bishop at Eucharist does not conform to reality. See "A Theology of the Local Church and Religious Life," *Review for Religious* 36 (1977) 668.

the answer to the problem behind the theme which the symposium was addressing, that of "unity and subsidiarity in the Church":

> The communion of churches did not mean [in the ancient Church] their uniformity. It was the expression of their mutual acceptance and fundamental unity of faith and discipline. But to say that local assemblies were "in communion" did not imply that they were identical, similarly governed, or that there was a formal structural relation among them. It was a communion in freedom. Local differences, regional practices, and community autonomy were respected, prized, and safeguarded. In other words, the concept of "communion" bridged the gap between the need for unity in the Church and the desire for self-direction and adaptation in the local churches.[50]

The role of the bishop of Rome in the ancient church was as servant of ecclesial communion. His authority was not considered apart from that of the other bishops, but more in terms of his role as principal custodian of the Church's unity, having power not *over* the Church but within and toward the whole ecclesial communion.[51]

Is this idea of *communio ecclesiarum* from the ancient church also in evidence in the teachings of Vatican II? How did the council view the relations among the local churches with each other and with the universal Church symbolized by its head, the pope? To answer these questions it might be profitable to look first at what the council meant when it used the term "Church." What are these *ecclesiae* that are *in communione*?

Actually, the use of the term *Ecclesia* by Vatican II was surprisingly clear and consistent. Whether in reference to the Church universal, the particular church, or groups of them, *ecclesia* expressly or indirectly is used only for the episcopally composed Church. The decisive criterion for what constitutes "Church" is that it be that community of believers in union with their bishop who is in apostolic succession.[52] In those sectors of Christianity where any of these elements are lacking, the council speaks of ecclesial communities (*communitates ecclesiales*). While the celebration

---

[50] *The Once and Future Church: A Communion of Freedom*, ed. James Coriden (New York: Alba House, 1971), pp. xi–xii.

[51] Eugenio Corecco, "The Bishop as Head of the Local Church and its Discipline," in *The Sacraments in Theology and Canon Law*, Concilium, 38 (New York: Paulist, 1968), p. 90.

[52] Winfrid Aymans, "Die Communio Ecclesiarum als Gestaltgesetz der einen Kirche," *Archiv für katholisches Kirchenrecht* 139 (1970) 73–74.

of the Eucharist is the primary manifestation of Church, it does not in itself
represent the Church in its fullness unless the celebration is "under the
sacred ministry of the bishop."[53]

While the council was clear in its conception of what constitutes
Ecclesia, namely a Eucharistic community with a bishop in apostolic
succession, the *relationship* between the whole Church and the particular
churches was not so distinct. *Communio ecclesiarum* was not an established theological concept at the council.[54] Only a single time, in its Decree
on the Church's Missionary Activity, did it speak of *ecclesiarum novel-
larum communio cum tota Ecclesia*.[55] Hence, the council did not deal
systematically with this ancient and important ecclesiological principle.
However, as Winfrid Aymans notes,[56] there is a masterfully brief and
precise expression of the relationship between the universal Church and
particular churches found in *Lumen gentium*, 23.

> The individual bishops are the visible source and foundation of
> unity in their own particular churches, which are constituted after
> the image of the universal Church; it is in these and formed from
> them [*in quibus et ex quibus*] that the one and unique Catholic
> Church exists.

The key phrase in the quotation is *in quibus et ex quibus*—the universal
Church exists both *in* the particular churches and *from* them.[57] There are
two elements in this description of the particular church/universal Church
relationship. The first element is that the universal Church exists in the
particular churches. They too are people of God, body of Christ, temple of
the Holy Spirit, etc. This is also expressed in *Lumen gentium*, 26 where the
universal Church is seen to exist in the local churches because it is there
that the mission of the Church finds concrete expression in word and
sacrament. Clearly, where there is a Eucharistic community and a bishop
in apostolic succession, there is *Ecclesia* from the council's point of view.

The second element of the *in quibus et ex quibus* duality is that the

---

[53] *LG*, 26. Cf. also *Sacrosanctum Concilium*, 42 where it states that groupings of the
faithful below the bishop [such as parishes] "represent" the visible Church; they do not
constitute it like the particular churches do.

[54] Corecco, "The Bishop as Head," p. 98.

[55] *Ad gentes divinitus*, 19; Aymans, "Die Communio Ecclesiarum," pp. 69–70, 76.

[56] Aymans, "Ecclesiological Implications," p. 88; idem, "Die hierarchische Organ-
isationsstruktur der Kirche," in *Handbuch des katholischen Kirchenrechts*, pp. 239–
242.

[57] This theological description of the relation between the particular churches and the
universal Church has been adopted by the revised code, c. 368.

universal Church is constituted *from* the particular churches. While a
particular church is fully *Ecclesia*, it is not the total *Ecclesia*. Vatican II
referred to the diocese as a *portio Ecclesiae universalis* or a *Populi Dei
portio*.[58] In this portion of the universal Church of God's people, the one
Church of Christ truly exists and is effective, but it is only a part of the
whole people of God. The particular churches are fully Church, but they
are not the whole Church. The whole Church consists in the sum total of
all the particular churches which are joined together in the relationship of
communio. No particular church can be isolated from the other churches
without ceasing to reflect the unity of Christ's body and, in effect, ceasing
to be part of the whole Church.[59] A particular church can only make visible
the universal Church when it is in communion with the other particular
churches. It is *from* this relationship of *communio* among the local
churches that the universal Church exists.

In reference to the role of law in the Church, one can draw two broad
conclusions based on the two elements of the *in quibus et ex quibus*
duality. From the fact that the universal Church is constituted from the
particular churches, an evident conclusion is that a universal law should
attempt to preserve and promote the communion of the particular churches
with each other. A principal way that canon law has done this in history,
at least since the Gregorian reform, has been by enhancing the position of
the papacy and thereby strengthening the ties of the local churches with
their head and symbol of unity.[60] Certainly there are adequate safeguards

[58] *LG*, 23, 28; Decree on the Pastoral Office of Bishops in the Church, *Christus
Dominus*, 11, 28. The revised code also defines a particular church as a *populi Dei portio*. See
cc. 369–372.

[59] The New Testament itself indicates that the body of Christ cannot be said to exist only
at the level of the local church or only at the level of the universal Church, but rather that both
are truly the body of Christ. In 1 Corinthians and Romans the body of Christ is the individual
community; in Colossians and Ephesians it is the whole Church. See Hans Küng, *The Church*
(New York: Sheed and Ward, 1967), pp. 227–234.

[60] John Lynch, "The History of Centralization: Papal Reservations," in *The Once and
Future Church*, pp. 57–109.

While tradition and doctrine both indicate the necessity of some form of Petrine ministry
to maintain this *communio*, its exact canonical structuring need not be forever that which is
specified in canon law today (cc. 360–367). After all, the modern day papacy is itself the
product of evolution. Moreover, if the non-Roman churches and ecclesial communities are
some day to be fully united with the Catholic Church, it seems certain that the present
canonical powers of the pope will have to be modified in light of developing insights into the
meanings of the doctrines of primacy and infallibility. See, e.g., the excellent study of
J.M.R. Tillard, "The Jurisdiction of the Bishop of Rome," *Theological Studies* 40 (1979)
3–22. Only after there is *plena communio* among all Christians will the imagery of the Church

in canon law for maintaining the communion of the particular churches with the see of Rome, including the penalties of automatic (*latae sententiae*) excommunication for the delicts of schism and the ordination of a bishop without authorization of the Holy See (cc. 1364, §1; 1382). However, the attitude of Roman authorities, and to some extent even that of the code, sometimes appears to be distrustful of independent activity by and relations among local churches.[61] Insofar as this is true, canon law is in need of reform to foster better the communion of particular churches with each other.[62]

Another general conclusion follows from the first element of the *in quibus et ex quibus* duality. Since the particular churches are truly and fully Church in their own right, canon law must acknowledge this reality by allowing particular churches to be Church. Cardinal Joseph Bernardin has spoken of the "creative tension" that inevitably exists between the bishop of Rome and the local churches seeking to develop their unique character and identity.[63] While canon law cannot eliminate such tension, which is human and natural, it can help to reduce it by fostering the principles of subsidiarity and collegiality.[64] The law must allow particular churches to have in disciplinary matters as much autonomy as possible while preserving

as the body of Christ point with clarity to an achieved reality.

[61] An example of this attitude is seen in the restrictions on the law-making powers of conferences of bishops and particular councils. See cc. 455, 456, 439, 441, and 446. Another example is c. 459, §2 which states that whenever any of the actions or programs of episcopal conferences have an international aspect, the Apostolic See must be consulted.

[62] Is it possible to use the term *communio ecclesiarum* analogously to describe other relations between churches and within them? It seems that this rich theological principle could be used in an analogous way to describe two relationships: that of parishes within a diocese with each other and that of local churches with other Christian churches and ecclesial communities. (1) In reality, "Church" exists at the level of the parish where the people of God actually gather to worship and thereby "become" Church. Rarely do the faithful, especially in larger dioceses, have the opportunity to celebrate Eucharist with their bishop who remains a rather remote if not insignificant part of their real experience of Church. (2) Since all the baptized belong to the Church of Christ and are *christifideles* (cc. 96, 204), one could also use analogously the concept of *communio* in describing the relations between the Catholic Church and other Christian communities. The significance of these uses of the term for the role of law is that it suggests that canon law must also foster *communio* among the structures within dioceses, and even between local churches and other non-Catholic Christian churches and ecclesial communities.

[63] Joseph Bernardin, "A Bishop's View," *Chicago Studies* 23 (1984) 39–40.

[64] See, e.g., the studies by Richard McBrien, "Collegiality: State of the Question," and William Bassett, "Subsidiarity, Order and Freedom in the Church," in *The Once and Future Church*, pp. 1–24 and 205–265. See also the volume, *Who Decides for the Church? Studies in Co-Responsibility*, ed. James Coriden (Hartford: CLSA, 1971).

the fundamental character and traditions of the Catholic Church (and not simply those of a Roman church). A universal law must leave room for the particular churches to express their unique cultural identities and spiritual needs in the framework of their own canonical order.[65] A universal law in a Church which is a communion of churches must uphold the principle of "diversity in unity," safeguarding the essential aspects of ecclesial unity but not imposing a rigid uniformity.[66] Canon law must let the Church be a "world Church." In Rahner's sense of the term, a world Church is not an Italian, or a European, or a Western church, but a Church that embraces the distinctive elements in the cultures of all the world's peoples.[67]

CONCLUSIONS

The Church is an institution unlike any other because it is not merely one more human society alongside other communities or civil states. Rather it is a community formed by the word of God and the indwelling presence of the Holy Spirit. Thus church law must somehow be different from other species of the legal science if it is to be true to the Church's nature.

This discussion of the role of canon law has been based on the ecclesiology of Vatican II, examining some principal images of the Church as people of God, body of Christ, temple of the Holy Spirit, and the nature of the Church as mystery and *communio*. From this partial overview of conciliar ecclesiology it is possible to formulate some conclusions for the role of law in the Church. They are not hard and fast conclusions that follow with inexorable logic from their theological premises, nor are they intended to be a taxative listing, but are rather more like general indications or patterns of how canon law ought to be fashioned in light of the mystery that is Church. The first seven conclusions apply to all church laws; the next two refer especially to the

---

[65] See Ronald Modras, "Roman Law in a Universal Church," *America* 149 (1983) 389–392.

[66] Giuseppe Baldanza, "L'Incidenza della Teologia conciliare nella riforma del diritto canonico," *Monitor Ecclesiasticus* 95 (1970) 280.

[67] Karl Rahner, *Concern For the Church*, Theological Investigations, 20 (New York: Crossroad, 1981), pp. 77–89.

It is a gross distortion of the meaning of *communio* to use it politically as a justification for Roman authorities to intervene in the legitimate affairs of local churches. On the contrary, *communio* implies local autonomy in most areas of the local church's life notwithstanding agreement with the other churches on the more essential matters of faith, morals, and discipline.

role of universal law; and the final conclusion concerns the interpreters of law, including the diocesan bishop.

Church Law

1.   The Church is the new people of God, chosen to manifest God's presence and activity in the world. Therefore canon law must reflect the goodness of its divine author and ought never be harmful, divisive, or needlessly discriminatory.

2.   God chose a community as his own, not isolated individuals. Like any human community, the Church needs laws to keep peace, promote justice and order, and preserve institutional values. But because the Church is a community of persons who are radically equal in dignity in virtue of their common baptism, canon law must also protect individual rights and freedoms and serve the life, ministries, and mission of all members of God's people.

3.   The Church exists in history as a pilgrim people with a mission to proclaim the kingdom of God which is present but yet to come. Since the Church is an imperfect, historical reality, its canon law must be open, adaptable, and tentative in nature in order to provide current and helpful structures that further the mission of God's people on the way to the kingdom.

4.   The Church is the body of Christ, a unity of members with Christ their head. The Eucharist is the principal sign and source of ecclesial unity. Canon law, too, has a role in preserving and fostering the unity of the Church. It also must be ecumenical, promoting unity among all baptized members of Christ's body.

5.   The Church is the temple of the Holy Spirit, a visible institution with an invisible, spiritual presence. Canon law, though properly part of the Church's visible side, must not neglect its spiritual dimension. Canon law especially must provide appropriate means for the expression of individual and communal charisms and avoid obstacles which prevent their expression.

6.   The Church is sacrament; it is mystery, a complex reality of the visible and invisible; but the two elements are distinct. There will always be some measure of tension between law and the Spirit because canon law is human and fallible and therefore cannot fully reflect the divine element of the Church's mysterious nature. Hence, the role of law in the Church is necessarily limited. It cannot solve all the Church's problems.

7.   The Church is the *communio fidelium*, a mysterious communion of God's life and love with his people. Canon law should have as its priority

the community itself, not its office-holders. It should provide structures which promote the sense of a communion of faith, hope, and love; which reflect the redemptive presence and activity of God; and which equip the community for effective service in the world.

8. The Church is a *communio ecclesiarum* constituted *from* the particular churches headed by the bishops who signify the apostolic succession of the Church. A task of canon law is to preserve and foster the *communio* of particular churches with each other and with the universal Church at whose center is the papal office.

9. The Church is a *communio* which is not only constituted from the particular churches, but which exists fully *in* each particular church. Canon law must be based on principles of subsidiarity, collegiality, and shared responsibility and must uphold the principle of diversity-in-unity, allowing local churches to express in their own discipline their spiritual needs and aspirations as experienced in their own cultures and localities.

Interpreters of Church Law

Sometimes the observance and enforcement of canon law on the level of the local church is a source of tension. How do members of the local church handle the law in such a situation? How do they resolve the problems and reduce the tensions that can arise between universal law and the needs of the local community? Above all else, it is necessary that there be good interpreters of law among all sectors of the people of God, and not just canonists and other professionals. Good law flows from sound theology, and good interpretation of law requires persons who are versed in the various theological disciplines, especially ecclesiology, in order to contextualize the law properly. It is not enough to master the technical principles of canonical interpretation found in the code, canons 14–21. The good interpreter must also have inculcated the spirit behind the law to ensure that the way it is observed is faithful to the nature of the Church itself. Pope John Paul II has affirmed that the revised Code of Canon Law must always be interpreted in view of Vatican II, and his words on the code are equally applicable to all church law, universal or particular.

> If, however, it is impossible to translate perfectly into *canonical* language the conciliar image of the Church, nevertheless the Code must always be referred to this image as the primary pattern whose outline the Code ought to express insofar as it can by its very nature.[68]

---

[68] *Sacrae disciplinae leges*, p. xiv.

The conciliar ecclesiology is the principal basis on which all canon law is to be formulated, and also the starting point for its interpretation.[69]

The diocesan bishop is a singularly important interpreter of universal law. He is the shepherd of the local church charged with the duty of enforcing universal law and safeguarding ecclesiastical discipline (c. 392). If he is to accomplish this task in a way that faithfully reflects the Church's true nature, he must be able to interpret the law not rigidly and legalistically but in accord with the theological vision of Church that underlies the law. Moreover, the governance of his diocese in all its aspects ought to manifest the Church's nature. Its policies, systems, and organization cannot be formulated and structured in a way that violates the principles underlying the proper role of law as developed above.

Whether the bishop and members of the particular church have the task of interpreting and implementing universal law, or formulating new laws and policies for diocesan governance, the product of their efforts ought to share in and reflect the Church's nature and mission to be like Christ, a light of the nations.

---

[69] The art of canonical interpretation has received significant attention in recent years as a result of the efforts of Ladislas Orsy. His reflections have produced an entirely new outlook and methodology for interpreting canon law. See esp. Ladislas Orsy, ''The Interpreter and His Art,'' *The Jurist* 40 (1980) 27–56; idem, ''The Interpretation of Laws: New Variations on an Old Theme,'' *Studia Canonica* 17 (1983) 95–134. See also John Huels, ''The Interpretation of Liturgical Law,'' *Worship* 55 (1981) 218–237; and James Coriden, ''Rules for Interpreters,'' *The Jurist* 42 (1982) 277–303.

DIOCESAN GOVERNANCE IN MODERN CATHOLIC THEOLOGY AND IN THE 1983 CODE OF CANON LAW

MICHAEL A. FAHEY, S.J.

The promulgation of the Code of Canon Law on January 25, 1983, brought to completion a triple project announced unexpectedly by Pope John XXIII on January 25, 1959: plans for a synod for the diocese of Rome, convocation of a general council eventually to be known as Vatican II, and revision of the 1917 Code of Canon Law. In fact this is a completion of phase one only. What now follows is the long process of implementation of Vatican II and reception by the Latin Church of its new code. The commentaries now in preparation, practical interpretations and symposia (of which this Canon Law Society of America symposium and its publication will be an example) all witness to the work that remains undone. To help plan for the future it is well to know more about the genesis of the code against the background of modern theological and pastoral concerns in the Roman Catholic Church.

It is unrealistic to expect to have embodied in the new code all theological insights regarding the local church or the episcopate arrived at since the 1950s by Roman Catholics and more recently by ecumenical dialogues. The new code has achieved only a modest résumé of recent thought. Still, the more I have studied the code in preparation for a university course entitled "The Ecclesial Implications of the 1983 Code of Canon Law," the more impressed I have been by the paradigmatic shift of ecclesiology it reflects especially in Book Two on "The People of God." The code has encapsulated in juridical form many of the major ecclesiological emphases of Vatican II. Eventually a computer-based study will be able to illustrate how much even of the terminology and exact phraseology of the code are products of the council.

My presentation is divided into four parts:

1. An overview of recent theological developments regarding the local church, the bishop and his ministry;
2. The main theological principles that have marked contemporary writing about episcopacy and diocesan governance;
3. The transposition of these insights into the 1983 code;

4. Some factors in the Church that shape present attitudes toward bishops.

RECENT THEOLOGICAL DEVELOPMENTS REGARDING THE LOCAL CHURCH AND THE BISHOP

To situate the recent shifts in ecclesiology it would be important to review the historical climate of the Catholic Church from the period 1850 to 1950. Here a nuanced study of its "ultramontanist" undercurrent dominating 19th century ecclesiology and practical church administration in the Latin Church would be needed. During this period a few theologians could be cited as exceptions: Johann Adam Möhler (1796–1838), John Henry Newman (1801–1890), and Adrien Gréa (1828–1917). They were among the few who articulated a vision of Church in an organic, sacramental and pneumatological context that ran counter to what had predominated since the Council of Trent and the controversialist theology of the Counter Reformation typified in the ecclesiology of Robert Bellarmine. Characteristic of the ultramontanist attitude, often as a defense against governmental interference in the Church, was a pronounced emphasis on papal authority even in the ordinary administration of the Church and the presupposition that churches should adopt the disciplinary traditions of the church of Rome (including even its liturgical practices). In the minds of some the Church was inappropriately seen as a vast diocese under the governance of the pope and his administrative assistants, the bishops.

Some shift of emphasis was beginning to emerge already at the time of Vatican I, as for instance in the draft schema on the Church which never reached the council floor because of the outbreak of war. Other shifts were beginning in Scriptural exegesis and church history, but some of these developments were hindered by Rome's highly cautious and severe disciplinary opposition to Modernism. Still the encyclicals of Pius XII, notably *Mystici Corporis Christi* (1943) and *Mediator Dei* (1947), were signs that theological and liturgical developments underway in Europe were having an impact. After World War II in parishes, monasteries and universities, notably in Germany, Austria, France and Belgium, various renewal movements were underway. This included a "return to the sources" especially the bible and the fathers of the Eastern Church.[1] The

---

[1] For an example of a patristic perception of bishops, see Engelbert Neuhäusler, *Der Bischof als geistlicher Vater* (Munich: Kösel, 1964). See original sources such as Gregory the Great, *Regula pastoralis* (ca. 591 A.D.) in *PL* 77: 13–128. Earlier sources include Gregory of Nazianus, *Apologeticus de fuga* (ca. 362) and John Chrysostom, *De sacerdotio* (ca. 386).

structures of church governance in the Eastern Churches, both Orthodox and Catholic, were studied to explain the distinctiveness and the relativity of certain ecclesial structures in the West. The presence in Western European cities, especially Paris, of Russian émigré theologians after the October Revolution helped expand the discussions. The Institut St. Serge of Paris became a center for a distinctive ecclesiology that placed stress on the local bishop (''Eucharistic ecclesiology'') as seen in Orthodox theologians such as Nicholas Afanassieff and Paul Evdokimov.

The renewal of the liturgy brought greater participation by the faithful in the celebration of the Eucharist and in Catholic Action. A so-called ''kerygmatic'' theology based mainly in Innsbruck and Vienna influenced how writers and preachers explained the Church. Since reforms in catechetical material took place on a national level, this contributed to a new assertiveness in the diocesan bishop and the national conferences of bishops. Modern theology studied initially not the bishop as such, not even the local church, but the lay person or groups of laity. The work of Yves Congar, the product of much soul searching and questioning during World War II, was published in 1953 as *Jalons pour une théologie du laïcat* (English translation: *Lay Persons in the Church*, 1965). This volume radically altered the way many Catholics regarded the Church.

Some of the new approaches to theology of the Church were shaped by concerns for the working class. In France the efforts of Cardinal Suhard and the priest-worker movement encouraged bishops to formulate a pastoral agenda for themselves and not to wait for directives from the Roman offices. Such pastoral renewal brought a clearer perception of diocesan responsibility. In Austria, even during the difficult war years from 1939 to 1944, Karl Rahner and Joseph Jungmann collaborated with others at the Vienna Pastoral Institute and formulated the theoretical ground work for the *Handbuch der Pastoraltheologie*, probably the single most important collaborative work that shaped ecclesiology in the 1960s. Rahner's first article on the episcopate appeared in the German review *Stimmen der Zeit* during 1958.[2] His concern was not the nature of the

[2]''Primat und Episkopat,'' *Stimmen der Zeit* 161 (1958) 321–336. English translation in Karl Rahner and Joseph Ratzinger, *The Episcopate and the Primacy* (New York: Herder and Herder, 1962), pp. 11–36. Another important contribution of Rahner is ''Pastoral Theological Observations on Episcopacy in the Teaching of Vatican II,'' *Theological Investigations*, vol. 6 (Baltimore: Helicon, 1969), pp. 361–368. For Rahner's earlier research which influenced Vatican II formulations on the episcopate, see: ''Die Träger des Selbstvollzugs der Kirche,'' *Handbuch der Pastoraltheologie*, ed. F.X. Arnold et al., Bd. I (Freiburg: Herder, 1964), pp. 149–215, and N. Greinacher, ''Der Vollzug der Kirche im Bistum,'' ibid, Bd. III (1968), pp. 59–110.

bishop's office as such, but ways to redress the imbalance between the papacy and the episcopacy. After the announcement of an ecumenical council to complete the unfinished work of Vatican I, a number of important theoretical studies on the episcopacy were published.[3]

A major encouragement to theological research came with the challenge to prepare coherent conciliar decrees on the status of bishops and on their pastoral role.[4] It is a sobering experience to read the initial drafts of the document on the Church, and even more so the drafts of two preparatory documents prepared by the Theological Preparatory Commission: "On Bishops and Diocesan Government" and "On the Care of Souls." These documents, heavily impregnated with the 1917 code and curial prejudices, were so out of touch with the real life of the diocesan churches that they came as a shock to bishops and *periti* alike. These schemata on bishops which are printed in the *Acta* of Vatican II were presented at the 60th general congregation (November 5, 1963) until the 68th general congregation (November 15, 1963). After their rejection and the formation of a new drafting committee, a revised draft, the basis of *Christus Dominus* and hence part of the inspiration of the 1983 code, was debated from the 83rd to 85th general congregations (September 18 to 22, 1964). The gap between the texts of 1963 and 1964 was far greater than that between the first drafts of the new code and its final form in 1983. It is informative to read the interventions by many bishops who opposed changes that would give some autonomy to local bishops or national episcopal conferences and lessen the authority of the Roman Pontiff. One common thread running through the bishops' interventions at the council was resentment toward the Roman Curia. Important insights came from

---

[3]Some important pre-Vatican II research includes J.P. Torrell, *La théologie de l'épiscopat au premier concile de Vatican*, Unam Sanctam, 37 (Paris: Cerf, 1961); *L'Episcopat et l'église universelle*, ed. Y. Congar and B.D. Dupuy, Unam Sanctam, 39 (Paris: Cerf, 1962); W. Stählin et al., *Das Amt der Einheit* (Stuttgart: Schwabenverlag, 1964), French version: *Eglises chrétiennes et épiscopat: Vues fondamentales sur la théologie de l'épiscopat* (Paris: Mame, 1966). Rahner's text is available in English: "The Episcopal Office," *Theological Investigations*, 6: 313–360.

[4]Among the better commentaries on the Vatican II texts about bishops, see Klaus Mörsdorf, "Decree on the Bishops' Pastoral Office in the Church," in *Commentary on the Documents of Vatican II*, ed. H. Vorgrimler, Vol. 2 (New York: Herder, 1968), pp, 165–300; *La Charge pastorale des évêques: Decret 'Christus Dominus'* Unam Sanctam, 74 (Paris: Cerf, 1969); *L'Eglise de Vatican II*, tome 3, Unam Sanctam, 51c (Paris: Cerf, 1966), especially the section: "La constitution hiérarchique de l'Eglise," pp. 721–914. See also, H. Holstein, *Hiérarchie et peuple de Dieu d'après Lumen Gentium* (Paris: Beauchesne, 1970).

bishops of former mission countries where concern for evangelization and inculturation predominated over questions of jurisdiction and protocol.

One of the best preparations for understanding the 1983 code is thus to reread the Vatican II decree on the Pastoral Ministry of Bishops, *Christus Dominus*, especially the sections (*CD*, 12–18) that treat the bishop's ministry in the local church. Drawing upon material from the separate schema "On the Care of Souls," the text describes the bishop's ministry and its relationship to the proclamation of the gospel (*CD*, 12), the promotion of dialogue and the adaptation of doctrine (*CD*, 13), the encouragement of new forms of catechetical instruction (*CD*, 14), sacramental administration (*CD*, 15), pastoral care in governance of groups with special needs (*CD*, 16–18). Apart from Chapter II of *Lumen gentium* "On the People of God" and Chapter III on "The Hierarchical Constitution of the Church and the Episcopacy in Particular," no other conciliar document influenced the new code more.

During the council a number of consultant theologians such as Karl Rahner and Joseph Ratzinger gave lectures that explained how the insights of modern theology could be brought to bear on the texts on the council. The greater realization by bishops that they had independent responsibilities separate from those of the Curia and the papal office raised interest in further research on the nature of the local church.

After the council several follow-up documents were published by Rome to implement the theoretical decisions reached earlier.[5] Then at the first International Bishops' Synod that met from September 30 to October 5, 1967, ten principles were formulated to be guidelines for the revision of the Code of Canon Law.[6] The work of reflection and application has continued to our day as exemplified in the recent meetings of the American bishops at Collegeville for a period of prayer and sharing.[7]

Another factor came into prominence after the close of Vatican II,

---

[5]Post-conciliar documents on the ministry of bishops include: Paul VI, motu proprio *Ecclesiae Sanctae*, August 6, 1966: English translation in *Vatican II: The Conciliar and Post Conciliar Documents*, ed. A. Flannery (Northport: Costello, 1975), pp. 591–610; Congregation for Bishops, *Directory on the Pastoral Ministry of Bishops* (Ottawa: Canadian Conference of Catholic Bishops, 1974); Congregations for Bishops and for Religious and Secular Institutes, Directives for Mutual Relations between Bishops and Religious in the Church, *Mutuae relationes*, April 23, 1978: English translation in *Vatican II: More Postconciliar Documents*, ed. A. Flannery, Vatican Collection, 2 (Northport: Costello, 1982), pp. 209–243.

[6]See the list in *Origins* 12 (February 3, 1983) 544.

[7]*The Ministry of Bishops: Papers from the Collegeville Assembly* (Washington: NCCB, 1982).

namely the establishment of theological bilateral consultations between various confessional bodies. For Roman Catholics this task was encouraged by the Secretariat for Promoting Christian Unity. Episcopacy was not the first question addressed by these dialogues. At first topics such as baptism and Eucharist were addressed. Only later came discussion of authority, primatial and diocesan, followed by explorations on ministry and the ordained ministry of bishop, presbyter, and deacon. Especially among those churches which preserve the historical tripartite division of ordained ministry (Orthodox, Roman Catholic, Anglican, and Lutheran) interest was strong on the role of the bishop. The most creative study ecumenically was one prepared in France by the Group of Les Dombes (a small village near the historic monasteries of Cluny and Taizé). This ecumenical group made up of Roman Catholics and Reformed Christians explored the concept *episkopē* in a text, *Le ministère épiscopal*.[8] Other bilateral international consultations also addressed episcopal ministry such as the Anglican/Roman Catholic International Commission and the Lutheran/Roman Catholic International Commission.[9] Many of the member churches of the World Council's Faith and Order Commission, including the Roman Catholic Church, worked toward the publication of the so-called Lima Document, *Baptism, Eucharist and Ministry* (1982) which included a section on the bishop's office.

One further stimulus for the clarification of episcopal ministry was the preparation and distribution of the earlier drafts of the code. The 1977 draft was evaluated by canon lawyers and ecclesiologists alike, especially in North America, and was criticized on a number of issues. Many improvements were eventually incorporated into the final code.[10]

---

[8]*Le ministère épiscopal* (Taizé: Presses de Taizé, 1976), English translation: "The Episcopal Ministry: Reflections and Proposals concerning the Ministry of Vigilance and Unity in the Particular Church," *One in Christ* 14 (1978) 267–288. The Group has published a follow-up statement entitled *Le ministère de communion dans l'Eglise universelle* (Paris: Le Centurion, 1986).

[9]The major international bilateral consensus statements have been published in *Growth in Agreement: Reports and Agreed Statements of Ecumenical Conversations on a World Level*, ed. H. Meyer and L. Vischer, Ecumenical Documents, 2 (New York: Paulist, 1984). See the Anglican/Roman Catholic *Final Report*, specifically the 1973 Canterbury Statement on "Ministry and Ordination," pp. 78–84 of *Growth*, and the 1981 International Lutheran/Roman Catholic text on "The Ministry in the Church," pp. 248–275 of *Growth*.

[10]See James H. Provost, "The Impact of the Proposed Book II 'De Populo Dei' on the Local Church," *Studia Canonica* 15 (1981) 371–398; Thomas J. Green, "The Revision of Canon Law: Theological Implications," *Theological Studies* 40 (1979) 593–679. For a comprehensive account of the various drafts for the new code, see René Metz, "La nouvelle codification du droit de l'Eglise (1959–1983)," *Revue de droit canonique* 33 (1983) 110–168.

At the end of this brief historical overview we are able to draw up a series of theological principles that characterize the theology of local church and episcopacy. That is the task we assume in our second section.

THEOLOGICAL PERSPECTIVES IN RECENT WRITINGS ON THE EPISCOPACY AND DIOCESAN GOVERNANCE

Some eight theological theses in the last twenty-five years seem to have characterized the way writers have described the local church and the bishop.

1. First, the Church of Christ is truly present in the local church.[11] This teaching of theologians of East and West alike is explicitly affirmed in Vatican II. It is the key for understanding the new ecclesiology which complemented the views of ultramontanism. Its formulation in *Lumen gentium* is perhaps the clearest: "This Church of Christ is really present in all legitimately organized local congregations of the faithful, which insofar as they are united to their pastors [bishops], are also quite appropriately called churches in the New Testament" (*LG*, 26). A similar formulation appears in the Constitution on the Liturgy. Christians, it says, "must be convinced that the principal manifestation of the Church consists in the full active participation of all God's holy people in the same liturgical celebrations, especially in the same Eucharist, in one prayer, at one altar, at which the bishop presides, surrounded by his college of priests and by his ministers" (*SC*, 41).

While not a new notion, the importance of the local church has been neglected by Catholics. In New Testament usage, it was stressed, the term church applied preeminently to the Church of Christ in a specific place.

---

[11]Among the best studies on the local or particular church, see Hervé Legrand, "La réalisation de l'Eglise en un lieu," in *Initiation à la pratique de la théologie*, ed. B. Lauret and F. Refoulé, Tome III: *Dogmatique 2* (Paris: Cerf, 1983), pp. 143–345. See also his commentary on *Christus Dominus*, nos. 11–24, "Nature de l'Eglise particulière et rôle de l'évêque dans l'Eglise," in *La Charge Pastorale* (see above, footnote 4), pp. 103–223. See also Henri de Lubac, *Les églises particulières dans l'Eglise universelle* (Paris: Aubier, 1971). For an Eastern Orthodox perspective: J.D. Zizioulas, "The Local Church in a Eucharistic Perspective," *In Each Place: Towards a Fellowship of Local Churches Truly United* (Geneva: WCC, 1977), pp. 5–61; and the acts of the May 10–June 3, 1980, Orthodox symposium on this theme: *Eglise locale et église universelle*, Etudes théologiques de Chambésy, 1 (Geneva: Centre Orthodoxe, 1981). The Roman Catholic Bishop of Saginaw, Michigan has written on practical ramifications of this teaching: Kenneth E. Untener, "Local Church and Universal Church," *America* 151 (October 13, 1984) 201–205.

Thus, the prerogative of catholicity belongs to each particular church. Catholicity implies a church's possessing all that is necessary to be Church: such as Scriptures, sacraments, ordained ministries, fellowship, common efforts to embody gospel values.

Vatican II had employed both expressions "local" church and "particular" church. The 1983 code prefers the term "particular" church used as an umbrella concept to include not only dioceses, but also territorial prelatures, territorial abbacies, apostolic vicariates, apostolic prefectures, apostolic administrations (c. 368). In practice, however, it becomes an equivalent for the diocesan church. The expression "local" church used in Vatican II (in *Lumen gentium*, 23, 26, 28 [bis]; *Unitatis redintegratio*, 14 [bis]; *Apostolicam actuositatem*, 30; *Ad gentes*, 19, 27, 32; and *Presbyterorum ordinis*, 6 [ter]) is the term that some theologians would have preferred to retain. At least "particulares" is preferable to the term used in the 1917 code, namely "peculiares."

2. Second, the meaning of the ministry of bishop, presbyter and deacon must be understood in the context of the general ministry of all the Christian faithful. This perspective is common to all the bilateral statements and the collective document of the Faith and Order Commission on *Baptism, Eucharist, and Ministry*; it was also affirmed by Vatican II, especially in the decision taken in *Lumen gentium* to place immediately after the first chapter on the mystery of the Church, a chapter on the People of God before chapter three on the ministry of the hierarchy. This arrangement has symbolic importance beyond words as was realized by those who formulated the new code.

3. Third, all Christians, by reason of baptism, possess a basic equality in dignity and in responsibility for the Church's mission. Leaders in the Church such as bishops must be attentive to the many charisms bestowed upon the faithful by the Spirit for the building up of the Church. Vatican II restored to Catholicism the importance of the Pauline concept of charism. The basic formulation of the true equality between laity and hierarchy is stated in *Lumen gentium*: "Although by Christ's will some are established as teachers, dispensers of the mysteries and pastors for the others, there remains, nevertheless, a true equality between all with regard to the dignity and to the activity which is common to all the faithful in the building up of the Body of Christ" (*LG*, 32).

4. The sense in which bishops may be said to be successors of the twelve or of the apostles needs to be carefully nuanced. Exegetes and church historians have recently noted that (a) the functions of the twelve do not correspond fully to those of the apostles in the New Testament; (b) some of the tasks of the apostles in the early church are unique and unrepeatable;

(c) apostolic succession is achieved in the Church not simply by continuity in episcopal ordination but also by the living, ancient faith of the whole Church. These ideas were popularized by the distinguished New Testament scholar Raymond Brown, who brought to the awareness of many the fact that the texts of Vatican II speak with less than scientific accuracy when they state categorically that bishops are the successors of the apostles.[12]

Lumen gentium, 20 is typical of the way that this nexus between apostle and bishop is understood: "For that very reason the Apostles were careful to appoint successors in this hierarchically constituted society." In Rahner's commentary on this passage for the supplement to the *Lexikon für Theologie und Kirche* he views this more as an assertion rather than a proof. He argues that the historical questions connected with this matter have been simplified in the Vatican II texts. The word *successor(es)* (singular or plural) is employed 37 times in the texts of Vatican II, 16 times to refer to the Roman Pontiff as successor to Peter, and 21 times to describe bishops as successors to the apostles. One cautionary remark in the *Nota Explicativa praevia* appended to *Lumen gentium* does note, however, that the statements about bishops do "not imply the transmission of the extraordinary powers of the Apostles to their successors" (*NE*, 1).

In general, it is clear that the texts of Vatican II on episcopacy do not possess the details or distinctions found in later ecumenical consensus statements or in some modern commentaries on the New Testament.

5. Authority and governance in the Church is a form of shepherding undertaken by the bishop in imitation of the Good Shepherd. Governance exists for service and is not a form of dominance.[13] The term for this ministry that had been used in the Latin tradition, common in the 1917 code and repeated in Vatican II, is *regimen*. Although generally translated as "governance," the original intention was to describe "shepherding." The verb from which *regimen* derives etymologically is *regere* used by the Latin Vulgate to translate the Greek *poimainein*. The Vulgate text of Acts 20:28 shows why bishops "shepherd." "Spiritus Sanctus posuit episcopos regere [*poimainein*] Ecclesiam." This ministry is the same assigned to Christ in texts such as Mt 2:6: "regat [*poimanei*] populum."

---

[12]Raymond Brown, *Priest and Bishop: Biblical Reflections* (New York: Paulist, 1970).

[13]On the biblical roots of shepherding especially in Ezekiel 34, see Walther Zimmerli, *Ezekiel 2: A Commentary on the Book of the Prophet Ezekiel Chapters 25–48* (Philadelphia: Fortress, 1983). See also V. Hemp, "Das Hirtenmotiv im Alten Testament," in *Episcopus: Studien über das Bischofsamt*, Festschrift M. Faulhaber (Regensburg: Gregorius, 1949), pp. 7–20. For a critique of erroneous concepts regarding hierarchical power, see Yves Congar, *Power and Poverty in the Church* (Baltimore: Helicon, 1964).

Some possible confusion may result if one mistakenly concludes to an etymological connection between the adjective *regalis* and the words *regimen* or *regere*. However, as the Latin text of 1 Pet 2:9 makes clear, *regale* corresponds to the Greek *basileion*. Christians because of their baptism are called a "chosen race, a royal *(regale)* priesthood, a holy people." Vatican II texts assert that all Christians share in the triple function of Christ as prophet, priest and king. But it is not clear exactly in what this "royal" function consists. It certainly does not imply that anyone besides clerics may exercise *regimen*. *Regimen* in Vatican II refers thirteen times to a spiritual governance of bishops: *Lumen gentium*, 14, 22, 23, 27; *Christus Dominus*, 3, 4 (quoting *LG* 22), 23, 25, 27 (bis); *Orientalium ecclesiarum*, 2, 11; *Presbyterorum ordinis*, 7.

6.   The triple role of the bishop (teaching, sanctifying and shepherding) derives directly from sacramental ordination and not by canonical mission from the pope. Hence the theoretical separation that existed in Catholic theology between *potestas ordinis* of the bishop and *potestas jurisdictionis* must be avoided.

7.   The local bishop possesses his right to governance in such a way that his canonical power is "ordinary, proper and immediate." In the administration of his diocese the bishop retains a certain autonomy from national episcopal conferences, from the Roman congregations, and even from the pope himself.

8.   Finally, by reason of sacramental ordination or consecration into the episcopal college, bishops share in "collegiality," a responsibility for fostering communion among churches throughout the wide world. Hence the ministry of the bishop, although focused primarily on the local diocese, is not restricted exclusively to his own particular church.

These eight theses that have been developed especially in the last twenty-five years seem to be the central insights that have dominated Catholic ecclesiology. We now proceed to see to what extent these principles where transposed into the 1983 Code of Canon law.

Transposition of These Ecclesiological Insights into the 1983 Code of Canon Law

Before commenting on how successful the Roman Catholic Church has been in incorporating these theological and pastoral principles into the 1983 code, it would be helpful briefly to review how the 1917 code envisaged episcopal governance. Instructions about the ministry of bishops were situated in Book Two "De Personis" which contained 639 canons out of the total 2414 (in other words, 27%). The order of the section *De*

Personis is the reverse of the 1983 code. It began with an introduction (22 canons, i.e., 4% of Book Two); clerics (379 canons, 59%), religious (195 canons, 30%), and laity (44 canons, 7%). The 1917 code began to discuss bishops in Titulus VIII, *De potestate episcopali deque iis qui de eadem participant.* The section was subdivided into eleven parts: (1) the bishop in general; (2) the coadjutor/auxiliary bishop; (3) diocesan synod; (4) diocesan curia; (5) chapter of canons; (6) diocesan consultors; (7) vacant sees; (8) vicars forane; (9) pastors (parish priests); (10) parish assistants; (11) rectors of churches.

The 1983 code also devotes Book Two to the same persons now described as "The People of God."[14] It contains 543 out of the total code's 1752 canons, i.e., 31%. The order of discussion is: the Christian faithful (126 canons, 23% of Book Two); hierarchy (243 canons, 45%); and institutes of consecrated life (173 canons, 32%). The section on "The Hierarchical Constitution of the Church" discusses first the supreme church authority (the Roman Pontiff and college of bishops) and then in section two "particular churches and their groupings." This part corresponds to the 1917 Titulus VIII and has three major subdivisions: particular churches and the authority established in them; groupings of particular churches; internal ordering of particular churches. This last section on "ordering" is further subdivided into: the diocesan synod; the diocesan curia; the presbyteral council (and college of consultors); the chapter of canons; the pastoral council; parishes and pastors; vicars forane; rectors of churches.

Before I evaluate how successfully the code was able to incorporate the major theological principles of the last twenty-five years relating to the bishop, I wish to recommend an important work on "The Diocesan Bishop in the Revised Code" by Thomas Green, canon lawyer at the Catholic University of America.[15] My evaluation is organized according to different criteria but there are many points of agreement between us.

---

[14]For a general introduction to the 1983 Code of Canon Law, see: Jean Beyer, "Le nouveau Code de droit canonique: esprit et structures," *Nouvelle revue théologique* 106 (1984) 360–382, 566–583; Richard Puza, "Strömungen und Tendenzen im neuen Kirchenrecht," *Tübingen Theologische Quartalschrift* 163 (1983) 163–178; Winfried Aymans, "Ecclesiological Implications of the New Legislation," *Studia Canonica* 17 (1983) 63–93; Michael D. Place, *A Pastoral Guide to the Revised Code* (Chicago: Chicago Studies, 1984) [reprinted from *Chicago Studies* 23 (1984)]; Roger Paralieu, *Petit guide du nouveau code de droit canonique* (Bourges: Tardy, 1983); Johannes Neumann, *Grundriss des katholischen Kirchenrechts* (Darmstadt: Wissenschaftliche Buchgesellschaft, 1981).

[15]Thomas J. Green, "The Diocesan Bishop in the Revised Code: Some Introductory Reflections," *The Jurist* 42 (1982) 320–347. See also Anthony Padavano, "A Theology of Church Government," *CLSA Proceedings* 33 (1971) 23–27; James K. Mallett, "Diocesan Structure and Governance," *CLSA Proceedings* 42 (1980) 151–160; James Provost, "The

1. What of the importance of the local church in the new code? The most obvious fact to note is that the particular church is mentioned even before the bishop. From the outset it is stated that it is particular churches "in which and from which exists the one and unique Catholic Church" (c. 368). It then clearly affirms the theology of the particular church in canon 369. (For this canon I cite the translation of the Canon Law Society of Great Britain and Ireland which is clearer.) "A diocese is a portion of the people of God, which is entrusted to a Bishop to be nurtured by him, with the co-operation of the *presbyterium*, in such a way that, remaining close to its pastor and gathered by him through the Gospel and the Eucharist in the Holy Spirit, it constitutes a particular church. In this church, the one, holy, catholic and apostolic Church of Christ truly exists and functions." In point of fact this canon 369 is an exact reproduction of *Christus Dominus*, 11, including its nuanced theological use of prepositions.

2. Is the ministry of the hierarchy contextualized within the ministry of the whole Church in the new code? Yes. This is done symbolically and explicitly. The symbolism is seen in the decision to place the canons about the *Christifideles* before those relating to the hierarchy.[16] Canon 207 situates the ordained ministry within the context of general ministry. "Among the Christian faithful by divine institution there exist in the Church sacred ministers, who are clerics in law, and other Christian faithful, who are also called laity." The laity are shown to have very specific rights and obligations as guaranteed in canons 224–231 (the remnants of the original *Lex fundamentalis*). Despite a patronizing tone it is clear that lay persons "who excel in the necessary knowledge, prudence, and uprightness are capable of assisting pastors of the Church as experts or advisors" (c. 228, § 2). But canon 230, § 1 retains a curious anomaly of restricting to laymen the conferral of lector and acolyte on a stable basis (c. 230, § 1) and allows women to serve as a lector only by temporary deputation (c. 230, § 2). In general there is no explicit mention of what specifically laypersons do to participate in the royal (*regale*) office of Christ mentioned in canon 204, § 1. Still there are a number of administrative functions that laypersons are now allowed to exercise.

Working Together of Consultative Bodies—Great Expectations?" *The Jurist* 40 (1980) 257–281; Robin P. Greenwood, "Towards a Church of the People: [Church Understanding and Practice of Church Government]," *Theology* 86 (1983) 416–425.

[16]Gustave Thils, *Les laïcs dans le nouveau code de droit canonique et au IIᵉ concile du Vatican*, Cahiers de la Revue théologique de Louvain, 10 (Louvain la Neuve: Faculté de théologie, 1983). See also Francis Morrisey, "The Laity in the New Code of Canon Law," *Studia Canonica* 17 (1983) 135–148.

3. Does the 1983 code assert a basic equality in dignity of all the faithful? Again, yes. Canon 208 (drawing upon the formulation of *Lumen gentium*, no. 32) states: "In virtue of their rebirth in Christ there exists among all the Christian faithful a true equality with regard to dignity and the activity whereby all cooperate in the building up of the Body of Christ *in accord with each one's own condition and function.*" The addition to the council formulation which I indicate by italics is probably intended to forestall any claim by the laity that the equality is undifferentiated.

Equality of mission in the particular church is also implicit in the code's requirements of participatory governance. The new code establishes principles of consent and counsel (consultation). Five structural organizations are established for the particular church, two of which are obligatory, three are recommended.[17] Obligatory are the presbyteral council which includes a college of consultors drawn from that council (cc. 495 and 502, § 1) and the finance council which can also include members of the laity (c. 492). The three consultative bodies recommended but not obligatory are the diocesan synod (c. 460), the diocesan pastoral council (c. 511) (both of which may include lay members), and the episcopal council or bishop's cabinet (c. 473, § 4).

No mention is given of a national pastoral council, an organization much discussed some ten years ago in the United States. Perhaps the difficulties experienced in the West German and Dutch churches with national pastoral councils may have made the Vatican cautious about recommending them. The experience in Great Britain seems to have been more successful especially in establishing pastoral priorities. National consultations may well be needed to avoid reduplication and neglect of talent. Also omitted from the new code is recommendation of a diocesan personnel board, but it is clearly within the spirit of the legislation for a bishop to establish one or to retain one already in operation.

4. Did the 1983 code nuance the way that bishops are said to be successors of the apostles? No. This is not surprising for a canonical document. Canon 375 repeats the same language of the council: "Through

---

[17]On the various diocesan consultative bodies, see *Code, Community, Ministry: Selected Studies for the Parish Minister Introducing the Revised Code of Canon Law*, ed. James Provost (Washington: CLSA, 1983), especially pp. 53–62. See also Richard Puza, "Die Diözesansynode: Ihre rechtliche Gestalt im neuen CIC (cc. 460–468)," *Tübingen Theologische Quartalschrift* 163 (1983) 223–226. For a historical overview, see L. Chevailler et al., *Le droit et les institutions de l'église catholique latine de la fin du XVIIIᵉ siècle à 1978: Organismes collégiaux et moyens de gouvernement*, Histoire du Droit et des Institutions de l'Eglise en Occident, 17 (Paris: Editions CUJAS, 1982).

the Holy Spirit who has been given to them, bishops are the successors of the Apostles by divine institution. . . . '' This is almost a repetition of the 1917 formulation (c. 329): "Episcopi sunt Apostolorum successores atque ex divina institutione peculiaribus ecclesiis praeficiuntur. . . . ''

5. In what way does the new code stress the ministry of the bishop as shepherding, or governing for service and not control? The new legislation tries to incorporate new terminology to describe the bishop's task such as "munus pastorale" (c. 381). Also the word *iurisdictio* recedes and gives way to *regimen*, a term, as we have seen, inspired by the Vulgate's *regere*, "acting as a (good) shepherd." Occasionally *potestas regiminis* appears as *potestas iurisdictionis*. The 1983 code states that one must be ordained to exercise *regimen* (c. 129). This may be a sound canonical principle, but it does not take into consideration the importance of the laity's cooperation in the governance of the Church. Another term for the governing function of the bishop is *gubernatio* (cf. c.375 §1), which seems to be an allusion to *gubernatio* or "steering" (*kybernesis*) mentioned by St. Paul in 1 Cor 12:28 as a specific charism in the Church.

The ambiguities found in Vatican II about how all Christians (including the laity) share in the triple role of Christ as prophet, priest and king remain in the code. The reflections of Edward Kilmartin on this troubling question will have to receive further attention and analysis.[18]

The function of *regimen* is also spelled out in canon 205 where it is stated that for a baptized Christian to be fully in communion with the Catholic Church one must be joined with Christ in its visible structures by bonds of profession of faith, of the sacraments, and of the ecclesiastical governance (*regiminis*).

6. Does the 1983 code affirm that the bishop's ministry proceeds directly from sacramental ordination and not from a canonical mission? Yes, this is the clear conclusion from canon 375, § 2 but the concept needs to be further expanded. A new notion is added to this, that of "possessio canonica" (e.g., cc. 380, 382, 388). The relationship of ordination and of canonical appointment needs more exploration.

7. Does the new code assure the bishop of autonomy in the adminis-tration of his diocese? Yes and no. Whereas it does state that "a diocesan

---

[18]Edward J. Kilmartin, "Lay Participation in the Apostolate of the Hierarchy," in *Official Ministry in a New Age*, ed. James Provost (Washington: CLSA, 1981), pp. 89–116 [reprint of *The Jurist* 41, no. 2 (1981)]. In the same volume, see James Provost, "Toward a Renewed Canonical Understanding of Official Ministry," pp. 194–225. Valuable historical material can be found in Garrett J. Roche, "Hierarchy: From Dionysius to Trent to Vatican II," *Studia Canonica* 16 (1982) 367–389.

bishop in the diocese committed to him possesses all the ordinary, proper and immediate power (*potestas*) which is required of his pastoral office . . . '' it continues with the rider '' . . . except for those cases which the law or a decree of the Supreme Pontiff reserves to the supreme authority of the Church or to some other ecclesiastical authority'' (c. 381). What would be crucial here is to determine if there are limits to what the Supreme Pontiff may reserve without compromising episcopal autonomy. Also it would be helpful to have a further explanation of who might be "some other ecclesiastical authority" cited in the canon.

8. Finally, how does the concept of collegiality find embodiment in the new code?[19] This aspect of the bishop's ministry is stressed in the reaffirmation of the conference of bishops (c. 447) in which a bishop is expected to participate. Bishops are said to "jointly exercise certain pastoral functions on behalf of the Christian faithful of their territory in view of promoting that greater good which the Church offers humankind, especially through forms and programs of the apostolate which are fittingly adapted to the circumstances of the time and place" (c. 447). Rather than having the Vatican draw up the constitutions of the conferences of bishops "each conference is to prepare its own statutes" (c. 451) which must be reviewed, however, by the Holy See. Once legitimately erected it "enjoys a juridic personality by the law itself" (c. 449, § 2). Another form of sharing collegiality is recognized in canon 459 which encourages mutual relationships between the conferences of bishops of different regions, especially those who are neighbors.

A global response to the question whether the 1983 code sufficiently incorporates the insights of modern theological research on episcopal ministry would be a cautious yes. In general, the code is as inclusive as Vatican II, recognizing that the council did not accept as its own some of the currents of theological research at that time.

Some Factors in the Church that Shape Present Attitudes Toward Bishops

Despite the careful planning that preceded the new code's elaboration of Book Two on the "People of God," there remain problem areas of

---

[19]Michael J. Sheehan, "'Is There Any Life in the Church Beyond the Diocese?' Supra-diocesan Structures and Church Governance," *CLSA Proceedings* 42 (1980) 132–150; Willy Onclin, "Le pouvoir de l'Eglise et le principe de la collégialité," in *La Chiesa dopo il Concilio*, Atti del congresso internazionale di diritto canonico, Roma, 14–19 Gennario, 1970, Vol. I (Milan: Giuffré, 1972), pp. 135–161; Jérôme Hamer, "La responsabilité collégiale de chaque évêque," *Nouvelle revue théologique* 105 (1983) 641–654.

considerable moment. I wish to identify briefly ten factors that shape the present view of bishops. The first two are attitudinal changes in the Church, the following eight are weaknesses rooted in the new code.

1. The attitude of many Roman Catholics toward authority has shifted notably in the last two decades. Nowhere does the code suggest that bishops are facing opposition or indifference because of what some perceive as abuse or ineffective use of authority by leaders in the Church. The mood of some Catholics, whose number is difficult to estimate, is characterized by frustration, indifference, or even anger. Some, especially women, resent that they are not listened to or consulted. Others feel they have been marginalized by authoritarian statements from the pope, various congregations, chancery officials, or local clergy. The feeling is expressed that "authorities" have abused authority by premature judgments or exaggerated condemnations especially in sexual morality (remarriage, contraception, homosexuality, premarital sex, in vitro fertilization). Opposition to women's access to ordained ministry is seen by some as patriarchal and authoritarian. Hence, even the most open bishop is called upon to exercise his governance amidst a climate hostile to church spokesmen.

2. The role of the local bishop or even the national conference of bishops seems obscured by what is judged to be interference by higher or even the "supreme" authority. Some are convinced that the bishop's governance is unduly hampered by Vatican congregations or even direct interventions of the papacy. Examples of this would include objections by the Congregation for the Doctrine of the Faith concerning forms of liberation theology, aggressive investigations or "conversations" with various theologians in a setting that hardly inspires a sense of fair play or due process. Some point to actions by the Vatican to remove imprimaturs especially from catechisms as another example. Others point to investigations of diocesan bishops. Others cite the mandated study of the American seminaries underway at the request of the Vatican, or the mandated study on religious congregations especially of women. Others are convinced that the Vatican is not well informed about local or national matters because of one-sided advocacy groups. Such actions create the impression that local autonomy is merely tolerated within narrowly defined parameters.

3. The selection process for bishops remains a problem area in the judgment of some. Lay persons sometimes feel a sense of helplessness regarding their views on the choice of a new bishop. Such powerlessness is hardly dissipated by the unfortunate wording of canon 377, § 3: "if he [the bishop] judges it expedient" certain members of the laity can be

consulted if they "are outstanding for their wisdom." The problem of selecting bishops is not as acute when the choice is a talented, sensitive, fearless person. But if the choice is problematic, then people, including priests, feel powerless and wish they had more to say about his successor. The role of the apostolic delegate or papal legate in the selection of candidates is viewed with uneasiness. The norms for the selection of bishops published on March 25, 1972 do not allay concerns, in fact the norms are seen as a retreat from broad consultation. It is widely reported and believed that only candidates who have responded satisfactorily to controverted questions regarding contraception, ordination of women, etc., will be serious contenders for the bishop's office.

4. The size of dioceses, especially in large urban areas, is a source of much concern and discussion. The 1983 code does not give attention to this problem. Some feel that dioceses are kept disproportionately large and administered by a large number of auxiliary bishops for reasons that are more political than pastoral. The code's call for direct personal pastoral care by the diocesan bishop does not ring true in the experience of Catholics in large urban settings. Some may never have been able even to assist at a Eucharist presided over by the bishop.

5. Procedures for accountability of bishops are weak in the new code. Once a person has been appointed to an office it is not clear how his performance is to be evaluated. The formal *ad limina* visits to Rome are not always seen as effective procedures. More consultation in a diocese is laudable, but structurally there must be mechanisms for sororial or fraternal correction of the bishop. Presumably the bishop's spiritual director, close friends, or psychological counsellor, if he has one, will provide helpful suggestions. Canon 212, § 2 states: "The Christian faithful are free to make known their needs, especially spiritual ones, and their desires to the pastors of the Church." What is not clear is how to find effective ways for expressing those needs.

6. Conceivably from the perspective of the year 2083 it may be judged that the 1983 code concentrated too much on the role of the *episcopus* rather than the *parochus* (the "pastor" in American usage, the "parish priest" in Canadian and British usage). In practice, it is the pastor who for most persons exercises *regimen* in the particular church. If the faithful experience sanctifying, teaching and shepherding in the modern church it is more likely because of contacts with the pastor.

7. Despite the remarks made in passing in the 1983 code about the need for concern about other Christian churches, attention to ecumenism is somewhat scant. One applauds the suggestion of canon 463, § 3 to invite

non-Catholics to a diocesan synod; one agrees with canon 383, § 3 about the need for the bishop "to act with kindness and charity toward those who are not in full communion with the Catholic Church." But a more formal directive in the code about Catholic bishops co-operating directly with Orthodox, Anglican, Lutheran bishops, or even leaders in other churches who exercise oversight would have been helpful. The scope of local cooperation among priests and ministers is often good. The need for improvement resides mostly at episcopal levels for ethical, social, educational, and liturgical concerns.

8. One further area of neglect, which may be inevitable in the literary genre of a legal codification, is to relate the three areas of pastoral care of the bishop. Statements about governance and administration made in Book II about the bishop need to be integrated more forcefully with the obligations of the bishop in Book III (on the teaching office of the Church) and in Book IV (on the office of sanctifying in the Church). This excessive compartmentalization can be reduced by finding other ways for describing the bishop's ministry besides the triple division of teaching, sanctifying, and governing.

9. Another omission is frank admission that there may arise situations where tension will exist between decisions of a diocesan bishop and those of the national episcopal conference. This was a large concern of the bishops who spoke against episcopal conferences during Vatican II. Understanding this tension may help the interpreter explain why there was a notable shift away from the authority of episcopal conferences in the earlier drafts of the code to the final text. A similar, perhaps more serious source of tension, is conflict that could arise between a bishop's priorities and those of the international Synod of Bishops.

10. Finally, history may judge that the code of 1983 did not achieve its goal because it did not envisage the possibility of a limited term of office as bishop.[20] Perhaps the idea is still too premature in the Roman Catholic context. It has been suggested, however, by some groups of theologians. What is meant is not the provision for retirement at the age of 75 or because of serious illness (both of which are envisaged in c. 401). Rather what has

---

[20]On a limited term of office for the diocesan bishop see the proposal by the Catholic Theological Faculty of Tübingen in L. Swidler and A. Swidler, edd., *Bishops and People* (Philadelphia: Westminster, 1970), pp. 22–37 [originally appeared in *Tübingen Theologische Quartalschrift* Vol. 148, no. 2 (1968)]. See also *Reform und Anerkennung kirchlicher Ämter: Ein Memorandum der Arbeitsgemeinschaft ökumenischer Universitätsinstitute* (Munich: Kaiser; Mainz: Matthias Grünewald, 1973). The main statement is translated in *Journal of Ecumenical Studies* 10 (1973) 390–401.

been suggested is the pastoral effectiveness of a possible term of office for all bishops limited to eight or ten years. The experience of other Christian churches might be of assistance on this matter.

CONCLUSION

After some hesitations the Roman Catholic Church learned not to use the 1917 Code of Canon Law as a source book for theological reflection. Catholics came to recognize that code as a particular embodiment of a specific view of Church and governance very much the child of its time. A similar judgment is at work regarding the 1983 code. It will help us appreciate the achievement of Vatican II and structural improvements in our community since the council's closing in 1965. But the experience of Vatican II has not been only the elaboration of texts or creation of new procedures. Behind it all lay a conversion of heart, a shift of horizon, a vision shared by many under grace. Behind the new code rests communal efforts to comprehend and to judge, a struggle to discern pastoral wisdom, a dedication to serve, hopes not yet fulfilled. If we listen attentively and prudently to the voices speaking in our Church, we shall be guided for now and for the future.

THE EVOLVING CHURCH AND CHURCH GOVERNANCE

Eugene F. Hemrick

"Do you feel you might have knowledge about the Church from the research you have conducted that we bishops do not have?" The question was asked of me during an administrative meeting of the bishops.

It was not the first time a question of this nature has been asked of me. The National Task Force on Church Personnel raised it because of concern over the dwindling numbers of priests and religious. The question was also brought up by the New England Conference of Councils of Priests (NECOPS) at their fall meeting of 1984. What follows has been shared with the above concerned parties.

During the last seven years we have conducted research in many areas of ministry. There are now sufficient data to piece together a mosaic on church services. Although the mosaic could use more pieces of information, the data we do have has definitely produced valuable indicators on the state of affairs.

For the purpose of this paper I have selected specific findings from several pertinent studies. They are cited not to bore the reader with numbers, but in hopes that as one statistic follows the other they will heighten our consciousness of the dramatic movements the Church is experiencing. They are the heart of the mosaic which defines the key problems as well as the opportunities for growth, that challenge those in governing positions. We will focus on the status of religious life, the permanent diaconate, lay volunteerism, religious education, diocesan pastoral councils, and offices of planning and research.

RELIGIOUS LIFE

Vocations

We turn first to the statistics on vocations to the priesthood and religious life.

In the last fifteen years, enrollment at the high school and college

140

seminary level declined 74%, religious novitiates 68% and theologates 50%.[1]

Recent declines in religious seminarians have been slightly greater than in diocesan seminaries. The declines in the religious brotherhood have been somewhat greater than in the priesthood.[2] Projections for ordinations, when combined with projections for resignations, retirements, and deaths, lead to a projected 50% decline in the population of active diocesan clergy by the year 2000.[3] It should be noted that these projections are presently being updated by the Office of Research NCCB/USCC to see if any substantial changes have taken place since they were made.

In the 1960s the typical first-year theology student was twenty-two or twenty-three years old. Today's seminarian tends to be older. One large seminary found that in the last few years at least 20% of the first-year theologians were thirty years old or older. There are more "second career" or "delayed" vocations today than previously.[4]

Information compiled by the Centro Catolico para Hispanos del Nordeste shows that in 1982 the total number of Hispanics preparing for the priesthood was 961, or 7.9% of all United States seminarians. Hispanics are still underrepresented in the seminary population relative to their numbers in the total Catholic population of the United States—which is estimated at 25%.[5]

A recent study found approximately 163 black seminarians at the college and theology level. Only about 270 of the 58,000 priests in the United States are black, even though an estimated 2% of American laity are black.[6]

---

[1]Adrian Fuerst, "Commentary on Seminary College Statistics for 1983," *Cara Seminary Forum* 10–11 (Winter 1982—Spring 1983) 1.

[2]William Ferree, "An Atlas on the Way Out of the Vocation Crisis," (University of Dayton: Institute of Consecrated Life, 1983), p. 5. (Photocopied)

[3]Richard Schoenherr and Annemette Sorensen, *Decline and Change in the U.S. Catholic Church: From the Second Vatican to the Second Millenium*, CROS Report, 5 (Madison: CROS/University of Wisconsin, 1981), p. 36.

[4]Thomas R. Ulshafer, "The Diocesan Seminarian of the '80s," National Conference of Diocesan Vocation Directors *News* (May-June-July 1983), p. 2; Christopher J. Pino, "Interpersonal needs, counselor style, and personality change among seminarians during the 1970s," *Review for Religious Research* 21 (1980) 354; Richard M. McGuinness, "Rootedness" (Emmitsburg, MD: Mount St. Mary Seminary, 1981), p. 1.

[5]*Seminary News* (1981) 2; (1982) 4–5.

[6]Task Group for Black Seminarians and The Catholic University of America Center for

When it is asked, "What type of seminarian do we have today?" researcher William McCready says, "There is some preliminary evidence beginning to emerge that today's seminarians are people in need of a great deal of personal affirmation who come from troubled familial settings."[7] Other observers indicate that the characteristics of today's seminarian include independence, lack of commitment and self-knowledge, less altruism, more conservatism, and more prestige orientation.[8] On the other hand several other observers see increased maturity, more interest in sacred functions of the priesthood, and more individuality.[9]

If we ask, "what is being done to foster vocations?" "A large nationwide study of active priests in 1970 found that there was indeed a trend away from active encouragement to a hands-off approach. Among these priests, 34% said they were less encouraging concerning vocations. Younger priests, those likely to be the most attractive role models for young men considering the priesthood, were least likely to encourage vocations actively."[10] Although it was shown in one study that 74% of parents thought vocation talks for elementary school children were a good thing, 58% of the parents did not think they should actively promote vocations for their own son or daughter.[11]

These findings prompted the Assembly of Ordinaries and Rector-Presidents of seminaries in collaboration with the National Catholic Education Association, the Office of Research NCCB/USCC, and the Bishops' Committee on Priestly Formation to undertake a national study in 1985 of all theologians. The study will look at their background, what prompted them to enter a seminary, and how they view the Church and their role in it.

the Study of Youth Development, "A National Survey of Black Catholic Seminarians" (Washington: The Catholic University of America, 1983), p. 1.

[7]William McCready, "Presentation," in *Laborers for the Vineyard*, Proceedings of a FADICA Conference on Church Vocations, December 1983 (Washington: USCC, 1984), p. 48.

[8]Thomas J. Morgan, "Screening Applicants for the Priesthood," *The Priest* 36 (February 1980) 12–15; Matthias Newman, "Assessing Priestly Formation Today," *The Priest* 37 (October 1981) 39–45.

[9]Mary Fay Bourgoin, "Seminarians an Endangered Species," *National Catholic Reporter* 19 (February 25, 1983) 7, 24.

[10]National Opinion Research Center [NORC], *The Catholic Priest in the United States: Sociological Investigations* (Washington: USCC, 1972), p. 269.

[11]Joseph Fichter, *Catholic Parents and Church Vocations* (Washington: CARA, 1967), pp. 12–13, 84.

Sisters

Taking a brief look at vocations to the sisterhood we learn from a study conducted by Sister Marie Augusta Neale:[12]

> Overall membership is now 60% of what it was in 1966. The number of sisters in final vows is down 30%; in initial commitment down 86%; novices down 89%; affiliates down 85%; candidates down 83%.
>
> An average congregation had 410 members in 1966. It had 309 in 1982.
>
> Each retained an average of thirty-two candidates in 1966, two in 1982. This, of course, reflects the smaller numbers entering.
>
> From 1950 to 1955, 70% of those who entered stayed; from 1966 to 1970, 51%; from 1975 onward 76%. That means that those who enter are staying, but not so many are entering.
>
> The high point for new candidates leaving before making final vows was 1970. Then, an average of fifteen per congregation left, as compared to three in 1980. This, of course, is related again to the lower number entering.
>
> In 1966, 16% of the membership were under perpetual vows; today, 3.7%. In 1966, 19% were over 65; today, 37%.
>
> In 1966, 8% were inactive due to illness or old age; today, 23%. Therefore, the overall decrease in numbers in initial formation is 86%. The overall increase in inactives is 72%. So the replacement potential is down 159%.

Religious Brothers

In the report, *Catholic Church Personnel in the United States*, the statistics on religious brothers speak for themselves.[13]

Year	Brothers
1960	10,445
1965	12,250
1970	11,597
1975	8,612
1980	7,626
1983	7,658

[12]Marie Augusta Neale, "Presentation," in *Laborers for the Vineyard*, p. 54.
[13]Task Force Report, "Catholic Church Personnel in the United States," (1984), p. 5.

Retirement Concerns

In the 1982 survey of retirement concerns of religious institutes conducted by NCCB/USCC Office of Research, the Leadership Conference of Women Religious, and the Conference of Major Superiors of Men, three findings in particular immediately catch our attention.[14]

> Sixty-five percent of the membership of the Leadership Conference of Women Religious and the Conference of Major Superiors of Men is aged 50 and above. The current median age of the members is 57 and is expected to increase in an exponential, not linear fashion.
> A high percent of members foresee a financial crisis in responding to the costs of caring for aged and infirmed religious institute members.
> Fifty-six percent of the members have not had an actuarial study, and of the total membership of both Conferences only 10% plan to have one conducted.

The results of this study have ended in actuarial help being given to some of the religious orders who indicated an immediate need for it. One diocese has called together all of its religious orders to identify those in most trouble. It has also approached foundations interested in funding a cause like this and asked for their assistance.

There are many more statistics that could be cited. It is sufficient here to say there will definitely be less of a presence of those in religious life in the Church from now until the year 2000. Many changes will be experienced in the next few years. Religious life will have an older appearance. A number of religious communities will be consumed more with maintaining their aged and infirmed than with growing in numbers and new programs. Some religious communities and dioceses will reflect holding patterns rather than projecting a progressive image. In other places we will also see a remnant which will give the Church new types of vitality unexperienced before.

It would seem that the moral, spiritual and physical support that priests, sisters and brothers generally give to each other in terms of numbers will be far less than in the past. Parish rectories or community recreation rooms, for example, where there are several persons sharing experiences

---

[14]National Task Force on Religious Retirement Cases, *Survey of Retirement Concerns of Religious Institutes in the United States* (Washington: USCC, 1982), p. 14.

with each other, will be more of an exception than norm. One thing for certain is that the life style of parishes, to say nothing of religious communities may bear little resemblance to what we have experienced.

In a few dioceses we have samples of such changes in life style. In Hartford, for example, Archbishop Whealon has established a lay-clerical team to run St. James Church in Rocky Hill. He describes the team as a ''brave experiment'' made possible by the revised Code of Canon Law. Although both ordained permanent deacons and lay people have served under priests in many parishes the appointment of a deacon, lay person and priest at St. James as a joint team is considered unique in the official administration of a parish.

In addition to this uniqueness, before the lay-clerical team was approved each member was carefully screened by both church officials and a psychologist. Imagine what a priest who was named a pastor twenty years ago would have said to psychological testing in order to be compatible with a lay person and permanent deacon as co-equals.

In other parts of the country dioceses are clustering their priests together in one place and having them serve many parishes that no longer can afford a priest. Deacons, their wives and lay persons are becoming the administrators of parishes. There are one or two dioceses that have sisters as chancellors. Some dioceses are replacing chancery office clergy with lay personnel and women religious in order to conserve their priests for parish work, and they are also reducing 2 or 3 priests parishes to a one priest parish. Diocesan priests wishing to continue their studies are being limited. In some dioceses there is the trend of priests reverting back to being an associate pastor, rather than desiring to be a pastor, or opting for smaller parishers rather than big ones.

On the national scene a national task force on future personnel needs of the Church has recently recommended that the question of redistribution of priests be addressed seriously.[15]

And then there is the new presence of married priests and their wives who once belonged to the Anglicans. Whether some want to admit it or not, these few statistics and observations alone tell us religious life is going through a dramatic evolution.

The Permanent Diaconate

In 1980 the NCCB Bishops' Committee on the Permanent Diaconate commissioned the NCCB/USCC Office of Research to conduct a national

---

[15]"Catholic Church Personnel in the United States," p. 10.

study of the permanent diaconate in the United States. One purpose for the study was to establish a better understanding of this new ministry in order to update the original guidelines of the permanent diaconate.

Today, we have more than 6000 permanent deacons with another 2,500 in formation. In *A National Study of the Permanent Diaconate in the United States*[16] we learn:

> The majority of permanent deacons, 70%, are between 41 and 60 with the median age being 49. Almost all are married, average 4 children, and 75% say they have one or two children currently residing at home (p. 13).
>
> Deacons devote an average of 14 hours per week to their ministry. Over half, however, do not have a role description and 75% of their supervisors have not had training for their role (p. 15).
>
> Eighty-eight percent of deacons say they would definitely seek ordination again if asked to do it over. Ninety-four percent report they are very to moderately satisfied with the diaconate (pp. 15–16).
>
> Wives of deacons report that their husband's new role as deacon has had a good impact on their spiritual and married life and their relationship to the Church (pp. 28–30).
>
> Of the 196 bishops, 65% are generally positive toward the restoration of the diaconate. Twenty-six percent accept the restoration of the diaconate with reservation, and only 5% report a negative reaction to it (pp. 36, 41.)
>
> With regard to overall orientation of formation programs, 44.5% describe them as primarily academic, 26.6% as primarily pastoral, 20% as primarily spiritual, and 85% as mixed in orientation (pp. 16–17).
>
> Respondents rank scriptural, theological and spiritual training as the most adequate elements of their formation. Counseling, field experience, hospital ministry, canon law and training for prison ministry are rated least adequate (pp. 16–17).
>
> The vast majority of deacons receive no salary (p. 14).
>
> On the subject of continuing education and annual retreats, 62.6% say they have participated in formal continuing education courses, and 84% report that they make an annual retreat (p. 17).
>
> With regard to financial assistance for ongoing education and

---

[16]The Bishops' Committee on the Permanent Diaconate, *National Study of the Permanent Diaconate in the United States* (Washington: USCC, 1981).

retreats 73.5% receive no financial assistance for continuing education, 67.8% receive no financial assistance for participating in seminars (p. 14).

Comparing the Church of today with that of twenty years ago it is clear it has a new force of ordained men. It should be noted that many of the wives of these deacons have also become a very active force in church service working side by side with their husbands.

Most deacons appear to be very happy with the diaconate. Likewise, their bishops and supervisors are positive about their existence. The permanent diaconate is one of the most recent ministries the Church has for increasing her services.

If the diaconate is to grow stronger several areas need to be reassessed. For example, how much can we realistically expect of a man in serving the Church who is working full time and raising a family? If many deacons' supervisors are not prepared to direct them what needs to be done in this area?

As of yet, we have no indepth research on the effectiveness of diaconal formation programs. For instance, what are the various screening methods employed to guarantee a sound choice of candidates? Are deacons being trained for the local needs of a particular diocese, or the universal Church? What are the advantages of a curriculum that concentrates either on the practical, or academic, or spiritual? How well are the needs of the Church being matched with the gifts of these men?

A very big question that confronts the Church is, "Will there be a practice in the near future of asking deacons to be full time administrators of parishes?" If so, what provisions are formation programs making for this new stage in the evolution of the Church?

Finally, if the wives of deacons fulfill an important role in their ministry will there be a need in the future for some type of recognition of this role?

Again, the few statistics we have cited raise big questions for those in governance about the continued evolution of the permanent diaconate.

LAY VOLUNTEERISM

About 145 lay volunteer programs exist presently. Many of these programs are too new to have statistics on trends, but Maryknoll lay missions may serve as an indicator of recent trends on lay volunteers. Between 1975 and 1982 the annual number of inquiries about the lay mission program increased tenfold—from 300 to 3,320. The number of missioners actually contracted was very small by comparison. It fluctuated from 12 in 1975 to 26 in 1977, and 22 in 1982. The dramatic increase in inquiries during the last 10 years suggests that interest in short-term religious service is growing.[17]

Volunteers are generally satisfied with their experience in volunteer programs and feel they are well-received at their work sites. The main goal of the volunteers seems to be to grow as a Christian through service, primarily to the poor. Most volunteers feel that the experience did help them achieve this growth.[18]

Many religious communities appear to view lay volunteer programs as beneficial for all concerned in their own right and as important sources of potential candidates for the religious life. Since personal contact with religious "living the life" is viewed as one of the most important facets of recruiting, summer work programs are seen as an ideal means of introducing potential candidates to the religious life. One order noted that it typically gets two candidates a summer from an eight-week program of service and community living for men between 18 and 30 years of age. The director of a similar program notes that summer programs serve as feeders for the longer term programs, and they also enable young men who are doubtful of their ability to make a permanent commitment to religious life to test their ideals and hopes and "at least to see the possibility of a permanent commitment in service, faith and community."[19]

Recently International Liaison, the national office for lay volunteerism, contacted the NCCB/USCC Office of Research in order to conduct a national study on lay volunteerism. It is hoped that the new study will help us better understand why lay volunteerism is growing so quickly and who are involved. It is also hoped that this study will shed some light on vocations to the religious life.

Religious Education

In 1977 NCCB/USCC Office of Research conducted the study, *The National Inventory of Parish Catechetical Programs*, which studied all directors of religious education, whether full or part time, professional or volunteer, and their programs.[20] The results of this study led to a second

---

[17]Dean R. Hoge, Raymond H. Potvin, and Kathleen M. Ferry, *Research on Men's Vocations to the Priesthood and the Religious Life* (Washington: USCC, 1984), pp. 59–60.

[18]Arlene E. Brooks, *Profile of the Church-Related Volunteer* (Washington: International Liaison, 1980), pp. 164–165.

[19]Kevin O'Malley, "Volunteer Programs and Religious Communities," *Review for Religious* 34 (1975) 734.

[20]Eugene F. Hemrick, *A National Inventory of Parish Catechetical Programs* (Wash-

study titled, *National Profile of Professional Religious Education Coordinators/Directors.*[21] This study was concerned only with professional directors of religious education and the level of quality that religious education has reached since the establishment of directors of religious education in this country.

It is estimated there are over 5000 professional DREs in the United States. According to the National Catechetical Directory a professional DRE is defined:

> A person with a master's degree in theology, religious education, or an equivalency, and at least three years of administration or teaching experience who has demonstrated skills in organization and is a salaried, full-time member of a parish staff.

The *National Profile of Professional Religious Education Coordinators* reports:

> Women DREs outnumber men DREs 83% to 17%. Of the female DREs 53% are religous sisters, and 47% laywomen. Seventy-four percent of all DREs range in age from 31 to 50 years (pp. 10–11). Written job descriptions are had by 84%, and 80% believe their job description is "nearly" to "very" accurate, while only 63% believe that it is "somewhat realistic" to "realistic" in terms of what one person can achieve in the position (pp. 17–18).
>
> Seventy-three percent have written contracts. However, the majority (86%) of the contracts extend for only one year (pp. 17–18). The majority of directors work 45 hours or more a week. Thirty-six percent would definitely encourage others to be coordinators and another 61 percent said they would encourage others, but with reservations (pp. 39, 77).
>
> Ninety-two percent have a high to moderate degree of satisfaction with their work (p. 76).
>
> There seems to be a good stability among directors in that they average eight years in total number of years they have held the position (p. 15).
>
> Thirty-seven percent of the religious education directors see the effectiveness of educating non-parochial school students as basi-

ington: USCC, 1978).

[21]Thomas P. Walter, *National Profile of Professional Religious Education Coordinators/Directors* (Washington: National Conference of Diocesan Directors of Religious Education, 1983).

cally to totally ineffective (p. 56).

(Unfortunately, there was no follow-up question to learn what exactly was meant by ineffectiveness. One guess is that DREs have not found a way of fully involving students on the secondary level in religous education programs. We are not getting to our high schoolers.)

Forty-two percent are somewhat to totally dissatisfied with their salaries (p. 63).

In 1980 we still had 2,508,642 children on the elementary level and 3,297,350 youth on the secondary level, or 43.5% of both grade levels, not receiving formal religious education.[22]

In light of the positive and negative aspects of religious education it must be asked, "Are DREs here to stay and will they grow in numbers and effectiveness?" Or, will they repeat the history of the Protestant professional religious educators who once were very prominent and then disappeared because of financial, organizational, and doctrinal problems within their church? These questions present some serious considerations for the future to those in positions of church governance.

DIOCESAN PASTORAL COUNCILS

In 1982 the NCCB Bishops' Committee on the Laity commissioned the NCCB/USCC Office of Research to conduct a study on diocesan pastoral councils. The results of the study produced the book, *Building the Local Church: Shared Responsibility in Diocesan Pastoral Councils*.[23] The study also became the basis for three regional meetings around the country to understand better the role of these councils and their future in the Church.

From a paper given on that study[24] we learn:

Sixty-nine dioceses have a council, 9 plan to have one within the next year or two, and an additional 11 are in an early planning stage to have one.

The median age of existing councils is 9 years.

---

[22]Eugene F. Hemrick and Andrew Thompson, *The Last Fifteen Years* (Washington: USCC, 1982).

[23]Eugene F. Hemrick and Mary P. Burke, *Building the Local Church: Shared Responsibility in Diocesan Councils* (Washington: USCC, 1984).

[24]Eugene F. Hemrick, "Our Diocesan Pastoral Councils," paper given at the Annual Meeting of Parish and Diocesan Councils Network [PADICON], Houston, Texas, March 1984, pp. 1–7.

When DPCs were asked about their strength they ranked first the statement, "Laity are represented on the council."
Laity account for about two-thirds of the council membership.
The main activities DPCs sponsor are: (1) establishing task forces for special projects; (2) sponsoring studies for data on needs, issues, and priorities; (3) promoting meetings at the regional, vicariate, or deanery level.
Some of the roles that DPCs fulfill consist of, "caller to action," "listener," "promoter of better communication," "futurologist," and "counsellor."

For example, as caller to action, a DPC establishes task forces on special projects. It listens by sponsoring research. In promoting regional or deanery level meetings it promotes better communication, and by helping to set goals it acts as futurologist. DPCs greatest impact is on the setting of diocesan goals; next is in the area of parish renewal, and third, the development of diocesan mission statements. DPCs report good support from the bishop, but very little relationship or consultation with other diocesan offices. The greatest frustration of DPCs is a lack of understanding of what the council does and a lack of appreciation by the clergy.

OFFICES OF PLANNING AND RSEARCH

In 1980 the NCCB Office of Research in collaboration with the National Pastoral Planning Conference conducted a study on the existing diocesan offices of planning and research. The study produced the book, *Diocesan Pastoral Planning in the '80s*.[25] From that study we learn that since 1966, 47 of such offices have been established in dioceses across the country. These offices provide the following services:[26]

On the diocesan level, services consist in taking diocesan census profiles, setting goals, conducting leadership programs, constructing budgets, etc.
At the parish level, offices report they service parish councils, help establish parish committees, engage in research projects, and offer in-parish training to parish leaders.
On the interoffice level, offices help other diocesan offices plan

---

[25]Ruth N. Doyle, Eugene F. Hemrick, and Patrick Hughes, *National Pastoral Planning in the 1980s* (Newark, NJ: National Pastoral Planners Conference, 1983).
[26]Ibid., p. 7.

and conduct research projects and coordinate programs of the various offices.
Within the office itself, offices report studying the feasibility of computer systems and developing better planning techniques.

Although most offices move in and out of all four levels of service it would seem they tend to be engaged most in total diocesan-level projects.
In response to a request to describe two major goals of the office five respective categories emerged.[27]

First, diocesan offices are concerned with goal setting and planning processes within the diocesan structure.
Second, they act as consultants for the diocese.
Third, they are involved with the coordination, management and financial planning of diocesan programs.
Fourth, they are involved with conducting research in the planning process.
Finally, they are concerned with other areas of church services such as offering leadership training and establishing parish councils.

When asked to rate their success they felt they were most successful in carrying out the goals of their office.
Information was also gathered concerning the persons who staff these offices.[28]

Fifty-four percent of the personnel who service these offices are lay persons, twenty-eight percent, priests, 16% religious sisters, and 2% religious brothers. Most of the lay personnel fall into the categories of secretaries and clerical staff.
Whereas 31% report no advanced degree, 22% who have such a degree have it in theology, 22% in business or administration, and only 5% in sociology.
Twenty-five percent say they work 20 or less hours. Forty-two percent work from 20 to 40 hours and 33% work more than 40 hours per week.
The average number of personnel per office is 2.6 persons.
Thirty directors are priests, 7 are laypersons, 7 are sisters, and one is a brother.

[27]Ibid., p. 9.
[28]Ibid., pp. 15–17.

Of the 30 priests directors, 8 have a doctorate, 10 have done post masters work, 8 have an MA/MS, and 4 have done post graduate work.
Sixty-nine percent of the directors say they have duties in addition to their directorship.

IMPLICATIONS

The statistics on professional DREs, permanent deacons, lay volunteers, offices of planning and research, and diocesan pastoral councils highlight the various stages in the Church's evolution. Twenty years ago all the above were virtually non-existent. We now have thousands of persons who have invested enormous amounts of time, energy and finances to be specially educated to serve the Church. Dioceses have established numerous new offices to service these people and their ministries. Parish budgets no longer center solely on maintaining a church or school. They include categories for full time lay ministers, DREs, deacons, youth ministers, adult education programs, programs for the elderly, and a variety of other services once unheard of.

Although these ministries can always improve, one very refreshing outcome is that they have fulfilled one of Vatican II's most precious dreams—to have greater participation not only in the liturgy, but in all dimensions of church service.

Having reviewed the more salient statistics on the Church's evolution the big questions must be asked.

1. If vocations to the religious life of the Church are the heart of its sacramental life, and if the present number of priests and religious will dwindle without sufficient replacements, what does one who is in a position of governance do, whether he or she be a religious superior, bishop, pastor, or director of a program? How do we define the problems and get a positive, operative handle on them?

2. If we now have a new force of persons deeply involved in church service, how does one who governs continue to increase and improve participation, foster zeal, and head off frustrations that could turn participation into confrontation, and reverse the positive effects of zeal?

A Call for Renewal

To answer these questions I believe our best resource person is Pope Paul VI and his encyclical, *Ecclesiam Suam*.[29] He deals with three themes: (1) the awareness Church has of itself, and the need for this to increase; (2) internal renewal in the Church, and external expressions of it; (3) the dialogue the Church must conduct within herself and with all persons.

On the topic of awareness Paul said:

> We think that it is a duty today for the Church to deepen the awareness that it must have of itself, of the treasure of truth of which it is heir and custodian, and of its mission in the world. . . . The Church in this moment must reflect on it to find strength in knowledge of its place in the divine plan; to find again greater light, new energy and fuller joy in the fulfillment of its own mission; and to determine the best means for making more immediate, more efficacious and more beneficial its contacts with mankind to which it belongs, even though the Church is distinguished from it by unique and unmistakable characteristics.[30]

It is appropriate to re-examine the ideal behind these words. The Church is reminded that it must deepen the awareness of itself, its treasure of truth, and its mission. Through reflection, which is the foundation of awareness, comes deeper knowledge. Knowledge is seen as the prime mover which enables the Church better to understand its place in the divine plan. Finally, because of a clearer picture greater determination can be generated to make closer contact with and touch more profoundly the world in which the Church exists.

Reflection begets deeper awareness, which in turn increases knowledge about the meaning of the Church in the world. It is this knowledge that moves the Church to draw closer to those it hopes to serve.

How is awareness, reflection, knowledge and determination generated? One way is by adapting an attitude of dialogue whose characteristics are: (1) clarity, (2) meekness, (3) truth, and (4) pedagogical prudence. Clarity reminds us to review every angle of our language in order to guarantee that it is understandable, acceptable, and well-chosen. Meekness reiterates the principle that the authority of dialogue is intrinsic to the truth it explains.

---

[29]Paul VI, encyclical letter *Ecclesiam Suam*, August 6, 1964; translation from *National Catholic Almanac* (Garden City, NY: Doubleday and Co., 1965).

[30]Ibid., p. 182.

The dialogue is not an imposition. It is peaceful. It avoids violent methods. It is patient and generous.

Trust promotes confidence and friendship. It binds hearts in mutual adherence to the good which excludes all self-seeking. Pedagogical prudence esteems highly the psychological and moral circumstances of the listener. It strives to learn the sensitivities of the hearer and requires that we adapt ourselves and the manner of our presentation in a reasonable way lest we be displeasing and incomprehensible to the listener.[31]

The rationale for awareness, renewal and dialogue is vigilance, in order that we not be overwhelmed by "vertiginous confusion and bewilderment" which can result from transformations, upheavals and new developments which are profoundly changing not only our modes of life, but also our ways of thinking.[32]

These are some of the basic elements Paul VI gave to us on how to foster renewal. They can be applied to the reality of the Church today in light of the facts described above.

Operationalizing Renewal

The statistics we have reviewed reveal that a certain confusion does exist and that definitely there are transformations, upheavals, and new developments evolving. How do those who govern not only practice vigilance, but generate renewal in the midst of this evolution?

I believe we must return to the question asked by that bishop who inquired whether there is some knowledge gained by research which he and his brother bishops did not have. Yes, we have mosaics, but at present they are sparse. The ones we do have need to be greatly enlarged and improved. The prime movers behind renewal—increased dialogue and knowledge— need to be upgraded to equal the task of keeping abreast with evolution.

If the number of persons going into religious life is decreasing how many dioceses or parishes are conducting studies to learn about parental attitudes toward having a child enter such a life? Is there any truth, as one study shows, that parishes served by priests who spend a long period of time in a parish tend to attract more candidates to religious life than those in which priests are transferred frequently? We know from studies that priests, sisters and brothers are very influential in cultivating religious

---

[31]Ibid., p. 195.
[32]Ibid., pp. 182–183.

vocations. What means of dialogue are being employed to find out where their encouragement has dropped off, and why?

An equally important question that needs to be asked is, what type of studies are needed to understand the future of the Church's internal structure because of fewer persons in religious life and the new roles the laity are fulfilling? Where is on-going research being conducted to solve the age old problem of effective religious education programs? With the lay movement and permanent diaconate in full swing, who is doing an on-going study of their progress? With the increase of diocesan pastoral councils, from where should they ascertain reliable information in order to make their consultation realistic and apropos to the grass-roots level?

Going beyond the studies cited here, who is tracking the evangelization of the growing number of Hispanics in this country, and the American church's ability to supply missionaries and avoid becoming a mission country itself? Furthermore, who is going beyond counting numbers and researching the attitudes and images that can either increase or decrease the numbers of religious? What are the images of Church the laity and religious have today? How do they compare with the images they had twenty or thirty years ago? How wide-spread is the practice of sounding out parishioners about their desired expectations of a parish, and the reality they are experiencing?

Another question frequently raised is who is following through on the worth-while studies that have been produced on the national level, or dissertations which have studied the Church?

If the vision of renewal is to come true it would seem those in positions of governance need to practice pedagogical prudence and enter more fully into the psychological and moral circumstances of those with whom they collaborate. This is necessary in order to compose a mosaic aimed at heightening awareness of mission, dispelling the confusion that accompanies change, and generating more light and the energy it inspires. This leads us to ask what more needs to be done to accomplish this. One hopeful possibility is for those who govern to take a closer look at the functions of planning, research and renewal, and realize the close relationship between them.

Often research is seen solely as the gathering of statistics, graphs, and the use of computers. Research types usually are stereotyped as being math wizzards, computer geniuses, and at worst, boring people who see the world in unimaginative numbers and who put people into categories. There are also persons who feel research is a tedious process. Why wait one or two years when you can get the advice of a few persons well-versed in the problems, make a decision, and move quickly on solving them? Why go through the labor and financial costs of establishing a research team? Seldom do many of us who read the statistics or know of a research office realize the value behind the gathering of numbers, the institution of such an office, and their relationship to renewal. Nor do those who gather the statistics take full advantage of the process.

To conduct an effective study requires, first, the coming together of concerned parties to pray about and define the importance of an issue. This may entail a pastor and selected parishioners, a DRE and the parish council, or a bishop and his DPC sitting down together. Assumptions on what the problems are must be probed and clearly defined in order to formulate intelligent questions that will return valid information. Pre-testing and outside consultation must be conducted to guarantee the research team is on target.

Before a study is launched, if the process is followed correctly, prayer, study, reflection and dialogue, the foundations for renewal, are already well in place. The process also leads to a well-defined focus which enables those involved in the study to explore an issue indepth and become more aware of its many dimensions. This awareness, if accepted in the spirit of meekness necessary for dialogue, increases one's tolerance and respect for the large range of problems inherent in any issue. It can likewise surface many hopeful possibilities for a positive change.

At this stage there should also be a dream about hoped-for-outcomes. It should be about a struggle not only to produce a final report, but through the report to have those served by it join the struggle for increased knowledge and become part of a continuing education process.

Next comes stage two: audience response to the questions raised in the study. By their nature, good questions cause those for whom a study is intended to reflect and dialogue in much the same manner as those who initiated them. Good questions have the power to convert bystanders into active participants.

In stage three the report is developed and all concerned parties come together to learn what new light has been shed. Is the new knowledge valid and sufficient? If so, where does the action begin?

Three stages, when properly conducted, make research and subsequent planning an excellent forum for renewal.

A Challenge to Those who Govern

Today one of the biggest challenges that face those who govern is their use of consultation and especially the depth it takes. In light of the complexities of modern society they face, those in governing positions have to ask themselves if they are willing to employ a research and planning team as part of their consultation processes and to lend it the support it needs to function at its highest level. This is no easy question to answer. It implies more than a passing nod. If espoused, it raises some very weighty questions.

First, there are the qualifications the team should possess. On whatever level research and planning is established it should employ personnel with a well-balanced blend of theological, sociological, and psychological training.

Sociological training insures a disciplined methodology and the use of well-founded theory necessary to conduct a respectable study. It helps avoid critical errors which often give research and planning a poor image. How often have we filled out questionnaires in which the questions were poorly formulated and revealed little real contact with the issue, and were the direct antithesis to pedagogical prudence?

Psychological training enables a study to go beyond demographics and to surface feelings, attitudes, and behaviors. It avoids the non-personal which often is a trademark of statistical findings. It is key to creating the effective involvement and communication necessary for research and planning. Furthermore, it is necessary for the management skills needed to carry out the stages of research.

A theological understanding avoids leaving a study at the marketing level which is only interested in learning causes in order to make changes. It is the theological mentality which asks how the Holy Spirit is revealing God's plan at this time in salvation history. It looks at Church and its ministries as the City of God, and adds to the thinking framework of a sociologist and psychologist the extra dimensions of the prophetic and eschatological. It looks for those educational opportunities in a study where catechesis should be included.

When the above team is found it must not reflect the statistics we presently have on the personnel in offices of planning and research. Rather, these teams should be employed full-time, have research and planning as their one and only task, receive a salary commensurate to their professional status, and have at their disposal the tools of their trade. If this is not plausible in the beginning then at least a part-time team should be considered. What is pleaded for here is that talent hunts be initiated and talent be encouraged, and that the best of strategies for funding a team of this type be employed.

This personnel role description is a tall order. Those in governance will have to determine if they are interested enough to build and support such a team. Can they appreciate the quality that is implied here and its possibilities for renewal, even though they themselves may be unfamiliar with the inner workings of the processes?

Once a research and planning team is in place, those in governance will also have to be willing to undergo the circumstances that may result from the team's work. Let us say that because of surveys, interviews and subsequent dialogues a parish really comes alive and wants to change its mood of operation. If the evidence is overwhelmingly in favor of change, do those who govern feel strong enough to flex and support the new changes? Are they big enough not to be threatened by the changes that research and planning inevitably suggest?

In his book, *The End of the Modern World*, Romano Guardini suggests three virtues that leaders must possess in order to get us safely beyond a nuclear holocaust into a post modern era. They are earnestness, gravity and asceticism.[33] Earnestness simply asks the question, "What is really at sake?" It cuts through the artificial, pseudo common-sense approaches to problems and endeavors to get at their essences. Gravity is the courage not to panic when all seems chaotic, but to stand and sort out the variables— to take control in the midst of confusion. Asceticism is self-discipline and self-mastery.

Just as Pope Paul VI's encyclical *Ecclesiam Suam* closely relates with the functions of research and planning, so too do Guardini's proposed virtues. Hopefully, those who are responsible for church governance will also see this relationship and employ them in their quest for renewal in a post-modern world.

[33]Romano Guardini, *The End of the Modern World* (Chicago: Henry Regnery, 1968), pp. 112–113.

MINISTRY, GOVERNANCE, AND RELATIONAL GROWTH

ROBERT J. WILLIS

The 1983 revision of the Code of Canon Law characterizes bishops, rather unusually, as "ministers of governance" (*gubernationis ministri*— c. 375). Governance, indeed, is not unusual nor at issue here; the Catholic faithful customarily accept their bishop as ruling "the particular church committed to him with legislative, executive and judicial power in accord with the norm of law" (c. 391). What does invite explanation and expansion is *regere* for bishops and *praestant in regimine* for those assisting him when *minister* is modified by *gubernatio*.[1]

Although this appellation appears only in canon 375, the code, its framers and interpreters, undoubtedly desire governance to be exercised in the context of service. John Paul II in *Sacrae disciplinae leges* calls "hierarchical authority as service" an element which characterizes "the true and genuine image of the Church."[2] The preface to the code claims that in the new code "the exercise of authority appears more clearly as service,"[3] as a means of taking "cognizance of the conditions and needs of the contemporary world."[4]

In its book of studies introducing the revised code, the Canon Law Society of America quotes John Courtney Murray's understanding of authority and freedom as standing "in the service of community."[5] Kenneth Lasch straightforwardly agrees when he maintains that "the bishop has a primary concern for all the people of God entrusted to him. His

---

[1]See cc. 391, 469, and 475. For a discussion of the meaning of *regimen* in the code, see Michael Fahey, "Diocesan Governance in Modern Catholic Theology and in the 1983 Code of Canon Law," above. For a detailed look at the relationship of power and authority in the Church, see Agnes Cunningham, "Power and Authority in the Church," above.

[2]John Paul II, apostolic constitution *Sacrae disciplinae leges*, January 25, 1983; English translation from *Code of Canon Law, Latin-English Edition* (Washington: CLSA, 1983), p. xv.

[3]Ibid., p. xxi.

[4]Ibid., p. xxviii.

[5]James H. Provost, ed., *Code, Community, Ministry* (Washington: CLSA, 1983), p. 4.

position is not one of honor, but of service."[6] Bertram Griffin, moreover, clearly raises for us the difficulty in understanding this "ministry of governance." In discussing canon 204's statement that "the faithful participate in the priestly, prophetic, and royal *munus* of Christ," he points to the confusion around translating *munus* as it is sometimes "translated as 'office' or 'role,' sometimes as 'mission' or 'service,' and sometimes as 'ministry'. . . . "[7] In this broad understanding, *munus, minister* or *ministerium*, and *gubernatio* are arguably seen as necessarily united.

Given this intended union of governance with service, we need to confront the possibility that in actual practice some governance may *not* serve, and to explore how it may best do so. We must also address the task of elucidating the conditions that may signify, support, and strengthen this "ministry of governance." In this study may we, from a psychological and developmental perspective, at least begin the latter task.

Common sense daily forces upon us the recognition that service truly serves only when, in the modern jargon, it "touches us where we're at!" To be invited to eat still more when full, to be served only brussel sprouts when we dislike the whole wintry family, to be admonished to eat or drink or sleep—in service to our health when none such is at the moment required or desired—such actions are rejected as intrusive exercises of a non-serving dictatorship. So too, no matter the motivation, the serving up of the following: information already had or not understandable; directions deemed superfluous or not desired; judgments offered gratuitously, warnings given irrelevantly, decisions made preemptorily. The managerial cliché that "the leader who marches too far ahead of his army is no leader but simply a lonely marcher" graphically illustrates how governance, let alone governance seeking to serve, must keep in appropriate contact with the recipients of its actions.

Common sense, however, may not alone suffice in determining how governance must change according to the people governed. Clearly, common sense would and does take account of growth and development. The revised code, echoing this common-sensical assessment of the influence of age, does speak of the "seven ages of man: infants, children, youth, young adults, mature adults, older adults, and retired ministers."[8] But this view takes account of age only in the context of minimum and maximum thresholds; e.g., we do not teach a six year old to drive our car,

---

[6]Ibid., p. 89. See also the discussion of power and authority as service during the Middle Ages, Cunningham, above.

[7]*Code, Community, Ministry*, p. 19.

[8]Ibid., p. 21.

nor do we require a fragile retiree just recovering from a stroke to try out for our football team!

In order to supplement common sense, the code, and the differing requirements of age thresholds, it seems worthwhile to call upon the theoretical and experimental endeavors of modern psychology, and in particular developmental psychology. Much evidence exists to support the thesis that the human being does indeed grow and develop through quite predictable stages—and this relative to various human capacities. We need only mention the names of Piaget and Erickson, Kohlberg and Maslow, Freud himself, and more recently, Fowler to illustrate this thesis.[9] For the "minister of governance," service and governance need more than a knowledge of the minimal capacities of each age; they may well mandate an assessment of the developmental capacity of the person and the group to be governed.

Since the code presents the Church as "the people of God . . . a *communion*"[10] and looks to the "organic development in the life of both the ecclesial society and the individual persons who belong to it,"[11] a developmental theory that addresses the stages of relational growth would seem most useful in understanding how governance may best take account of the differing capacities of those it serves. Although the developmental theorists mentioned do implicitly consider relational growth, they explicitly emphasize the stages of the developing life of the individual. While helpful methodologically and contextually, they do not directly address the changing relationship between the Church and its people, the governing and the governed. Their usefulness is therefore limited.

In the following pages a theory of relational growth rather than individual growth will be offered in the first four of its six stages. As each stage unfolds, two specific topics will be treated: first, the characteristics

[9]For representative work, consult the following: Jean Piaget, *Six Psychological Studies* (New York: Random House, 1967); Erik H. Erickson, *Childhood and Society* (New York: W. W. Norton and Company, 1963); Barbara Munsey, ed., *Moral Development, Moral Education, and Kohlberg* (Birmingham: Religious Education Press, 1980); Abraham Maslow, *Toward a Psychology of Being* (New York: Harper and Row, 2nd ed. 1970); Sigmund Freud, "An Outline of Psychoanalysis," *Standard Edition*, Vol. 23, ed. and trans. James Strachey (London: The Hogarth Press, 1964); James H. Fowler, *Stages of Faith* (San Francisco: Harper and Row, 1981).

[10]*Sacrae disciplinae leges*, p. xv. For a discussion of the Church as *communio* in the documents of Vatican II, see John Huels, "The Role of Canon Law in Light of *Lumen Gentium*," above.

[11]*Sacrae disciplinae leges*, p. xiv.

of the particular stage; second, the mode of church governance most appropriate for persons or groups resting primarily in that stage.

SOME THEORETICAL PRESUPPOSITIONS

Before considering directly these stages and their implications for diocesan governance, the following presuppositions should be put forth because of their influential role in shaping this developmental theory.

> 1. Human growth is primarily and intrinsically interpersonal; it is secondarily individual, yet, even then, individual in an interpersonal context.

The validity of considering interpersonal development as primary to human growth lies in the theoretical conviction that "the ego, the person, the self develop only in relationship."[12] An impressive body of psychological evidence supports this contention—evidence quite diverse in itself, but converging in this important recognition.

When babies in hospitals in Nazi territories received physical care but no loving touching, they died.[13] When young children become separated from human society, are raised by animals, only to be "captured" and "civilized," they are at least assured of a lifelong struggle to attain even the most rudimentary experience of what it is to be human.[14] When children perceive their relational world as insecure, spasmodic, untrustworthy, they may respond drastically by fixating on nonhuman objects, avoiding all human contact and communication, setting up rhythmically predictable patterns of self-stimulation: the result is autism, the fear-filled denial of interpersonal existence.[15] Lest one be tempted to conclude from

---

[12]Luise Eichenbaum and Susan Orbach, *Understanding Women: A Feminist Psychoanalytic Approach* (New York: Basic Books, 1982), p. 32.

[13]For controlled studies of the minimally attached infant, the causes and results of this state, we must turn either to animal studies or studies of institutionalized children. In the former category, the classic study was done by Harry Harlow, "Learning to Love," *American Scientist* 54 (1966) 244–272. As a sample study of socially deprived children, see Sally A. Provence and Rose C. Lipton, *Infants in Institutions* (New York: International Universities Press, 1962).

[14]The time-honored anthropological study is that done by Jean Marc Gaspard Itard in the last century. See Jean Itard and Lucien Malson, *Wolf Children and the Problem of Human Nature*, and *The Wild Boy of Aveyron* (New York: Monthly Review Press, 1972). For another more general look at this phenomenon and, in particular, a discussion of isolated children, see J. A. L. Singh and Robert M. Zingg, *Wolf-Children and Feral Man* (New York: Harper and Row, Archon Books, 1966).

[15]The classical work in the study of childhood autism is that of Bruno Bettelheim, *The*

the above that children alone are in need of relationships, think of the psychic disintegration attendant upon schizoid withdrawal or psychotic depression,[16] or recall the panic experienced when the familiar interpersonal world cannot be intelligibly ordered by the victim of severe emotional exhaustion[17] or by the born-blind but now newly-sighted adult.[18]

This demonstrable need for human relationships as the very basis of human existence rests, moreover, on a firm if disputed philosophical base. Contrary to the assertions of essentialistic philosophers who by and large consider human life to be a given and essentially finished reality, existential philosophers look on it as an ongoing project of creation. For the former, any change is "accidental," a matter of quantitative and qualitative additions to what is already present; for the latter, such logical distinctions totally miss the human experience of becoming an ever-new and unfolding person through decisions made and stances taken which reverberate throughout the whole of one's being.

Specific to our examination of church governance, one's philosophical position regarding human life may well determine its exercise. Is faith essentially a set of beliefs, a creed, a "deposit" to be handed on and adhered to? If so, then governance would rightly emphasize the orthodox transmission of dogma with the eye to preserving and explaining, defending and celebrating, an experience once had between God and God's people. Or is faith in its very core, as Fowler asserts, "*always* relational; there is always *another* in faith"?[19] To emphasize faith as relationship would be to consider the transmitting of an ongoing and deepening and changing experience of God as the primary task of church governance.

Empty Fortress (New York: Free Press, 1967).

[16]So much has been written on depression—its causes, symptoms, effects, treatment—that it is difficult to choose representative resources. For a psychiatric discussion, see Fredric F. Flach and Suzanne C. Draghi, eds., *The Nature and Treatment of Depression* (New York: John Wiley and Sons, 1975). For a current psychological approach, see Aaron T. Beck et al., *Cognitive Therapy of Depression* (New York: The Guilford Press, 1979). For a time-honored existential approach to the problem of depression in the more general context of death, see Ernest Becker, *The Denial of Death* (New York: Free Press, 1973). Of special interest in this instance is chapter 10: "A General View of Mental Illness."

[17]Symptoms associated with this transitional stress disorder are perceptual distortions (e.g., skin hypersensitivity, "tunnel" hearing, vision as through the wrong end of a telescope), lack of control (e.g., hysterical crying), fear ("I'm going to die!"), strangeness and inability to contact the normal world, physical exhaustion, and lack of motivation.

[18]For a representative treatment of the emotional reactions to blindness, see Richard M. Restak, *The Brain: the Last Frontier* (Garden City, NY: Doubleday and Company, 1979), chapter 18.

[19]Fowler, p. 16.

Turning to morality, the essentialistic view would demand individual conformity to laws and norms consistent with the original religious experience. As moral teachers church leaders would look for evidence of "right action," of conforming behavior as indicators of religious conviction. Moral behavior may, however, be considered at its core to be relational. Such would appear to be Kohlberg's position when he asserts that "the other assumption is of the interactional origins of morality."[20] In this view "right action" occurs when one acts in such a manner as to further, according to the ever-changing possibilities and capabilities of our developing life experience, the human race's approach to God.

As we move through our discussion of the various stages of human relational growth, it will become, one hopes, clearer how the understanding and practice of church governance must change according to a deepening capacity for faithful and moral action.

> 2. Human development is a process moving from the unchosen unity of the embryonic world to the chosen separateness of independent individuality and on to the chosen unity of an essentially relational existence.

Much of twentieth century psychology has dealt with the life project of "making an adult out of a child," of helping the individual "stand on his own two feet," of creating the "well-balanced person." Independence, self-assertion, self-esteem, and personal responsibility are its canonical goals; the movement from dependency to independency its professed task.[21]

Within the last quarter century both the theory and the practice of psychology have increasingly shown this vision of life to be at least questionable, if not myopic. Many influences have combined to open our eyes to horizons beyond our conventional idea of human maturity: Abraham Maslow's writings about self actualization and peak experiences[22] as well as his creative action in starting "Transpersonal Psychol-

---

[20]Munsey, p. 38.

[21]For a revealing list of the assumptions of Western psychology seen over against the "spiritual psychologies" of the East, see Charles T. Tart, "Some Assumptions of Orthodox Western Psychology," in *Transpersonal Psychologies*, ed. Charles T. Tart (New York: Harper and Row, 1975), pp. 61–111.

[22]For a detailed look at the process of self-actualization and the "secular religious" peak experiences, see Abraham Maslow, *Religions, Values, and Peak Experiences* (New York: Penguin Books, 2nd ed. 1976).

ogy'';[23] the scientific examination of a widespread use of hallucinogenics, first tried by enterprising young people but then increasingly by adults, that produced states often sounding ecstatic and mystical;[24] the introduction of meditative practices into our society, not as formally religious actions but rather as ones linked to human growth and development;[25] the turning to mind-expanding, mind-altering practices, often in esoteric contexts, by people no longer touched by the common practices of mainstream religion;[26] the introduction of Eastern religions, religions that are essentially esoteric psychologies, to a Western society desperately in need of practical instruction in the ascent to the infinite.[27]

Under these influences humanistic and transpersonal psychologists—a growing force in American psychology—now see that an individual's life task is completed only when one moves ''on to his or her tiptoes,'' that to be well-balanced is to be ''off-balanced in a direction,'' that independence must give way to integration into a Life force much greater than individual life, yet in which individual life is more fully realized.

3. Human development happens through an interaction of life and death occuring on two different but intersecting planes: on a vertical plane, *Life* is experienced as a positive, enhancing force

[23]For an overall and ongoing view of Transpersonal Psychology, refer to the *Journal of Transpersonal Psychology*, a journal started by Abraham Maslow and Tony Sutich in 1969.

[24]For a careful account of the relationship of hallucinogenics and mystical states, see the chapter on ''Transpersonal Experiences in LSD Sessions'' in Stanislaus Grof, M.D., *Realms of the Human Unconscious: Observations from LSD Research* (New York: E. P. Dutton and Company, 1976). A discussion of Grof's work from a religious perspective may be found in David R. Crownfield, ''Religion in the Cartography of the Unconscious: A Discussion of Stanislaus Grof's *Realms of the Human Unconscious*,'' *Journal of the American Academy of Religion* 14 (1976) 309–315.

[25]For a psychological discussion on how meditative practices may be used as a force for human growth and development, even in the context of psychotherapy, see Patricia Carrington, *Freedom in Meditation* (Garden City, NY: Anchor Press, 1977).

[26]For an overview of such esoteric religions in modern American life, see Jacob Needleman, *The New Religions* (Garden City, NY: Doubleday and Company, 1970). For some of the dangers associated with their abuse in our time, see Harvey Cox, *The Seduction of the Spirit: The Use and Misuse of Peoples' Religion* (New York: Simon and Schuster, 1973).

[27]As a psychologist, in the 1960's and early 1970's I dealt in large part with questions of alienation and loneliness. Since the mid-1970's this has changed to assisting people grappling with feelings of confusion and inner emptiness. Underneath it all lies the specter of meaninglessness, of a lack of purpose to human existence. The title of a popular song of that era, ''Is That All There Is?'' reflects well this state of societal loss; the appalling statistics pointing to an epidemic of teenage suicide dramatically answers this not-just-musical question, an answer being placed by growing numbers of our fellow citizens and church members.

engaged in an unending struggle with the negative, destructive tyranny of Death; on a horizontal plane, life grasped at and made secure out of fear of Death becomes its unwitting, unwilling ally, while death accepted as the trusting risk of Life's essential goodness brings about its developing realization and integration.

Graphically, this presupposition looks like this:[28]

LIFE (+)
life (−)   death (+)
Death (−)

Until the advent of the personal and transpersonal revolutions in psychology, most of Western psychology viewed death as a hopeless disaster and as an evil experienced whenever there appeared a regression from the logical, independent, self-directed place of chosen separateness. Thus Freud, a spokesman for psychodynamic theorists, viewed mysticism at its best as a "regression in the service of the ego," the temporary losing of the hard-fought egoic ground as one fell back into the chaotic, undifferentiated state of an unfree and unchosen childish world.[29] Behavioral psychologists would, for the most part, echo Skinner's denial that interiority is either meaningful or available to the conditioned human animals we are.[30] To them, behaviors can be seen, reinforced, or extinguished; symptoms can be modified and changed; and all this may be done by the quite logical process of manipulation of rewards and punishments. Life is thereby maintained and enhanced through control, not through the willing relinquishing of control.

To psychologists who follow Freud in this respect, one can only say: "The child's experience of unchosen unity is non-relational, before any recognition of other, before the possibility of choice. For one moving

---

[28]I am indebted to Ken Wilbur for first introducing me to this simple, graphic way of describing the twofold interaction of Life-Death and life-death. See Ken Wilbur, "The Pre-Trans Fallacy," *ReVision* 3/2 (Fall, 1980) 66.

[29]As an antidote to this traditional Western psychological view of mysticism, see Lawrence Leshan's intriguing study of the relationship of mystical practices to psychic healing in *The Medium, The Mystic, and The Physicist* (New York: Viking Press, 1974). For Freud's discussion of the origin of the religious attitude in infantile needs, and the desire for the "oceanic feeling" to still those needs, see his *Civilization and Its Discontents*, ed. and trans. James Strachey (New York: W.W. Norton and Company, 1962), pp. 13–19.

[30]The classical treatment of behavioral conditioning in a relational context may be found in B. F. Skinner, *Walden Two* (New York: Macmillan, 1976). The denial that interiority has any scientific interest is best seen in his *Beyond Freedom and Dignity* (New York: Knopf, 1971).

toward chosen unity, relationship, choice and the other are paramount: by choosing to release control over my separate life I find it more alive in integration with another."[31]

To Skinner's followers, one may only assert: "Your experience of life is narrow. The moment of gift, of trust and faith, of risk and letting go, is the gateway of life and happiness and peace."[32]

In the course of this discussion of developmental stages, we will consider how growth happens through letting go of a previous self identification and by trusting a new experience of selfhood. At the critical junctures between stages, the struggle often feels like a confrontation between Life and Death, and it is. Victory, peace, and growth come only if and when Life joins hands with death through the conscious and trusting choice to leave a former known and secure personal place in a courageous search for a fuller Life. "Unless the grain of wheat dies. . . . "

> 4. Age ordinarily offers a minimum threshold for the experiences of a given growth stage; it, however, does not assure its attainment. And a stage attained does not exclude recurrences of actions more appropriate to previous stages.

Human life stands as a potential to be realized. Some levels of development may or may not happen; some may more or less happen. Physical predispositions and emotional capacity must join hands with intellectual and spiritual capabilities—and all this in a relational context— to form the real possibility of entrance into any given stage. Any loosening of this inner integration, any negative relational forces, may occasion a developmental "slippage" into a stage once left but at this time, in this situation, very much revisited.[33]

This explains, for example, why an adult returning to a parent's home may feel and act "just like a child"; why a secure, non-violent adult may become a competitive, whining and insecure "adolescent" in the presence of siblings; why a self-possessed and interiorly "centered" person can be

---

[31]Ken Wilbur quite deftly and pointedly exposes this confusion in his article, "The Pre-Trans Fallacy," pp. 51–71.

[32]For a classical confrontation between an interpersonal and a behavioral view of human development, see the report of a symposium featuring Carl Rogers and B. F. Skinner, "Some Issues Concerning the Control of Human Behavior," *Science* 124 (1956) 1057–1066.

[33]It is commonly asserted by developmental theorists that psychological trauma can "fixate" a person at a given developmental level, or that under sufficient internal and/or external stress a person may "regress" to a previous level until the stress is reduced. As an example, see Erickson's discussion of the "Eight Ages of Man," chapter 7 in *Childhood and Society*.

sent into a fracturing and disorienting rage over the slighting remark of a loved one.

To put it succinctly: a stage attained is not a stage possessed. When we are in equilibrium, internal and external, we find ourselves in the stage attained. When for the moment we lose equilibrium, we will move to the stage offering the best protection to our threatened egos.

A Theory of Interpersonal Development

Because of an emphasis on individual development, theorists such as Erickson and Piaget begin their examination of life stages from the moment of birth. Generally speaking, Erickson's first stage of Basic Trust vs. Basic Mistrust[34] and Piaget's Sensorimotor stage[35] cover the infancy years up to the age of 1 1/2. This period marks the struggle of the newborn toward some experience of differentiation and autonomous existence, an experience that flourishes in an interpersonal context while not being in itself interpersonal; interpersonal stage development begins later. The budding interpersonal years of early childhood (ca. 2–6) mark the first truly interpersonal stage. Kohlberg as a moralist calls this stage one of Heteronomous Morality;[36] Fowler as a theologian refers to it as Intuitive-Projective Faith.[37] As a psychologist, I call it Extrinsic Evaluation. Our examination begins there.

Stage I: Extrinsic Evaluation

Identifying Characteristics

To be extrinsically self-evaluating is to find meaning, worth, and ultimately identity through meeting standards imposed by others. Through the punishments and rewards of an adult world the small child begins to find personal meaning. The wide-eyed explorations of the "terrible two's," so destructive of adult order and patience, may soon lead to the equating (by child *and* adult!) of, say, breaking a vase with "bad boy!" Scoldings, raised voices, painful spankings reinforce this dawning recognition that "doing what you're told" opens the way to personal worth and acceptability. Not only does the child learn to "look primarily to external cues to determine the rightness and wrongness, goodness and badness of

[34]Ibid., p. 274.
[35]Piaget, pp. 8–17.
[36]Munsey, p. 91.
[37]Fowler, p. 133.

actions . . . in terms of anticipated punishment and reward'';[38] the child more importantly finds that rightness and goodness and rewards lead directly to "*I* am good," their opposites to "*I* am bad."

Life stages, while dependent upon maturation and time, are not tied to them. "Movement from one . . . stage to another is not automatic or irresistible."[39] An only-in-years adult may organize the sense of self just as the young child does. However, this extrinsic evaluation does not flow simply from direct reward and punishment; the ability to control one's world through meeting agreed-upon societal standards ordinarily becomes the measure of worth and furnishes a sense of personal identity. "My life is worthwhile since my ordination . . . because I am tenured . . . now that my third book has hit the best seller lists." The name plate prominently displayed on the executive desk, or the name-brand suit flaunted at the reception, or the Mercedes left conspicuously in the driveway bespeak an ability "to make it," to have become "a somebody." The loss of a job, forced retirement, bankruptcy are financial disasters that too routinely end in suicide for many because the disaster is really experienced as the loss of an extrinsically manufactured self.

Mode of Church Governance

The power to govern finds a distressingly good match when confronting the powerless.[40] If the object of governing is realized when order is achieved, conformity is assured, and destructiveness is minimized, then the powerful and consistent doling out of rewards and punishments presages success. At a most primitive level the threat of ultimate damnation and the promise of unending beatitude serve as admirable means for the training and formation of "a good conscience." At a more sophisticated level, institutional rewards for "being a good Catholic"—be they positions of honor or influence—will motivate the extrinsically evaluated adult to follow the dictates of church authority.

The effect upon such persons of governance by domination is mixed. Erich Fromm, in speaking about "authoritarian religion," underlines it this way:

The main virtue of this type of religion is obedience, its cardinal

---

[38]Ibid., p. 58.

[39]Ibid., p. 50.

[40]In this section, power is treated as domination. Authentic religious power, *dunamis*, united to authority, *exousia*, is not domination. See Cunningham, above.

> sin is disobedience. Just as the deity is conceived as omnipotent or omniscient, man is conceived as being powerless and insignificant. Only as he can gain grace or help from the deity by complete surrender can he feel strength. Submission to a powerful authority is one of the avenues by which man escapes from his feeling of aloneness and limitation. In the act of surrender he loses his independence and integrity as an individual but he gains the feeling of being protected by an awe-inspiring power of which, as it were, he becomes part.[41]

The feeling of protection and the sense of union with the all-powerful strongly motivate persons empty and powerless in themselves. But the price is deprivation of a sense of, and independent growth of, the self.

In its place such governance helps to instill, not a conscience, but a superego which "springs from a frantic compulsion to experience oneself as lovable."[42] *No one* in itself, the superego must find approval and acceptance through the blind conformity of its actions to the commands of the powerful. The greatest disaster lies in the possibility of the withdrawal of love, a withdrawal that would signal banishment into the interior darkness of no-being.

This superego parades as conscience. Conscience, unlike the superego, flows from the perception of something or someone as lovable and valuable, inviting both response and commitment.[43] The confusion of the two and the ascendency of the superego leads ultimately to the destruction of both individuality and the Christian vision:

> A second reason why the image of God the punisher has flourished in the Christian and even post-Christian imagination is drawn from personal pathology. The idea of God as judge on a throne, meting out punishment, corresponds to a self-destructive trend of the human psyche. On a previous page, we have mentioned man's primitive conscience or, as Freud called it, his superego. The person who is dominated by his superego—and no one is able to escape it altogether—has the accuser, judge, and tormentor all wrapt up in one, built into his own psychic makeup. When such a person hears the Christian message with the accent

---

[41]Erich Fromm, *Man For Himself* (New York: Rinehart and Company, 1947), p. 35.

[42]John W. Glaser, "Conscience and Superego: A Key Distinction," *Theological Studies* 32 (1971) 32. This article would be well worth reading in connection with the present discussion of Extrinsic Evaluation.

[43]Ibid., p. 38.

on God the judge, he can project his superego on the divinity and then use religion as an instrument to subject himself to this court and, unknown to himself, to promote his own unconscious self-hatred. As we mentioned more than once in these pages, Jesus has come to save men from their superego. God is not punisher; God saves.[44]

This self-hatred effectively halts the maturing of conscience, confuses a loving God "with the hot and cold, arbitrary tyrant of the superego,"[45] sends frightened and unhappy adults in frantic pursuit of security, and stifles the natural development of the human person.

Given a person—be it child or adult—whose self-development ordinarily rests in this most basic interpersonal stage, the "minister of governance" best serves the individual and the church community in the following ways:

He or she will not

— use the fear of punishment or the hope of reward as the way of assuring order and conformity;
— portray the loving God as a judge and punisher in order to assert extrinsic control over the faithful;
— attribute personal mortal sin—with the consequent withdrawal of God's love—to individuals virtually incapable of interior, personal moral acts;
— identify objectively wrong or bad actions with subjective evil;
— contribute to the formation of a tyranous superego by confusing its frantic voice begging for love with the voice of God drawing the person in love;
— substitute conscience training that conditions the person into extrinsic conformity for conscience education that opens the person to choose what is ultimately valuable.

The "minister of governance" will instead

— value the life and personal potential of the individual, no matter the disruptive or amoral behavior;
— support the efforts of an emerging and fragile ego by a constant, consistent, and nurturing love;

---

[44]Gregory Baum, *Man Becoming* (New York: Herder and Herder, 1970), pp. 223–224.
[45]Glaser, p. 39.

— offer clear limits and guidelines which may lead the individual toward the realization of living values that may constitute a responsible inner life;
— through example model the kind of behavior that flows from a mature Christian conscience;
— value interior responsibility over external conformity.

Such church governance, though sounding perhaps easy, may in reality not be so. "Many religious groups similiarly reinforce a conventionally held and maintained faith system, sanctifying one's remaining in the dependence on external authority. . . . "[46] Even today Christianity may well earn its share of a judgment attributed to the Christianity of Martin Luther's era:

> [It] tended to promise freedom from the body at the price of the absolute power of a negative external conscience: negative in that it was based on a sense of sin, and external in that it was defined and redefined by a punitive agency which alone was aware of the rationale of morality and the consequences of disobedience.[47]

The very codification of laws which occasions this collection of essays runs the risk faced by all religious groups of externalizing "themselves to such an extent that the authentic religious element in them—the living relationship to and direct confrontation with their extramundane point of reference—has been thrust into the background."[48] This living relationship, indeed, depends upon a human concern and love daring to touch the extrinsically evaluated individual with a call to personal, internal growth. This is the primary task of church governance.[49]

---

[46]Fowler, p. 178. See also Michael Fahey's consideration of Catholic attitudes toward church authority since Vatican II, above, pp. xx–xx.

[47]Erik H. Erickson, *Young Man Luther* (New York: W. W. Norton and Company, 1962), p. 193.

[48]Carl G. Jung, *Modern Man in Search of a Soul*, trans. W. S. Dell & Cary F. Baynes, (New York: Harcourt, Brace and World, 1933), p. 31. See also Avery Dulles, S.J., "Imaging the Church for the 1980's," in *A Church to Believe In* (New York: Crossroad, 1982), pp. 3–4. Without using the term, Dulles outlines clearly the effects of an institutional Church acting out of the realm of the superego.

[49]See Eugene Hemrick, "The Evolving Church and Church Governance," above, for some rather staggering statistics on the decline of priestly and religious vocations in the United States. This decline may be attributed to many factors, but a positive reason may be the growth of our Catholic people out of the domination of the superego and into an authentic Christian conscience. In this regard, see Glaser, pp. 44–47.

STAGE II: MUTUAL DEPENDENCY

Identifying Characteristics

When the young child leaves the comparative safety of home to enter school, a new life task arises. Previously, "measuring up" meant meeting the standards imposed by an adult world; now, being accepted by one's peers becomes at least as important. Parental approval must now compete with that of "the other kids"; adult standards of success motivate less while being "one of the gang" assumes an exaggerated centrality to a sense of one's well-being.

Any adult who lives or works with children from early grade school years through adolescence has heard innumerable, if not daily, snatches of conversation like the following:

> "Dad, may I go to the hockey game after school, please?"
> "Hockey game! What's up? You don't even like hockey?"
> "Oh, Dad, *everybody's* going to be there!"

or

> "Did Jerry call?"
> "Not that I know."
> "Oh, I'll just die if he doesn't ask me to the party!"

Exaggerations, of course! But they point to a significant psychological truth: when one's identity and security are lacking from within, they *will* be sought through an external over-identification. Erickson, in speaking about one instance of this—adolescent love—puts it well:

> To keep themselves together they temporarily over-identify, to the point of apparent loss of identity, with the heroes of cliques and crowds. This initiates the stage of "falling in love" which is by no means entirely, or even primarily, a sexual matter—except where the mores demand it. To a considerable extent adolescent love is an attempt to arrive at a definition of one's identity by projecting one's diffused ego image on another and by seeing it thus reflected and gradually clarified. This is why so much of young love is conversation.[50]

"I am no one without you"; "I love you because I *need* you"; "I'll die

---

[50]Erickson, *Childhood and Society*, p. 262.

if you leave me"; "if I don't make the team, my life will be ruined." To the casual, objective observer such statements ring melodramatically and are often as not shrugged off with "they'll soon grow out of it." Maybe not. This stage

> typically has its rise and ascendency in adolescence, but for many adults it becomes a permanent place of equilibrium. It structures the ultimate environment in interpersonal terms. Its images of unifying values and power derive from the extension of qualities experienced in interpersonal relationships. It is a "conformist" stage in the sense that it is actually tuned to the expectations and judgments of significant others and as yet does not have a sure enough grasp on its own identity and autonomous judgment to construct and maintain an independent perspective.[51]

Clearly many adults ape this adolescent world when being "one of the boys at the club" rivals duties to work or family, when being an acquaintance of the "greatest scholar . . . politician . . . pastor . . . surgeon" becomes the means of an unearned self-importance, when being in the "in-group" leads to the progressive alienation of self from personal values, meanings, and life goals. The result is not pleasant:

> Although this second stage of mutual dependency is clearly a step above extrinsic evaluation because of its interpersonal emphasis . . . [what] is essentially constructed is an interpersonal prison formed by fear of being no one, maintained by guilt when one dares to be a someone on one's own, and made secure by the threat of personal exclusion, or even official expulsion, leading to isolation and interpersonal nothingness.[52]

Mode of Church Governance

The history of Western Christianity may well be characterized (among other characterizations) as the living out of the tension between St. Paul's proclamation that "ye are gods!" and Thomas à Kempis's dour reminder that "you are nothing." A fallen race, humankind grapples daily with the reality of sin and death; a redeemed people, we rejoice constantly in the

---

[51]Fowler, p. 172.

[52]Robert J. Willis, "Growth and Religious Diversity," *Human Development* 5/1 (Spring, 1984) 22. This article outlines all six developmental stages and relates each to prayer, morality, and community.

righteousness of God who saves.[53] Unhappily, the former state surrounds us with abundant concrete evidence of personal weakness and failure, sickness and suffering: we need only have enough openness to let reality intrude even a little to be convinced. The latter state, however, demands either a mature faith founded upon a solid sense of one's personal meaning, or upon a belief derived from human wishes that is a necessary illusion for any sense of ultimate personal security and meaning. Seeing this, if narrowly, Freud explains: "Thus we call a belief an illusion when a wish-fulfilment is a prominent factor in its motivation, and in doing so we disregard its relation to reality, just as the illusion itself sets no store by verification."[54]

Faced with this dichotomy between personal faith and personal fragility, church governance can tend to focus on attaining its ends through exploiting the fragility.

Individuals whose level of psychological growth drives them to seek personal meaning through acceptance are most susceptible to manipulation and exploitation, especially in the name of God. For the ones governing this may take the form of identification with institutional domination; for those governed it may appear as conformity accepted as the assurance of eternal salvation.

Like any large institution the hierarchical Church organizes itself so as to strive toward the realization of its goals. Institutional power—flowing ultimately from God—moves purposefully downward through the various levels of ecclesiastical authority. It seeks to create a secure order, to reinforce a ready obedience, and to develop effective and capable ministers of its directives. For those sharing in this mission, most certainly there is a satisfaction in contributing to a valuable task; however, there may also be an identification with power that substitutes for personal identity. Church authority, not unlike secular authority, invests some with power, inducts these powerful into prestigious inner circles, readily contributes to an illusion of personal worth caused by positions held, and provides roles that symbolically promise not only worth but final salvation. The "minister of governance" may find in the mutually dependent individual a readily conforming instrument: "I'll do whatever you desire if, in exchange, you'll give me meaning and insure my worth."

Unlike secular institutions, however, the Church's power over the

---

[53]Cf. Romans 5: 6–17.
[54]Sigmund Freud, "The Future of an Illusion," *Complete Psychological Works*, Vol. 21 trans. James Strachey (London: The Hogarth Press, 1961), p. 31.

dependent individual does not stop with the appurtenances of societal acceptance. Whatever the ultimate worth to his Church and to humankind of Christ's blessing of Peter and his descendants with the keys to the kingdom of heaven, with the power to declare forgiveness in the name of an appeased God, church governance could have no stronger means of tying the mutually dependent one to itself and assuring thereby a derived worth. Indeed, all other shared power and meaning and endowed identity pale before the power to declare the gates of heaven for this one or that one now open—or closed.[55]

All people, no matter what their psychological maturity, look for external, concrete signs of identity. The principal reason that human beings are interpersonal creatures lies in the necessary connection between such self-expression in an interpersonal context and the development of personal identity. Dependent people, however, need more than signs telling them *about* themselves; they desperately require symbols that transform them *into* themselves.

These symbols, especially sacred symbols like the sacrament of penance, transform not "in a kind of fundamentalism of symbolic forms. Rather, symbols of the sacred—their own and others'—are related to in ways which honor them as inseparably connected to the sacred. Therefore, worthy symbols are themselves sacred."[56] The mutually dependent in the first instant substitutes the sacred symbol (e.g., penance) for personal worth and identity found in and through connection with God. It is, however, only a short psychological step then to substitute the connecting symbol for the saving God: absolution, not God, saves and is savior. (Anyone who has tried in the name of a merciful God to disabuse the scrupulous from constantly revisiting the confessional knows how God's will and mercy have nowhere near the influence upon them that the sacred, saving absolution enjoys.)

If church governance is to support the life task of maturing as a person and as a person of faith, the dignity of the person must be reinforced rather than personal insecurity manipulated for institutional order or control. Theologically, this means emphasizing God's grace rather than our fallen state, divine love rather than the wrath we deserve, Christ's resurrection rather than our part in his death. Such is not to deny our participation in sin and our involvement in its effects, but to recognize the severely

---

[55]For a discussion of the effect of the penitential controversies in the West on the exercise of power in the Church, see Cunningham, above.

[56]Fowler, p. 163.

diminished responsibility the mutually dependent individual has because of an ego so weak that it *must* make decisions that offer to it a share in the power of group acceptance. These powerless truly lack responsibility to the extent they lack the freedom to accept their separateness as a possible good.

Psychologically, the "minister of governance" will be a force for personal growth when

— each individual is treated as powerful, not because of position or role, but because of Life shared;

— love is shared, not because of conformity to the plans and goals of others, but because of the intrinsic worth of the developing person;

— acceptance is offered and acceptability proclaimed, not because of identification with the socially powerful or influential, but because of potential influence for good inherent in all living things;

— roles and positions are recognized, not as measures of individual value, but as necessary means of contributing to the effective functioning of the church society;

— unity in faith is preached, not as a force for uniformity nor as a demand for conformity, but as a declaration to all—and especially the dependent— that God's love may be trusted as the divine declaration of human worth.

Because of the understandable pressures within any organization— including the Church—to maintain itself and to further its goals, organizations often act as if their own perpetuation takes precedence over everything else. Orthodoxy, originally meant to preserve for humankind a genuine experience of God, may easily lose that experience and substitute the preservation of the orthodox system itself. Orthodoxy thus serves orthodoxy, not God or God's people.[57] This author's personal experience of American religion would flag this as a danger that could bear serious and honest evaluation. Fowler, in describing his stage of faith development that has some characteristics in common with the stage under discussion, points to this same danger:

> Many critics of religion and religious institutions assume, mistakenly, that to be religious in an institution means to be Synthetic-Conventional. This mistake by critics is understandable. Much of

---

[57]See John Lynch, "Church Government: the Protestant Experience," above, for a discussion of the development of this tension in the Church.

church and synagogue life in this country can be accurately described as dominantly Synthetic-Conventional.[58]

My observations lead me to judge that the modal developmental level in most middle-class American churches and synagogues is best described in terms of Synthetic-Conventional faith or perhaps just beyond it.[59]

STAGE III: SHARED INDEPENDENCY

Identifying Characteristics

Some time between the ages of seventeen and twenty-two young people in our society regularly face the necessity of making independent life decisions. Questions of school and work, travel and vocation demand immediate, thoughtful, and personal stances. Group acceptance, group values and choices decrease in importance as the individual confronts the task of fashioning a personal and unique life. The "tyranny of the they" needs to give way to the development of the "executive ego."[60]

This emerging ego, like any new growth striving to depend on itself, is noteworthy for a surface independence which to others may seem brash and rebellious but to oneself feels like an exciting shuttle between growth and fear. The life possibilities created out of freedom and responsibility intoxicate; at the same time they confront the young person with the psychological straits of failure on the right and regression on the left: the new life may either shatter on the shoals of competition or be swept away and down into the seductive, whirling waters of protective dependency.

This venture into independent adulthood steadies itself in two major ways: an emphasis upon objective social norms, and a zealous demand for equality.

A stable, reliable social order gives a welcome support to one stepping out for the first time—alone. Stability, not the previous search for reward or the requirement of inclusion, leads to an "orientation toward authority, fixed rules, and the maintenance of the social order. Right behavior consists of doing one's duty, showing respect for authority, and maintaining the given social order for its own sake."[61] This authoritative position

---

[58]Fowler, p. 164.
[59]Ibid., p. 294.
[60]Ibid., p. 179.
[61]Munsey, p. 92.

throughout society assures the emerging adult that the competition will be fair. One truly may rely on personal abilities and hard work; lack of experience and absence of "connections" in themselves cannot foreclose a share in society's goods so long as socially acknowledged authority assures their availability to the independently responsible and resourceful.

Independence, however, does not alone suffice. Practical reality includes others and demands sharing with them appropriate to the life desired. Psychological growth, moreover, requires that this sharing be such as to touch the inner world of hopes and struggles, fears and risks, values and intuitions. The individual, no matter how independent, will not "make it" alone. In the stage under discussion, the tension between the twin needs of independence and sharing is distinctively marked by *quid pro quo* relating; those feeling this tension suffer from the inability to commit themselves to another in trust.

Because of the emphasis on fairness, the need for equality, and the horror of falling back into a dependency just recently conquered, Shared Independency *shares* only while zealously guarding its *independence*. Commitment, no matter what its face or fervor, is always qualified. Listen to random remarks like the following that are regularly attributed to supposedly committed people in this growth stage:

> "I called you last time; it's your turn now."
> "I'd get married but I'm afraid of being tied down."
> "If the order forces me to come back home, I'll transfer provinces or join another order or leave."
> "We have a close relationship but we're both free to go out with others as we want."
> "We like living together without the pressures and obligations of marriage."
> "With temporary vows I can always get dispensed if it doesn't work out."

Weighing, balancing, an eye to one's own worth, the demand for equality, *quid pro quo*, a conditional commitment—all dwell here like a huge, if unspoken, question mark. "I'll love you, share intimately with you, be committed, yes, as long as you respect me and my freedom." Young adults find the movement into Shared Independency "as a natural accompaniment of leaving home and of the construction of a first, provisional adult life situation."[62] But young adults are not alone in experiencing and even

---

[62]Fowler, pp. 181–182.

dwelling in this stage:

> Many people never leave this third psychological stage. Their lives reveal a constant tension between a desire to share and a demand for independence. Think of a friend who moves from job to job "because they don't value me," or who uproots the family time and again in search of new growth opportunities and the assurance of personal freedom. Experience or recreation often serve as the reason for vacations taken without one's spouse; or back-packing trips enjoyed alone; or extramarital affairs entered into easily, if not often; or jobs pursued that demand extensive time away from one's partner, community, or family. Below these changing surfaces one may well find, while "in relationship," the drive to assert personal freedom.[63]

Mode of Church Governance

In his apostolic constitution *Sacrae disciplinae leges*, John Paul II emphasizes among "the elements which characterize the true and genuine image of the Church . . . the doctrine in which the Church is presented as the people of God and hierarchical authority as service. . . . "[64] To the themes of "people," "hierarchy," and "service," the preface to the code adds "equality" when it includes as one of the principles nearly unanimously approved by the Synod of Bishops in October, 1967, the following: "6. On account of the fundamental equality of all members of the Christian faithful . . . it is expedient that the rights of persons be appropriately defined and safeguarded."[65]

Canon 208 confirms the equality of all church members "in virtue of their rebirth in Christ . . . with regard to dignity and the activity whereby all cooperate in the building up of the Body of Christ in accord with each one's condition and function." In practice, this equality is canonically mandated through the optional holding of a diocesan synod (cc. 460, 463) and the requirement to have a presbyteral council (c. 495) in every diocese. The code also advises that in "each diocese, to the extent that pastoral circumstances recommend it, a pastoral council is to be established" (c. 511).

The tension between the Church as hierarchy and as people of God, between authority as power and authority as service, becomes evident

---

[63]Willis, p. 22.
[64]*Sacrae disciplinae leges*, p. xv.
[65]Ibid., p. xxi.

when the code goes on to state that in all three collegial bodies mentioned above the vote is only consultative:

> The diocesan bishop is the sole legislator at a diocesan synod(c. 466).
>
> The presbyteral council enjoys only a consultative vote; the bishop is to listen to it in matters of greater moment, but he needs its consent only in cases expressly defined by law (c. 500).
>
> The pastoral council enjoys only a consultative vote; it is for the bishop alone to make public what has been done in the council (c. 514).

According to law it seems clear that the bishop would fulfill his obligation by establishing such collegial-consultative bodies and by considering their eventual recommendations.[66] However, for a "minister of governance" such may not be sufficient when dealing with people in the growth stage under discussion.

These individuals, more than any others, need to have clear signs that they are respected and valued as equals. Members of a consultative body may initially find themselves so treated; however, should their consultations either routinely or in matters closely touching their experience or special expertise be disregarded and not visibly influence subsequent decisions, they would receive precisely the opposite signals. Only the immature and dependent are open to be manipulated and used through "the appearance of consultation." For these persons it would be better not to seek their consultation than to do so simply as a legal requirement or as a pretence of collegiality. What could be a means of personal and communal growth through such futile exercises quickly becomes a source of personal doubt and community disintegration. One may certainly expect the erstwhile consultor to turn disdained experience, frustrated energy, and shaky allegiance away from the Church. The struggle for assurance of personal dignity and worth through the earning of equality and respect takes precedence over institutional commitment.

Another area of church governance closely touching upon this psychological stage of Shared Independency is commitment. When speaking of elevation to the priesthood (c. 1031), the contracting of marriage (c. 1083), and the making of perpetual vows (c. 658), the code recognizes minimum age requirements as necessary conditions for validity. Age alone, however, does not suffice. With regard to matrimony

---

[66]For further discussion of this tension in the code, see Fahey, above.

the code judges incapable of making the contract those "who lack the sufficient use of reason" and "who are not capable of assuming the essential obligations of matrimony due to causes of a psychic nature" (c. 1045). Moreover, bishops are to promote to orders only those who, among other requirements, enjoy "the psychological qualities which are appropriate to the order to be received" (c. 1029). Only those "who have the suitable use of reason are capable of making a vow" (c. 1191). At issue here is how "sufficient" and "suitable" and "appropriate" relate to the stage of Shared Independency.

People enjoying this degree of psychological maturity may meet the requirement of minimum age easily and ordinarily are capable of reasonably making *to some extent* a "deliberate and free promise" (c. 1191). They do not, however, have the psychological capability of making an *unconditional* commitment. Such requires a personal identity stable and secure enough to relinquish control and to place the future trustingly in the hands of another.[67] Because of fear of a dependent state recently left, a person here must have control over the possibility of dependent regression; because of a necessary narcissism attendant on the striving to establish, finally, personal values and meanings and directions, personal identity is neither developed enough nor secure enough to be offered as a permanent gift to another—including God.

What does this say to the "minister of governance"? The following decisions might reasonably flow from the foregoing analysis:

1. Age, the "age of reason," and the appearance of the ability to make a "deliberate and free promise" are necessary but not sufficient conditions for making a perpetual commitment.
2. Expert psychological assessment must be obtained relative to the ability to make a public permanent commitment before such will be approved.
3. A person judged to have the psychological development described in one or other of these first three stages will be allowed to make only temporary commitments.
4. If one accepts that the "modal developmental level in most middle-class American churches . . . is best described in terms of

---

[67]In this regard it might be helpful to consider how contemporary theologicans are looking at the commitment needed to be a religious. For just such a discussion, see Elizabeth A. Johnson, C.S.J., "Discipleship: Root Model of the Life called 'Religious,'" *Review for Religious* 42 (1983) 864–872.

Synthetic-Conventional Faith or just beyond it,''[68] and if one agrees with the contention that ''human beings in the mass are far less emotionally mature than they suppose themselves to be,''[69] then the ''minister of governance'' must seriously assess whether marriage and priesthood and religious vows as permanent commitments are possible to the majority of people at this period of human history and development.

5. If for social and/or moral reasons various life states are publicly considered to be permanent commitments, and if persons psychologically incapable of such are for good reason allowed to enter them under the public form of a permanent commitment, then the ''minister of governance'' must build in community supports that will appropriately assist the individual to live out a commitment truly beyond that individual's ability. In the internal forum, understanding, sensitive direction, and personal support are particularly needed when failures in living out this permanent commitment quite expectedly occur.

STAGE IV: SHARED INTERDEPENDENCY

Identifying Characteristics

The previous stages may well be considered a continuum of dependency based on the need to establish a developed personal identity. With this fourth stage a new continuum of relating emerges. A stabilized personal sense of self allows one to make three significant psychological shifts: from an extrinsic orientation to an intrinsic stance, from a certainty that assures one's self-esteem through external measuring to a trust in one's inherent worth, from the calculating trappings of security to the willingness to risk growth in and through relationship.

These shifts make a profound difference individually and relationally. The individual may now move from the struggle to establish a self to the life task of transcending that self: ''Existence fails unless it is lived in terms of transcendence toward something beyond itself.''[70] In previous stages,

---

[68]Fowler, p. 294.

[69]Harry Guntrip, *Schizoid Phenomena, Object Relations, and the Self* (London: The Hogarth Press, 1980), p. 47.

[70]Viktor Frankl, *Personality and Social Encounter* (Boston: Beacon Press, 1960), p. 103.

all one's psychological effort worked for the formation of the "I"; for the first time, the gift of "I" looks to the birth of "We."

In Shared Interdependency this shift, this new effort, is strikingly seen in the mode of relating intimately. In previous stages only the appearance of love existed and it paraded as love:

> It is not true as the idea of romantic love would have it that there is only *the* one person in the world whom one could love and that it is the great chance of one's life to find that one person. Nor is it true, if that person be found, that love for him (or her) results in a withdrawal of love from others. Love which can only be experienced with regard to one person demonstrates by this very fact that it is not love, but a symbiotic attachment.[71]

Mature love differs from dependent attachment in these ways:

1. Each relationship is unique but not exclusive.
2. Life shared flows from the relationship outward to include others.
3. Energy shared in one relationship energizes all relationships.
4. Commitment is made to the relationship as an extension and expression of one's life.
5. The relationship becomes an enlivening source of personal and interpersonal life.
6. Continuity with one's inner life, not any required activity or response from another person, sustains the relationship.

Note the following statements as illustrative of the change taking place here, a change so obvious when compared to previous life stages:

> "I need" (stage 1); "I love you because I *need* you" (stage 2); "I *need* you because I love you" (stage 3); "I love myself loving you"(stage 4).
>
> "It is" (stage 1); "the relationship is" (stage 2); "I am" (stage 3); "we are" (stage 4).
>
> "I am no one" (stage 1); "I am someone with you;" (stage 2); "I am someone as long as I am careful" (stage 3); "I am someone" (stage 4).

In each instance, stage 4 results from a self presence and acceptance that issues in the gift of self to another.

How commonly does such mature love happen in our society? Psychological investigation until recently has been hampered in assessing this

---

[71]Fromm, pp. 129–130.

because of a Freudian prejudice that equated "losing one's self" or "merging with another" with a regression to an infantile symbiotic state:

> It has taken psychoanalysis some time to realize that the ability to lose oneself in the meeting of bodies and minds leads to a gradual expansion of ego-interests and to a libidinal investment in that which is being generated.[72]

This Freudian prejudice has continued because much of traditional psychological theorizing has come out of the reflections of psychotherapists concerning their patients and not out of reflections upon the lives of developmentally mature people. Personal pathology has until recently been the measure of not what love is, but of what it is not.

The following statement by two practicing psychotherapists of a psychoanalytic persuasion illustrates a perceptual shift in recognizing the difference between the mature love of Shared Interdependency and the symbiosis of Mutual Dependency. It moreover underlines the risk in generalizing from a narrow and troubled population to one of the optimum states of human life:

> Rather two "whole" people come together, share love and intimacy, and merge emotionally, physically, and sexually without fear. What this means is, ideally again, that each person has the ability to open up, merge, and separate without fear of loss of self or loss of the other person.
>
> This model of the "healthy" couple is one that is not very familiar to us; few couples have achieved this state. What we find in couples who are having difficulties and therefore seek counseling is a diffused sense of boundaries, a lack of secure sense of self; each is seeking in the other the longed-for loving person he or she wants, or the longed-for self that she or he cannot be.[73]

Leaving aside judgments flowing from theoretical prejudice or a skewed professional sample, the following may be at least reasonably hypothesized. If the psychological growth of Western society is in the main, as previously asserted, a reflection of dependency, then a most conservative estimate would say that the mature love of Shared Interdependency is neither the average nor the modal way of relating among us.

---

[72]Erickson, *Childhood and Society*, p. 267.
[73]Eichenbaum and Orbach, pp. 183–184.

Mode of Church Governance

In recent years it has become in some Catholic quarters theologically sophisticated to speak of "Christianity in these post-Christian times" (cf., for example, Gregory Baum's statement quoted above). This rather strange, ironic phrase seems to refer either (1) to the fractured relationship of Church and State appearing with the demise of the medieval world and abetted by the Renaissance, the Enlightenment, and the Protestant Reformation; or (2) to the minority status of Christians in an essentially non-Christian world, a world described in terms of Old Testament realities like the "diaspora" and "the remnant people"; or (3) to the diminishing influence on and appeal to modern technological and information societies of biblical values such as humility and suffering, religious obedience and filial fear. The first two references may be lamented but must be accepted as quite evident facts; the third seeks reasons for the apparent incompatability of this modern age with the Christian vision.

In terms of this chapter's analysis, the estrangement may stem not so much from these *post*-Christian times, as from these *pre*-Christian ones![74] Shaw's oft-quoted judgment that "the only problem with Christianity is that so few try it" may need the further explanation "because so few are developmentally capable of doing so." As we have seen, humility and fear, obedience and suffering for the majority do more to highlight immature need than to express mature Christian values. Church governance in exhorting people to embrace Christian values such as these may be reinforcing, quite unwittingly, on the one hand dependency through compliance, on the other dependency through failure.

An example may be useful. Since Vatican II religious men and women have been urged, incessantly and insistently, to "form community." Such would seem quite reasonable for a "people of God." God alone may know how many hours and conversations and meetings around this topic have consumed religious life these past twenty years. God alone may be able to plumb the depth of anguish so many religious feel as words remain words, exhortations sail on unhindered by reality, and "Christian community" rarely, even at its optimum, becomes more than a benevolent aggregate.

---

[74]It might be objected that classifying our times as "pre-Christian" would in an evolutionary framework make all previous eras and/or civilizations even less capable of Christianity than our own is. Such an evolutionary model is neither intended nor accepted, nor such a judgment made. The judgment is, indeed, made only about our current Western culture.

The result?—failure, disillusionment, and a deepening and destructive self-hatred. "If I am a religious as well as a Christian, then *I should* be a model of Christian love and *we should* be the light of Christian community to the whole Church." (This example could be expanded to include "living the vows," "being committed," and "living a prayerful life.")

Church governance fosters this tortuous state when it fails to distinguish clearly between Christian values progressively to be actualized according to our limited ability, and Christian duties expected to be done absolutely, if not perfectly. "Be ye perfect as your heavenly Father is perfect" is how often preached literally, even if it is literally impossible, even if this perfection is really referring to the righteousness of a God who faithfully fulfills promises and who is merely asking us to be open to receive the divine salvific Love! Love and chastity, prayer and community dwell within us as goals to be aspired to and worked toward; they do not flourish simply through baptism or assure impeccability through some formal entrance into contemporary Christian adulthood (be that through confirmation, religious vows, orders, or matrimony).

In a developmentally pre-Christian world, the "minister of governance" best serves the Christian people by modeling for them and to them Christian love.[75] Whatever its theological definition, its psychological characteristics match those of this stage of Shared Interdependency. For the dependent, this will make visible the goal toward which they may aspire; for those capable of this love, it will be a desperately needed guide in an unloving world. As the Japanese *Zenrin* shrewdly notes, "If you wish to know the road up the mountain, you must ask the man who goes back and forth on it."[76] If the person psychologically capable of Shared Interdependency is to inform this stage explicitly with the vision of Christ, then someone ("minister of governance" or no) must facilitate that in-formation through a practical and practicing love. What is required is no more, no less than what Jesus gave to the two aspiring disciples:

> Jesus turned, and saw them following, and said to them, "What do you seek?" And they said to him, "Rabbi" (which means

---

[75]Of the three roles assigned by the code to bishops (teaching, sanctifying, and governing: c. 375), a "minister of governance" would most appropriately, for people in this developmental stage, put emphasis on teaching and sanctifying through the example of Christian love both seen and gratefully experienced. Note in this regard the division of the code: Book III, *Munus Docendi*, and Book IV, *Munus Sanctificandi*.

[76]Robert Sohl and Audrey Carr, eds., *The Gospel According to Zen* (New York: New American Library, 1970), p. 28.

Teacher), ''Where are you staying?'' He said to them, ''Come and see.'' (John 1:38–39.)

CONCLUSION

As a conclusion and summary, the following chart is offered:

Developmental Stages

	Extrinsic Evaluation	Mutual Dependency	Shared Independency	Shared Interdependency
Identity	Outside self	In relationship	In self	In gift of self
Mathematical equivalent	$0+\frac{1}{2}=\frac{1}{2}$	$\frac{1}{2}+\frac{1}{2}=1$	$1+1=2$	$1+1=3$
Objective Description	''It is''	''Relationship is''	''I am''	''We are''
Subjective Description	''I need''	''I love you because I need you''	''I need you because I love you''	''I love myself loving you''
Mode of relating	Instrumental	Symbiotic	Measured	Committed
Source of Motivation	Need for security	Need for acceptance	Need for stability	Valued self expression
Dominating authority	Rewards, punishments	Threat of rejection	Demand for commitment	Demand for perfection
Christ-like authority	Personal Affirmation	Unconditional acceptance	Sensitive guidance	Love

From the previous analyses the various categories and stage identifications charted here should be clear except, perhaps, that of ''Mathematical equivalent.'' A brief explanation may help.

In the first two stages the dependent person strives to find identity outside of self; the "½" is meant to convey this lack of a solid internal identity. In Stage 1 the search for identity is constantly and forever frustrated as identity does not exist in the meeting of external standards or laws. The "0" signals the fruitlessness of this search, one destined always to end up in "½." Stage 2 at least finds the appearance of an identity in the "1"; the problem here lies in a relationship based on need where both are desperately seeking from another the identity each interiorly lacks. The "½" of each must, therefore, cling to the other in order for the drive for meaning and identity to be quieted. And so it is, but at the price of a loss of freedom and with the spectre of future disintegration forever lurking.

In Stage 3 the individual does experience a tenuous sense of personal identity—thus the "1." But this identity is fragile, open to being shattered by extrinsic forces. Relationships, therefore, are measured, marked by the demand for equality ("1 + "), and do not generate the additional life that comes with a free, unmeasured, trusting gift of self. For this reason, Stage 3 never is more than the sum of its parts ("1 + 1" must always equal "2"). In Stage 4, on the other hand, the whole *is* greater than the sum of its parts ("1 + 1" will always equal more than "2") because of the energy and life created in the relationship through a trusting and hopeful gift of love. This is indicated by the numeral "3."

This chart and analysis, indeed this study's whole discussion, does not pretend to exhaust the rich subject of the relationship between church governance and human development. Stages 5 and 6 of this interpersonal developmental theory have, indeed, not even been included.[77] The omission, if great, is deliberate. These stages deal with a contemplative integration and expressive life which (1) are not ordinary experiences for most members of our civilization or Church, (2) are of sufficient complexity and unfamiliarity that they would require much more explanation than the other stages and would make this study both too long and relatively "top heavy" in emphasis, (3) are dependent for true understanding upon personal experience of either an artistic and aesthetic, intuitive and ecstatic, or contemplative and unitive nature that are not readily shared solely through logical analysis.

This omission should not, however, be taken as an implicit statement that the "minister of governance" and church members experiencing in various moments and ways these contemplative stages need not relate. The very opposite must be strongly asserted.

[77]Cf. Willis, pp. 24–27.

Of all twentieth century psychologists, Carl Jung enjoys the greatest popularity among, and earns the most serious attention of, religious professionals. Recall for a moment the continued popularity among priests and religious of the "Myers-Briggs" personality test, a test based upon Jungian character types. Think back over the outpouring of articles that have filled religious journals in a continuing exploration of the implications of Jung's "anima" and "animus" for questions of chastity and love, of his "shadow" to human frailty and sinfulness, and of his "collective unconscious" to the natural religious urge of human beings, to human unity in Christ's Mystical Body. Yet Jung, more than any other respected and articulate modern psychologist, has criticized religious institutions precisely because of their relationship, or lack of relationship, to the esoteric, prophetic, and contemplative side of religion.

Why do so many today turn away from religion and toward psychology? Jung answers:

> The "psychological" interest of the present time shows that man expects something from psychic life which he has not received from the outer world: something which our religions, doubtless, ought to contain, but no longer do contain—at least for the modern man. The various forms of religion no longer appear to the modern man to come from within—to be expressions of his own psychic life; for him they are to be classed with the things of the outer world.[78]

Why have religions lost this interior resonance for people grappling with a frantic and intrusive modern existence? Jung maintains that religious institutions are hanging onto systems

> no longer based on their own inner experience but on *unreflecting belief*. People call faith the true religious experience, but they do not stop to think that actually it is a secondary phenomenon arising from the fact that something happened to us in the first place which instilled *pistis* into us—that is—trust and loyalty.[79]

What must Christianity do to become relevant to individual lives in our time? Can such happen? Yes, says Jung, if. . . .

It is not Christianity, but our conception and interpretation of it,

---

[78]Jung, *Modern Man in Search of a Soul*, p. 206.
[79]Carl G. Jung, *The Undiscovered Self*, trans. R. F. C. Hall (New York: New American Library, Mentor Books, 1959), pp. 47–48.

that has become antiquated in face of the present world situation. The Christian symbol is a living thing that carries in itself the seeds of further development. It can go on developing; it depends only on us, whether we can make up our minds to meditate again, and more thoroughly, on the Christian premises.[80]

Why, if only from a psychological perspective, should the "minister of governance" bend sensitive and constant efforts to further and direct the contemplative experience of people? Jung says flatly, if for nothing else, for psychological health:

> Among all my patients in the second half of life . . . there has not been one whose problem in the last resort was not that of finding a religious outlook on life. It is safe to say that every one of them fell ill because he had lost that which the living religions of every age have given their followers, and none of them has really been healed who did not regain his religious outlook.[81]

We need not agree with Jung's analysis of religion's "failure" in respect to communicating and facilitating an experience of God; we would, however, be unwise not to hear his plea—it has echoes throughout our civilization—that church governance not be consumed by institutional and organizational problems. "Modern man [and woman] in search of a soul" desperately seek religious leaders who may be companions, models, and guides in that search.

In closing, what was stated in the introduction bears restating. The task undertaken here has been to begin a discussion "from a psychological and developmental perspective" of "the conditions that may signify, support, and strengthen this 'ministry of governance.'" General developmental outlines have been drawn. A few issues that touch upon the relationship of the "minister of governance" to the Christian people have been raised. It is hoped that this collection of essays, the result of many hours of individual and communal effort, may further a process of exploration, specification, and expansion of these beginnings. The ultimate goal?—some real, worthwhile assistance to the bishop, to diocesan officials, to pastors as they seek to fulfill the rather awesome role of "minister of governance" bestowed on them in the revised Code of Canon Law.

[80]Ibid., pp. 74–75.
[81]Jung, *Modern Man in Search of a Soul*, p. 229.

DIOCESAN GOVERNANCE IN EUROPEAN DIOCESES
FOLLOWING THE 1983 CODE:
AN INITIAL INQUIRY

ROLAND-BERNHARD TRAUFFER, O.P.

This is a report on the first practical steps taken in Europe in light of the new code's provisions on the diocesan curia (cc. 469–494). The curia, which assists the bishop and in his name carries out the governance of the diocese (c. 469), is often called the "Secretariat" or "Ordinariat" in Europe. Technically it includes all the persons and institutes which assist the bishop in administrative and judicial matters, but this survey will be limited to the administrative aspect.

Before discussing the results of a survey of a sampling of European dioceses, it will be helpful to review certain provisions of the new code which touch on the diocesan curia. The individual survey topics will then be reviewed, and the report will end with some concluding remarks.

PROVISIONS OF THE NEW CODE

1.Vicar General

Although the diocesan bishop exercises legislative power personally, and this power cannot be delegated unless specifically stated by law (cc. 391, 135), the bishop's other powers of governance can be exercised by vicars. In executive or administrative matters the vicar general is the bishop's personal representative, acting with ordinary vicarious power. This is more than a personal representation or delegation; it is connected with his office, and according to the *regula iuris*, one who acts through another is as if he did it himself (*qui facit per alium est perinde, ac si faciat per se ipsum*—Regula 72 in VI°). Thus in administrative matters the vicar general is called the bishop's "alter ego."

The role of the vicar general has grown in practice, as the answers to the survey will demonstrate. In the 1917 code a vicar general need be appointed only when his leadership was needed in the diocese (1917 code, c. 366); now by law a vicar general must be named in each diocese (c, 475, §1). His power ceases when the diocesan see is vacant (c. 481, §1), and is suspended if the diocesan bishop is suspended (c. 481, §2).

The vicar general is bound to the diocesan bishop in carrying out his office. He is to maintain close communications with the bishop, informing him of what he learns, of anything of importance which occurs, and the measures he has taken. He is not to permit anything to happen against the will of the bishop (c. 480). Although his authority encompasses the jurisdiction of the entire diocese (c. 479, §1), the bishop can reserve certain matters to himself.

The position of vicar general enjoys great flexibility and has the possibility of being adapted to the needs of various particular churches, something which the survey indicates is happening in Europe. The new code envisages only one vicar general for each diocese, although it permits more than one in exceptional cases when diocesan or other pastoral needs require this (c. 475, §2). Such exceptions, however, should be rare because since Vatican II it has been possible to appoint episcopal vicars.

2. Episcopal Vicars

The episcopal vicar's office is determined either territorially, personally, or functionally. Like the vicar general, an episcopal vicar has permanent, ordinary, vicarious power but it is limited to the boundaries of his work. He may not go against the intentions of the diocesan bishop, is to keep the bishop informed of all his most important functions (c. 480), and is subject to any limitations the bishop may place on his office by reserving certain functions (c. 479, §2).

The relationship between the vicar general and episcopal vicars is not one of above or below the other; in this respect, episcopal vicars are not bound to the vicar general. An effort is therefore necessary to provide for unity in the diocesan administration. One representative of the diocesan bishop should not act against another, nor should one be used against another. Canon 65 on rescripts is one example of how this is to be avoided.

3. Coordination of Diocesan Administration

The new structure of diocesan administration increases the number of representatives of the bishop. The diocesan bishop is himself responsible to see to their coordination and to the unity of diocesan administration (c. 473, §§1–2), since ultimately it is the bishop himself who in answerable for the administration of the diocese.

One means of coordination provided in the new code is the new office of moderator of the curia (c. 473, §3). Normally the vicar general is to be appointed to this position, which entails supervising and coordinating the workers in the diocesan curia.

Another means of coordination is the episcopal council (c. 473, §4). This is the bishop's first advisory organ, to be consulted by him and also to provide a "horizontal" communications service to keep the vicar general and episcopal vicars informed about their activities and duties.

4. Other Positions in the Diocesan Curia

All other positions in the curia are subsidiary to the above. In this sense they are also coordinated and unified through the means described above, and the code leaves open the way to organize them effectively. For example, the office of chancellor can be organized according to various ways (c. 482, §1), and it is required that there be a finance officer but his duties can be further defined beyond the general responsibilities given in law (cf. c. 494, §§3–4). As is evident in the responses to the survey, European dioceses are still working out how these positions are to be organized.

Vatican II stated that "the diocesan curia should be so organized that it is an appropriate instrument for the bishop, not only for administering the diocese but also for carrying out the works of the apostolate" (CD, 27; Abbott, p. 416). It is not possible, therefore, to present one standard example of the organization of the leadership of a diocese. Moreover, there is considerable variety in practice. The survey demonstrates there is an abundance of organizational forms in European dioceses, responding to various sociological and pastoral conditions. The diocesan curia in European dioceses is also affected by the Church-State relations in individual nations, particularly on the level of trusteeship which is governed by specific legislation in the different countries. In some nations the bishop is the chief trustee; in others, questions of ownership and finance are handled by a Church-State panel and the bishop is at most in a position of being able to affirm and carry out their proposals.

Diocesan administration must always attend to pastoral considerations since there is always the danger of bureaucracy; hence, it must seek to assure contact with the people of the Church. The diocesan bishop does not depend solely on the curia for his leadership, and is aided in his contact with the people by various consultative bodies, some of which are required by law. Consultative bodies are both intra-curial (e.g., the episcopal council and the diocesan finance council), and extra-curial (e.g., presbyteral council and college of consultors, both required by law; and the diocesan pastoral council).

It is important that the bishop not overlook or underestimate these consultative organs. They are structures which embody the conciliar principle of participation, whereby all members of the Church share in the problems of the Church. The variety of consultative bodies, their number, membership, coordination and integration in the diocese, are beyond the scope of this paper. A separate survey and analysis would be needed for this.

It would also be a major study in itself to describe the competencies of various consultative bodies, partly because the law is not particularly clear in this respect. For example, the competencies of the diocesan pastoral council (c. 511) and the presbyteral council (c. 495, §1) are both said to relate to the effectiveness of pastoral work. Theoretically the pastoral council is supposed to focus on pastoral planning, so there should be no question as to which is essential for the governance of the particular church. Yet the results of the survey indicate these councils have not been formed everywhere, and where they have been established they do not function very well in practice.

THE SURVEY

A. Background

The questionnaire on which this report is based was sent to sixty different episcopal curias in the fall of 1984. The report itself was written in December 1984. Around fifty percent of those contacted replied, some of them with detailed reports. Great care was taken in selecting the various curia in order to achieve a cross-section of large (important), medium and small (less important) sees. All European countries except Great Britain and Ireland were included in the survey. The answers submitted come from the following countries: Austria, Belgium, France, Germany, Italy, the Netherlands, Portugal, Spain, Switzerland, and Yugoslavia. No answers were received from other East European countries or from Scandinavia.

It is impossible to repeat each individual reply. In the following report emphasis is placed on the general opinion before certain particularities are referred to. It should be noted that this inquiry was only meant to supply general information and not exact statistics.

B. The Report

1. *Who are the members of the staff of your Curia? What are their functions? Who, for example, are the members of the episcopal council or of the conference of the vicar general?*

    a. These titles were listed most frequently: vicar general, episcopal vicar, chancellor, secretary general of the curia.
    b. The following particularities are noteworthy.

    1) Especially in the answers from France, it appears that often there are several vicars general, not just one. In Germany and France the title ''chancellor'' is not used; instead, reference is usually made to a ''general secretary of the curia.''
    2) Only two of the responding dioceses have representatives of their seminaries listed among the responsible members of the episcopal curia.
    3) Some dioceses have ''delegates,'' along with episcopal vicars and office directors. For example, the Toledo (Spain) curia has one vicar general, two vice-vicars general, one judicial vicar, two episcopal vicars, seven episcopal delegates for diocesan commissions, and nine directors of the various offices.
    4) Other diocesan curias are organized into departments and have department directors.
    5) As a rule, the diocesan offices in Austrian dioceses are headed by ''official experts'' (*Referent*) who are also responsible for their department.

2. *What is the official title of the episcopal council (e.g. bishop's council, conference of the vicariate general, etc.)?*

The answers to this question are much more homogeneous than the previous one. Most diocesan curias have a ''bishop's council.'' Here is an example of the membership of one of the larger of these, taken from the diocese of Autun (France): the vicar general, auxiliary bishop, general secretary of the curia, four episcopal vicars, the delegate for women religious, the person responsible for seminaries, and three spiritual guides for the Catholic Action lay movement. In most dioceses, however, only the vicar(s) general, the auxiliary bishop(s), episcopal vicars, and possibly the chancellor belong to the bishop's council. However, the chancellor is seldom mentioned.

In the German-speaking dioceses of Europe there are many variations both in terminology and in composition. For example, the canons of the cathedral chapter are sometimes called the "general spiritual council"; in some dioceses, the cathedral chapter is called the "consistory." The vicar general and the directors of the various curial offices are said to belong to the "vicar general's conference" in some dioceses, to the "ordinary assembly" in others, or to the "office directors' conference" in still other dioceses. It goes without saying that the bishop belongs to all these advisory boards, regardless of the terminology.

3. *What is the function of the chancellor in your administration? Is it more in line with the 1917 code, the 1983 code, or is it defined in some other way, and if so, how?*

The answers to this question vary considerably. Many European curias do not have a "chancellor." As already mentioned, this office is occupied, for example in France, by "general secretaries of the curia."

An answer often reported was a combination of vicar general and chancellor. The administration of the curia as a rule is presided over by the vicar general when neither a chancellor nor a general secretary is mentioned.

Where a chancellor does exist, about twenty percent of the dioceses indicated the office was only provided with the competencies found in the 1917 code. The other eighty percent have adapted the office of chancellor to the new code.

Most dioceses answered the chancellor does have a specific function. This means that in the majority of those dioceses which have a chancellor, this office has been given additional powers over and above those specified in the code; e.g., diocesan financial administrator, or episcopal vicar responsible for diocesan property, director of personnel (*Personalchef*), archivist, or episcopal vicar "with special duties." Most chancellors entrusted with additional duties exercise these in the field of administration, finance, or organization.

4. *What is the function of the vicar general? Is he the "moderator of the curia"?*

It is noteworthy that many of the diocesan curia have not as yet made use of the new possibilities in the code. It was especially the Latin countries (France, Italy, Spain) that answered the vicar general is also entrusted with the office of moderator of the curia. A few other answers confirm that although on paper the vicar general is not listed as moderator of the curia, de facto he exercises this position. The majority, however, do not yet have a moderator.

5. *Have the rights of the vicar general been increased or decreased by the application of the new code in your dioceses? What are his rights and obligations in the running of the diocese?*

The majority answered that there has de facto been no change. One result of the new code was that the vacuum caused by the introduction of the office of episcopal vicar and the resulting competence problems have been eliminated. The competencies of the vicar general and of the episcopal vicars seem to be much clearer. The reply from Autun (France) can be understood in this sense:

> The vicar general is more or less general secretary. In order to understand his function, one must first realize that the diocese is divided into four regions encompassing eleven pastoral zones. Each region is directed by an episcopal vicar. The main function of the vicar general is to coordinate the work of these four episcopal vicars and at regular intervals to summon them to a conference.

The model of the diocese of Basle (Switzerland) is similar. The diocese is divided into ten different regions, each of which is administered by a regional dean. The vicar general presides over the regional deans' conference.

Some replies mention the fact that according to the new code an "extension of the field of office" of the vicar general has become possible. This is illustrated in the response from Freiburg-im-Breisgau (Germany) by a citation of the mandate given to the vicar general:

> The [full] powers and commissioning of the vicar general, through the bishop: "I hereby hand over to my vicar general, in accordance with canons 134, §3 and 479, §1 all powers for whose exercise, according to church law, my special mandate is necessary. Through this he is also empowered to represent the bishopric of Freiburg in all legal actions (c. 393).

Such an extension of course does not apply in cases where there is more than one vicar general. In these cases the various vicars general are entrusted with various competencies, which in other dioceses are performedby episcopal vicars.

With the general competence as the bishop's alter ego there is hardly any field not covered by the competence of a vicar general. Malines-Brussels (Belgium) provides a fairly common example:

> The rights and obligations due to the vicar general for the administration of the diocese:
>
> 1. He is the only vicar general of the whole diocese [there are four other vicars general (auxiliary bishops) responsible for a specific pastoral region].
> 2. He is responsible for the coordination and control of the whole curia and in this sense also moderator of the bishop's council.
> 3. He is also responsible for the supervision of pastoral duties, continuing education, and Christian education in the diocese.

Bamberg (Germany) provides a second example:

> He is responsible for transfers, granting leaves of absence, qualifications, certification exams, church dispensations, absolution from excommunication, admission to the Church, authority for consecrations and benedictions, questions referring to the administration of the sacraments, church services and church funerals, imprimatur, issuing documents and credentials. Apart from this he is also a member of the presbyteral council and the diocesan pastoral council, as well as a member of the examination board for the second priests' and laymen's examination.

Another example from a diocese with more than one vicar general comes from Liege (Belgium):

> We have three vicars general. They have jurisdiction over all affairs concerning the whole diocese, but in daily life each has his own field and except in cases of emergency they do not interfere with each other's affairs unless the responsible vicar general or episcopal vicar is absent. One vicar general is responsible for Catholic teaching in the diocese, another for Catholic Action and specialized pastoral duties, while the third occupies himself with parishes and pastoral regions.

The answer from Ljubljana (Yugoslavia) speaks for many others: ''The vicar general's rights have been extended by the new code. In the absence of the archbishop he has full authority. He is a member of nearly all councils and other boards (college of consultors, presbyteral council, pastoral council, etc.).''

6. *What is the function of the episcopal vicar(s) in your curia? Do they exercise their function directly as ordinaries? What are their competencies? What other rights and obligations do they have in the running of the diocese?*

The answers to this question also show that despite the number of years which have passed since the Vatican Council, all the possibilities which were opened up by the council have still not been put into practice. This question also reveals many different models: from one diocese with seven episcopal vicars (Autun, France) to dioceses with none at all (Linz, Austria or Lille, France, among others).

Many dioceses have only one episcopal vicar who is usually also an auxiliary bishop (e.g., Bamberg, Germany or Ljubljana, Yugoslavia). Many episcopal vicars are charged with the religious; i.e., they represent the bishop in all questions concerning religious and partly also other "church professions" (for example in Germany and Switzerland, the *Pastoralassistenten*).

Here are some examples of the distribution of an episcopal vicar's duties:

a. In Autun (France) there are seven episcopal vicars: the auxiliary bishop, the secretary general of the curia, the episcopal vicars responsible for the pastoral regions. "These are provided with ordinary power for their own region, and their work is coordinated with and by the vicar general; they also belong to the Bishop's Council and reside, of course, in their respective regions."

b. Venice (Italy) is an example of a diocese with only one episcopal vicar. He is "responsible for the missions in the diocese; he animates the missionary works." As director of this department he:

— coordinates all works having a missionary function or aim;
— encourages the development of the Pontifical Missionary Society, the Alliance of Missionary Priests, the Missionary
— Societies, the press, and all other boards engaged in the propagation of missions around the world;
— presides over the Center of Missionary Action and takes part in all conferences of the Missionary Commission of the diocese;
— is secretary of the diocesan collection "Bread for the Love of God";
— deals with regular and special collections for the missions and organizes the World Day for Missions;

— guides and coordinates parish activities for missionary works;
— keeps in contact with missionaries from the diocese and guarantees contact with their families at home;
— helps to propagate special missionary ideals in parishes, societies, and various diocesan institutions.

c. Finally, the Archdiocese of Vienna (Austria) is representative of the average European diocese.

There are three episcopal vicars for the territorial vicariates and a vicar for religious. They are provided with ordinary vicarious power for their territories as a vicar general is for the whole diocese, except that they only make use of this juridically in cases of emergency. Their main duty is to coordinate the pastoral conception of the diocese with the three different vicariates and to maintain personal contact with the clergy and lay people engaged in ministerial work.

Very often the responses to this question in the survey referred to regulations in the code, for example, canons 476, 479, §§ 2 and 3.

7. *Are there any lay people who exercise the function of an episcopal vicar? If so, who are they and what are their competencies?*

From the very beginning it was recognized that this question in the European context would be rather rhetorical, perhaps even provocative. It is also the only question answered univocally. All the answers received were negative.

Only one diocese, Lyon (France), reported: "A woman is delegate in the health care pastoral. However, she does not bear the title episcopal vicar." The diocese of Linz (Austria) responded that the director of "Caritas" and the school authority is also a layman.

There are, therefore, no lay people reported in the local church administration bearing the authority of an episcopal vicar.

8. *What is the function of the auxiliary bishop(s)? What are their tasks? Are they vicars general or episcopal vicars? What is their place (and importance) in the bishops' conference? Do they have interdiocesan tasks?*

A little more than half of the answers received reported that there are no auxiliary bishops in their dioceses. Many other responses indicated they have only one auxiliary bishop.

As to their tasks, the diocese of Bamberg (Germany) reported:

> The single auxiliary bishop is mainly engaged in supporting the bishop in the tasks demanding the competent authority of a bishop (confirmations, ordinations, consecrations, pontifical ceremonies). Along with his duty as a member of the general spiritual council [episcopal council] he also bears the office of ''Provost and 'Summus custos''' of the cathedral; he is president of the diocesan commission for recruiting and encouraging spiritual vocations, professions, and church services, vice-president of the presbyteral council commission for continuing education, as well as a member of the liturgical commission. In the archbishop's tribunal he fulfills the task of a promoter of justice.

This example is fairly representative since auxiliary bishops are engaged in many different duties. Where there are several auxiliary bishops they are organized like the episcopal vicars. For example, in Ljubljana (Yugoslavia), ''auxiliary bishops have their own duties—one is vicar general, the other is an episcopal vicar. They are both members of the college of consultors and the presbyteral council. The episcopal vicar is responsible for questions of family pastoral and is also Archdeacon of Ljubljana and surroundings.''

All responses indicated auxiliary bishops are at least episcopal vicars. In a few exceptional cases one or all of them are vicars general: Malines-Brussels (Belgium), Madrid (Spain), Vienna (Austria).

Within the conference of bishops as a rule they are full members. One exception is the Austrian conference of bishops: ''all auxiliary bishops are members of the conference of bishops with the right to vote except in financial matters.''

Interdiocesan duties are delegated to auxiliary bishops usually in virtue of being members of the conference of bishops. They are engaged in interdiocesan commissions and some have also been appointed members of Roman congregations. As an example of their engagement in commissions, the auxiliary bishops of Freiburg-im-Breisgau (Germany) are members of the German Bishops' Conference's commission for social and social-charity questions, pastoral commission, and commission for science and culture.

9. *Who is the financial administrator of your diocese? Is it a lay person or a priest? What are his professional qualifications?*

There is a very wide range of answers to this question. One third answered: "Not as yet decided." A further third answered a priest, but the answer was further qualified in most cases: "A priest who is also a qualified accountant and therefore fulfills the task of diocesan financial administrator" (Autun, France). A further third answered a lay person. Few dioceses have a lay person being trained for this task.

The general impression is still that of a priest as principal authority and responsible for financial questions. However, the many special juridical situations in Europe must be kept in mind, since every country has its own concordat. There are often very complicated relationships. Switzerland can be taken for an example. It has twenty-six cantons; within the federal system Church-State relationships are the responsibility of the individual cantons. The result is that Switzerland has twenty-six different Church-State relationships.

As a rule the bishop, in keeping with a concordat, has no specific financial competence. Finances are usually attended to by boards of the established (State-recognized) churches. In these cases the financial administrator is the accountant responsible for the budget which he has to justify before the state church board.

Finally, wherever a priest is delegated with this task, he is often also chancellor; e.g., Beauvais (France) or Lyon (France).

10. *Is there a council for the administration of diocesan properties and assets? How is it composed; i.e., what is its membership, who is its president?*

Here again about a third of the answers are negative, although some claim to be in the process of constituting such a council. An exceptional situation is found in France, where according to civil law a "Diocesan Association" must be formed. This is presided over by the bishop himself.

Austria has another solution. Here the consistory (i.e., the cathedral chapter) fulfills the duties of the diocesan finance council.

Not every diocese in Germany has a diocesan finance council as described in the code. But there is a "Church tax committee." In Freiburg-im-Breisgau (Germany) this is called a "Church tax agency" (*Kirchensteuervertretung*) and has forty members—nine elected priests, twenty-six elected lay people, and the diocesan finance council (i.e., the council of c. 492).

It is impossible to summarize such varied structures. The available answers make it clear that especially in this case, each diocese has found its own particular solution.

The answers to the additional question on the chairperson show that ninety percent of the finance councils are presided over by the bishop. There are, however, a few exceptions: Trier (Germany) or Malines-Brussels (Belgium), where the vicar general or an episcopal vicar presides over this council.

11. *Does the presbyteral council play a role in the running of the diocese? If so, how (give example).*

About half the answers point out that the presbyteral council has only an advisory function and that this function is fulfilled according to the code. Here, for example, is the response from Bamberg (Germany):

> There can be no talk of the presbyteral council really playing a role in the running of the diocese since this council has—according to the rules—only an advisory function. Important points of ministerial work are, however, handled at meetings of this council and discussed between the archbishop and the appointed and elected members of the council.
> Inasmuch as the deliberations of the presbyteral council influence in this manner the decisions of the diocesan administration, one could speak of a "share in the administration." Then there are certain cases where, according to church law, the presbyteral council has to be consulted (e.g., the establishment of parishes), although even in this case it is wrong to speak of a share in the administration since the bishop remains free to decide as he thinks—even against the will of the council.

Differently accentuated answers come from France. Here is the response from Besancon:

> This happened five years ago. On the basis of reflection and studies, the decision was taken to establish a new diocese—in agreement with the Holy See. The council also plays a role in the diocesan administration when it sets directives for the pastoral work which are then approved by the bishop: e.g., the foundation of parish councils, the renewal of the pastoral approach for confirmation, etc.

Larger dioceses often have more than one presbyteral council. For example, in Malines-Brussels (Belgium), there are four presbyteral councils corresponding to the four regional vicariates: for the Flemish, for the

Walloons, for French-speaking Catholics in Brussels, and for Dutch-speaking Catholics in Brussels.

Autun (France) points out how the presbyteral council performs "legislative" work in its pastoral reflection and by taking note of developments in the society in which the Church lives.

12. *Does the presbyteral council have competencies in matters which concern the priests of the diocese?*

Half the answers consist of a simple "yes." The other half insist that this is not the principal duty of the council. The council is mainly responsible for various pastoral questions posed to the diocese.

An individual reply from Germany noted, "The presbyteral council regards itself as representing the clergy. It therefore sees its duty in representing the priests' interest towards the bishop and the diocesan administration. There is no special presbyteral council commission which fulfills this duty."

13. *What other consultative bodies are there in your diocese?*

In some dioceses, no other consultative bodies exist; e.g., Lille (France) or Toledo (Spain). For others, there are a variety of bodies in existence. The following is a summary of the possible consultative bodies: cathedral chapter, college of consultors, workers' mission council, diocesan catechetical council, diocesan commission for permanent pastoral planning, diocesan council for women religious, diocesan pastoral council, clergy commission, archdeacon's council, personnel commission, deans' conference. In addition there are various commissions: liturgy, pastoral care of the elderly, church music, art and monument protection, ecumenism, etc.

The answers make it clear that in the North and in German-speaking regions there are more consultative commissions and bodies than in the South and in Latin-speaking countries.

The diocese of Basle (Switzerland) can serve as an example. It is organized as follows. Together with the cathedral chapter (which is mainly responsible for Church-State questions) and the permanent Episcopal Council, there are the following bodies:

    a. Regional Deans Conference—a regional dean from each of the ten regions together with the Episcopal Council. The regions consist of several deaneries. This conference meets monthly.

b. Conference of Deans—all the deaneries jointly with the Episcopal Council. This conference meets annually.
c. Personnel Commission—ten regional deans together with representatives of the Episcopal Council.
d. Diocesan Catechetical Commission.
e. Diocesan Liturgical Commission.
f. Diocesan Commission for Continuing Education of the Clergy.
g. Missionary Commission.
h. Finance Commission.

Not listed here are numerous interdiocesan commissions which can also have an important influence in the diocese.

14. *Is there a diocesan pastoral council?*

About half the answers are negative, especially from dioceses in France. Some other dioceses have long experience with a diocesan pastoral council. For example, Antwerp (Belgium) replied: "The Diocesan Pastoral Council has a majority of lay people. It gives important counsel and notes regarding pastoral questions." Salzburg (Austria) responded: "As a diocesan advisory—and administrative—board the Pastoral Council attends to the duties of the Church regarding ministry, society, culture, economy, and politics. The responsible and competent advice, information and comment represent a communication between the diocese and the archbishop."

15. *What is the relationship between the presbyteral council and the diocesan pastoral council?*

Of course only half the answering dioceses were able to answer this question, since only fifty percent of those responding have a presbyteral council. The most frequently named model is the "reciprocal representation" system: two members of the presbyteral council are also members of the diocesan pastoral council. Thus a connection is established between these two completely different consultative bodies—e.g., Freiburg-im-Breisgau (Germany), Salzburg (Austria), Basle (Switzerland).

Concluding Remarks

In the introduction to this report it was emphasized that on all levels of governance in the particular church, great importance must be attached to the exercise of the apostolate, to the pastoral needs of the particular church itself, and to realistic contact with the people of God. The question remains, after an examination of the answers to the survey, whether this perspective is being followed in practice.

The report in no way claims to be comprehensive. However, it is our opinion that it does give a good profile of what is being tried out in the different European diocesan curias as regards restructuring against the background of the new code. It seems that many diocesan administrators formerly found these questions unpleasant, and it is clear that questions about efficiency and structure are still raised too seldom in church circles.

It would certainly be interesting to conduct a comparative study on, for example, American and European models of diocesan administration. For the American reader it should not be too difficult already to establish the essential differences on the basis of the present report, despite its limitations. Hopefully in the future a more systematic and thorough comparative study can be undertaken.

CANONICAL REFLECTION ON SELECTED ISSUES
IN DIOCESAN GOVERNANCE

JAMES H. PROVOST

The ministry of governance has a long and noble history in the Church's legal tradition. Canonical provisions for governance have evolved as the Church has adapted to changing conditions; different styles have developed in varying contexts. The papers in this CLSA Symposium on Governance have explored the various factors affecting governance; this current study is designed to examine some of the canon law issues in structuring and conducting diocesan governance in the Catholic Church in the United States as we approach the twenty-first century.

At the outset of this paper some limitations need to be acknowledged. This study is not a summary or compendium of all there is to know about the canon law on diocesan governance; neither does it propose to be an exhaustive exploration of all the theoretical issues touching on the governance of a diocese today. The present discussion presumes the reader is familiar with the canonical doctrine on these matters or will easily find it in standard commentaries.[1] Instead, it sets out to explore some of the issues which are significant in light of the other papers in this symposium, and which may be of special interest to those involved in positions of government in American dioceses.

There are seven sections in this paper. The first explores why a renewed approach to diocesan governance is called for today. Next, two fundamen-

---

[1]See cc. 460–572; for commentaries, see Antonio Sousa Costa in *Commento al Codice di Diritto Canonico* [Urbaniana], ed. Pio V. Pinto (Rome: Urbaniana University Press, 1985), pp. 270–341; John A. Alesandro and Joseph A. Janicki in *The Code of Canon Law: A Text and Commentary* [CLSA], ed. James A. Coriden et al. (New York/Mahwah: Paulist, 1985), pp. 378–449; Juan Ignacio Arrieta and Juan Calvo in *Codigo de Derecho Canonico, Edicion anotada* [EUNSA], ed. Pedro Lombardía and Juan Ignacio Arrieta (Pamplona: EUNSA, 1983), pp. 327–389; Julio Manzanares, Juan Sánchez y Sánchez, and Lamberto de Echeverría in *Código de Derecho Canónico, Edición bilingüe comentada* [BAC], ed. Lamberto de Echerverría (Madrid: BAC, 5th rev. ed. 1985), pp. 252–304; Hubert Müller et al. in *Handbuch des katholischen Kirchenrechts* [*Handbuch*], ed. Joseph Listl et al. (Regensburg: Pustet, 1983), pp. 329–453. See also the general review of canonical provisions for diocesan governance in the companion volume in this series, *The Governance of Ministry*.

tal realities are addressed: the people of God, and the chief person responsible in diocesan governance, the diocesan bishop. Two sections examine others who are involved with the bishop: those who assist him personally, and consultative bodies in contemporary dioceses. Some practical issues facing diocesan governance are sketched, relating to personnel and finances. Finally, drawing on canonical tradition, twelve "rules" are proposed for contemporary diocesan governance.

RENEWED APPROACH TO DIOCESAN GOVERNANCE

New Way of Thinking in Canon Law

Since the time of the classical compilations in the Middle Ages, canon law has struggled with its identity. Is it a civil law written with ecclesiastical content? Should it set a paradigm for civil law? Or is it a properly theological discipline?

When Pius X and Cardinal Gasparri began drafting the 1917 Code of Canon Law, they proposed to formulate a comprehensive law patterned on contemporary civil codes.[2] The Church's law was to be such a perfect system of codified law that it would command the respect of the nations, and provide an example civil codes could emulate. This way of thinking was quite congenial to the ecclesiological concepts which developed in the nineteenth century, originally in the church-state polemic of that era when it was crucial for the Church to assert its legitimate autonomy. Drawing on then contemporary theories of governance, nineteenth century proponents of *ius publicum ecclesiasticum* proclaimed the Church to be a "perfect society," one which contained all the elements of a sovereign state but in the spiritual realm, supreme over all other sovereignties.[3]

Modern nineteenth century states had simplified centuries of accumulated laws by adopting unified civil codes. The bishops at Vatican I, impressed by the simplicity of their civil experience but oppressed by the complexity of laws within the Church, sought a similar simplification of

---

[2]See discussion in Stephan Kuttner, "The Code of Canon Law in Historical Perspective," *The Jurist* 28 (1968) 140–141.

[3]For an analysis of the historical development of "perfect society" theory in the Church see Marie Zimmermann, *Structure social et église: Doctrines et praxis des rapports Eglise-etat du XVIIIe siècle à Jean Paul II* (Strasbourg: CERDIC, 1981).

canon law.[4] To the drafters of this codification, the Church's spiritual supremacy needed to be reflected in the very product of their efforts.

There seems to be a different preoccupation underlying John XXIII's call for the *aggiornamento* of the Code of Canon Law.[5] His intent was primarily pastoral. Announcing at the same time an ecumenical council, he seems to have anticipated some pastoral adjustments would be required to implement the council's decisions, and these would obviously have to be integrated into the Church's laws. This understanding seems to be reflected also in an early decision of the commission of cardinals who were named to head up the work of revising the code; they decided to wait until the completion of the council before undertaking their work in earnest.[6]

More had happened by the close of Vatican II than a few practical adjustments in Catholic discipline. Paul VI spoke to the code commission of the new way of thinking, the new *habitus mentis* reflected in the council, and called for the revised code to reflect not only the practical changes but also this new way of thinking.[7] In promulgating the finished product, John Paul II reaffirmed that what is new in the new code is more than a few practical adjustments; it is the newness of Vatican II itself.[8]

It is not appropriate, therefore, to continue the previous way of thinking about canon law from before Vatican II. As John Paul II pointed out to the Roman Rota, even when the new code takes over verbatim canons from the old code, canons for which there is a noble and extensive tradition of interpretation, it is still necessary to consider them anew in light of the teaching of the Second Vatican Council.[9] This "new way of thinking" applies to more than those in judicial offices in the Church; it guides anyone who interprets canon law, even if only in applying it to a particular situation.

This "new way of thinking" is not a break with canonical tradition or

---

[4]The complaint of being buried in laws (*legibus obruimur*) was common. A special memorandum drawn up during Vatican I appealed to the pope to simplify the Church's law system in keeping with "modern" experience. See Kuttner, pp. 131–132.

[5]John XXIII, allocution, January 25, 1959: *AAS* 51 (1959) 68.

[6]For a history of the revision process see Alesandro in CLSA, pp. 4–8.

[7]Paul VI, allocution to code commission, November 20, 1965: *AAS* 57 (1965) 988. For an analysis of Paul VI's approach to canon law see Francis G. Morrisey, "The Spirit of Canon Law: Teachings of Pope Paul VI," *Origins* 8/3 (June 8, 1978) 33, 35–40; Jean Beyer, "Paul VI et le droit de l'Eglise," in *Liberté et Loi dans l'Eglise,* Les quatre fleuves 18 (Paris: Beauchesne, 1983), pp. 43–75.

[8]John Paul II, apostolic constitution *Sacrae disciplinae leges,* January 25, 1983: *AAS* 75/2 (1983) xii.

[9]John Paul II, allocution to Roman Rota, January 26, 1984: *AAS* 76 (1984) 645–646.

the past wisdom of the Church; neither is it a call to put aside the new code itself. Rather, it places the understanding and application of canon law in the context of the Church's renewed self-understanding as this comes to us through the magisterium, authentically expressed in the documents of Vatican II. As a result, even in the way it is taught canon law is being seen more in an ecclesiological context, rather than as an application of moral theology. But issues in canon law must still be dealt with in keeping with canonical tradition, for canon law is not a strictly theological discipline. As John Huels points out in his study above, canon law has its own principles and methods which must be respected.

Ways of Thinking in Diocesan Governance

There are various influences on how diocesan governance is approached in practice. In other studies in this book Thomas Curry, Gerald Fogarty and John Lynch illustrate historical, ethnic and civil law influences on diocesan governance in the United States. These have produced a distinct way of thinking about diocesan governance, especially when compared with the European approach reviewed by Roland Trauffer.

In the United States the Catholic Church has developed in the context of the separation of church and state characteristic of this country. Churches are treated as voluntary associations, funded by their members. Bishops have had to maintain a close personal involvement in the finances and administration of the Church, resulting in a business orientation on the part of many diocesan ordinaries. In effect, American dioceses are more accustomed to refer to diocesan "administration," as with a business, than diocesan "governance."

In Europe there has traditionally been a closer relationship of church and state. Under the *cuius regio, eius religio* norm, the religion of the prince determined the religion of the people, and the Church in many areas was a "necessary" society. European dioceses have been funded by patrimony and government subsidy, although the generosity of the faithful has been significant in many areas also. But the European tradition sees the archdeacon or vicar general as central to the running of the diocese, the diocesan bishop exercising a less immediate role in day-to-day diocesan operations. "Governmental" attitudes appear to be a more apt description of European thinking than business "administration."

The code reflects the traditional European approach to diocesan governance. Even in dealing with such new structures as presbyteral and diocesan finance councils, the focus is on governance. However, the code addresses only a few of the many new offices and agencies which have been developing in Catholic dioceses since the early 1960s, so local attitudes toward diocesan governance will continue to be a significant element in how dioceses are in fact governed.

Impact of New Way of Thinking

Whichever attitude—business administration or governmental—one adopts toward diocesan governance, it must reflect the new way of thinking which is to characterize the application of church law today. This includes a renewed sense of pastoring, the central importance of the people of God, and attending to new sources for the ministry of governing.

The concept of pastoral function (*munus pastorale*) is central to the teaching of Vatican II on the Church. Bishops succeed to the apostolic college in their *munus pastorale* (*LG*, 20). This pastoral function includes the three functions by which the Church continues the mission of Christ: teaching, sanctifying, and governing. Agnes Cunningham in her above study on power and authority in the Church highlights the etymological significance of "pastoring" in this context.

There are various implications for those who are pastors of dioceses, or who collaborate in this ministry. Their role is one of service,[10] not domination; their attitude must be that of Christ, seeking out the lost while nurturing those who are within the Church's communion. Neither secular business paradigms nor civil governmental models are adequate to describe the work of those who pastor a Catholic diocese.

Moreover, as with *Lumen gentium,* so with the new code, people are at the center of attention. This represents a shift in who is considered the central protagonist of the Church's law: the spotlight has moved from the institution to the people of God, even while both remain central players on the stage.[11] The law defines a diocese in terms of the people (a "portion of the people of God"—c. 369), a parish is a community of people (c. 515, §1). The institution is at the service of God's people.

The law encourages a collaborative style of pastoring. Early in the substantive part of the code (cc. 204, 209–211) it is affirmed that all the faithful share responsibility for the Church's communion and mission. The

---

[10]John Paul II emphasized that in the new code, hierarchical authority is to be seen as service; see *Sacrae disciplinae leges,* p. xii.

[11]See Eugenio Corecco, "Theological Justifications of the codification of the Latin Canon Law," in *Proceedings of the Fifth International Congress of Canon Law,* Ottawa, Canada, August 1984.

principle of subsidiarity underlies the revision process and hence provides a way of understanding the mind of the code's legislator.[12] Legitimate diversity, recently termed "pluriformity,"[13] is facilitated by the many canons which provide for local adaptation of the law.

Those involved in diocesan governance will find a number of sources to assist them in implementing this new way of thinking in their pastoral service. In addition to the documents of Vatican II and the 1983 code itself, the Apostolic See has provided among other resources the new liturgical *Ordines*, with their important introductions, and the *Pastoral Directory for Bishops*. The bishops' conferences have made further specification of the law for their territories; these, too, provide a pastoral direction for those in diocesan ministry, although for many of these conferences there are serious problems in how such decisions are promulgated and made available to the Catholic faithful.[14]

In addition, the NCCB has published a manual which organizes the provisions of the 1983 code in a way to facilitate an understanding of the bishop's rights and duties for those in diocesan positions.[15] It is hoped the "Oars and Sails" publications of this CLSA symposium on diocesan governance will also serve as resources for diocesan officials.

THE PEOPLE OF GOD

The people of God are central to diocesan governance. The ultimate goal of church ministry is salvation, the salvation of persons as God's people.[16] There are two evident implications of this priority: building the community of this people in mission is the proximate goal of diocesan governance; promoting and protecting the rights of persons are a central function of governing.

---

[12]See "Principia quae Codicis Iuris Canonici recognitionem dirigant," principle 5: *Communicationes* 1 (1969) 80–82; also, *Praefatio* to the 1983 code, *AAS* 75/2 (1983) xxii.

[13]1985 Synod of Bishops, "The Final Report," *Origins* 15/27 (December 19, 1985) 448.

[14]This problem was first signaled by Winfried Aymans, "Ab Apostolica Sede recognitum," *Archiv für katholisches Kirchenrecht* 139 (1970) 405–427.

[15]N.C.C.B., *A Manual for Bishops: Rights and Responsibilities of Diocesan Bishops in the Revised Code of Canon Law* (Washington: USCC, 1983); supplements are published periodically to update the *Manual* in light of decisions by the N.C.C.B.

[16]"The salvation of souls . . . is always the supreme law of the Church" (c. 1752).

Building the Community

The nature of the Church is a communion.[17] This is ultimately a theological reality: God is a communion of three Persons, revealed to us in the hypostatic (comm)union of the human and divine, dwelling in us through the power of the Spirit. The Church is the communion of persons in whom the Spirit dwells, and expresses itself most fully when the community gathers to celebrate the Eucharist, Holy Communion. These celebrations, these communities, are linked together through their pastors who are joined in a hierarchical communion, so that the Church is a communion of particular churches in and from which the one and unique Catholic Church exists (c. 368).

The diocese is an expression of this communion; it must also foster communion. It is not itself a "community" as such, but fosters various levels of communion ranging from the family to base communities (either formal or informal), associations, parishes, and groupings of parishes known as deaneries or vicariates. As Robert Willis points out above, diocesan governance is directed toward the effective and affective communion of persons within these various levels.

Making this work is not easy. It demands constant attention, a true spirituality on the part of those in governing positions, and the development of appropriate skills. As Eugene Hemrick argues above, pastoral planning has a central role in governance, for planning can bring all these things together and makes it possible to put them at the service of building communion.

Rights of Persons

Concern for rights is traditionally a central concern of governance; one of the purposes for courts, for example, is the vindication of rights (c. 1400, §1). But the understanding of precisely whose rights are being vindicated, of what rights are central to governance, has varied over the centuries.

The Catholic Church today has come to a renewed understanding of the rights of people within its communion. The social teaching of the Church

---

[17]There is extensive literature on the concept of the Church as communion; from a canonical perspective, see the results of the CLSA Permanent Seminar, *The Church as Communion,* ed. James H. Provost (Washington: CLSA, 1984). See also the final statement from the 1985 Synod of Bishops, "The Final Report," p. 448; and Walter Kasper, "The Church as 'Communio,'" *Communio: International Catholic Review* 13 (1986) 100–117.

has emphasized the importance of human rights.[18] The synods of bishops in 1971 and 1974 recognized that this teaching applies also within the Church and not just in a secular context.[19] The new code specifically addresses the rights and obligations common to all the Christian faithful (cc. 208–223).[20]

The meaning of these rights is subject to various interpretations.[21] However their centrality to the Church's legal system cannot be doubted, both in terms of the text and context of the law and because in promulgating the new code John Paul II called special attention to them.[22] Their impact on diocesan governance is both direct and indirect.

From a direct point of view, the rights of the faithful place limits on the exercise of the discretion of those in governance positions. Rights are claims which must be respected, particularly by those charged with urging the observance of ecclesiastical laws which guarantee such rights (c. 392, §1). Moreover, rights are an object of attention by those in governance positions. Their job includes promoting and protecting the rights of the faithful if they are to foster a genuine communion of persons in the Church. The vindication of rights includes adequate prior process in the exercise of discretion by those in governance roles, and the provision of means to resolve grievances.[23]

---

[18]For a review of the magisterium's teaching see David Hollenbach, *Claims in Conflict: Retrieving and Renewing the Catholic Human Rights Tradition* (New York: Paulist Press, 1979).

[19]See 1971 Synod of Bishops, *De Iustitia in Mundo,* "III. Effectio Iustitiae," *AAS* 63 (1971) 933; 1974 Synod of Bishops, "Human Rights and Reconciliation," *Origins* 4/20 (1974) 319.

[20]See the papers of the CLSA Permanent Seminar on the protection and promotion of rights in *The Jurist* 46/1 (1986). For commentary on cc. 208–223 see: Tarcisio Bertone in *Il Nuovo Codice di Diritto Canonico: Novità, motivazione e significato,* "Utriumque Ius" 9 (Rome: Libreria Editrice della Pontificia Università Lateranense, 1983), pp. 100–106; Giuseppe Dalla Torre in Urbaniana, pp. 114–139; Javier Hervada in EUNSA, pp. 173–186; Matthäus Kaiser in *Handbuch,* pp. 173–181; Julio Manzanares in BAC, pp. 137–146; James H. Provost in CLSA, pp. 134–231; Heinrich J.F. Reinhardt in *Münsterischer Kommentar zum Codex Iuris Canonici,* ed. Klaus Lüdicke (Essen: Ludgerus Verlag, 1985), pp. 208/1–231/2.

[21]James A. Coriden, "A Challenge: Make the Rights Real," *The Jurist* 45 (1985) 1–23, argues that the fundamental rights listed in the new code have a constitutional quality. On the other hand, Eugenio Corecco argues in "Il Catalogo dei doveri-diritti del fedele nel CIC," in *I Diritti Fondamentali della Persona Umana e la Libertà Religiosa,* ed. Franco Biffi (Vatican: Libreria Editrice Vaticana, 1985), pp. 118–120, that the code is listing "duties-rights" of the faithful and that these are not fundamental or constitutional.

[22]John Paul II, *Sacrae disciplinae leges,* p. xii; see also *Praefatio,* pp. xxi–xxii.

[23]See John P. Beal, "Confining and Structuring Administrative Discretion," *The Jurist* 46/1 (1986); John C. Meszaros, "Procedures of Administrative Recourse," ibid.

Indirectly, rights are a concern because of the Church's mission. Persons in governance positions have a directive role in regard to that mission (c. 394). Participating in this mission is a fundamental right of the baptized, assured them by the action of Christ in the sacraments by which they have been initiated into God's people (cc. 211, 225). Moreover, the charisms which the faithful receive in the Spirit are a source of rights and duties in the Church and in the world, which are to be tested and coordinated but not extinguished by those in authority (*AA*, 3).

The attention to rights in the new code is commendable, but it is still only a first step. The reality of a claim in a legal system is only so secure as the means to vindicate that right. The provisions in the code as finally promulgated are considered by many to be inadequate in this regard. While church courts exist for the vindication of rights, they are excluded from addressing cases in which the vindication of rights relates to the exercise of administrative power (c. 1400, §2). The only recourse in such cases is hierarchical, the objectivity of which is not readily apparent nor buttressed with reliable safeguards. Despite the early recognition that "it is necessary that particular attention be given to the organization of a procedure which envisions the protection of subjective rights,"[24] the proposed canons on administrative tribunals were stricken from the final text of the law.

The credibility of diocesan governance may well rest on the extent to which it is sensitive to the rights of people in the diocese and is able to provide adequate protection for them not only within the diocese, but within the wider Catholic communion.

Diocesan Bishop

The diocesan bishop governs the particular church committed to his care as a vicar and ambassador of Christ (*LG*, 27).[25] He is not a vicar of the Bishop of Rome, but a pastor in his own name—an *ordinarius proprius*. The Second Vatican Council attempted to provide renewed clarity to the diocesan bishop's role, and the 1983 code continues that effort. The bishop governs both personally and by sharing his power with others; both aspects deserve some attention here.

---

[24]Principle 7, "De ordinanda procedura ad tuenda iura subiectiva," *Communicationes* 1 (1969) 83; see also principles 1 and 6.

[25]See cc. 375–411; for commentaries, see Giuseppe Damizia in Urbaniana, pp. 226–245; Thomas J. Green in CLSA, pp. 311–341; José Luis Gutiérrez in EUNSA, pp. 279–301; Julio Manzanares in BAC, pp. 218–233; Hubert Müller, Heribert Schmitz and Joseph Listl in *Handbuch*, pp. 329–352.

Power of the Diocesan Bishop

In the diocese committed to him the bishop possesses all the power which is required for the exercise of his pastoral office, except for cases which are reserved to the supreme authority of the Church or to some other ecclesiastical authority (c. 381, §1). This is a significant presumption in the bishop's favor.

His power is termed "ordinary, proper and immediate" in the canon. That is, it comes with his office, it is a power he exercises in his own name and not in the name of some other church or civil authority, and he can exercise this power directly without having to use any intermediaries. Yet it is limited. Some cases are reserved, either by law or by action of the Supreme Pontiff, to supreme church authority or to some other ecclesiastical authority, such as a metropolitan, regional meeting of bishops, conference of bishops, or particular council.

There is a theoretical question here. What is it that is limited—the bishop's power itself, or his discretion to exercise it? The power in question is that power which is required for the bishop to exercise his pastoral office, not a power related to something beyond the scope of his competence.

Damizia clearly states that the power itself cannot be limited by anyone, since it comes from God.[26] Schmitz and Green both stress the change this canon reflects from the system of faculties and concessions, to a system of reservations.[27] The faculties and concessions approach saw the diocesan bishop as lacking certain powers, which were then conceded to him through faculties granted by the Apostolic See. The reservations system recognizes the bishop possesses all the power needed for his office, but that for the good of the Church the exercise of this power in certain cases is reserved to other authorities. Schmitz and Green seem to agree with Damizia that the power itself is not limited, only its exercise. Neither of the Spanish commentaries address the question directly but stress instead the need to preserve papal primacy.[28]

There are two practical implications of this question. The first relates to the dispensing power of the bishop, the second to his personal responsibility for his power. In regard to the first, if the bishop's power itself is

---

[26]"Il Vescovo . . . possiede tutta la *postestas sacra,* che in se stessa non può essere limitata da alcuno, perché proviene da Dio" (p. 230).

[27] Green, p. 325; Schmitz, p. 341.

[28]Manzanares (p. 221) acknowledges the canon wishes to reduce reserved cases to a minimum. See also Guitérrez, p. 284.

limited, and not just his discretion to exercise it, then he could not dispense validly in those areas which are restricted. On the other hand, if it is the exercise of his power which is restricted but not the power itself, he could conceivably dispense validly even in the restricted areas. His action would be illicit, however, unless there were other factors present whereby the law restricting him would not bind in the particular case.

The code does not seem to provide much clarification in this regard. It does state that the diocesan bishop may dispense from both universal and particular disciplinary laws established for his territory or for his subjects, provided he judges this will contribute to their spiritual welfare (c. 87, §1). There are some restrictions, however: he is not to do so if the dispensation would be from procedural law, penal law, laws whose dispensation is reserved to some other authority, or constitutive laws (cc. 86 and 87, §1). Under certain circumstances he can dispense even some of these restricted cases provided the Holy See is wont to dispense from them (c. 87, §2).

Does this last exception mean the bishop retains the fullness of power needed to pastor the diocese, and is restricted only in its exercise? Not necessarily; the exception applies to any ordinary, not just bishops. Moreover, the power to dispense can be given by the law even to people who are otherwise incapable of issuing dispensations because they lack the executive power of governance (c. 85). So the power to dispense, and the exception which applies in more urgent cases, would not seem to resolve the theoretical question, nor the practical one of the extent to which a bishop's dispensation of the restricted laws would nevertheless be valid.[29]

This discussion does point out, however, that the power to dispense which is now enjoyed by a diocesan bishop is quite broad even if considered within the limits of canons 86 and 87.[30] In governing the diocese the bishop is able to make considerable adjustments in the disciplinary law of the Church in pursuit of his pastoral responsibilities, provided these dispensations are for the good of souls.[31]

---

[29]For a fuller discussion, and arguments in favor of a broad interpretation of the bishop's dispensing power, see Richard A. Ryan, "The Dispensing Authority of the Residential Bishop of the Latin Rite Regarding the General Laws of the Church," *The Jurist* 35 (1975) 175–211.

[30]For commentaries on the power to dispense (cc. 85–93) see: Teodoro I. Jiménez Urresti in BAC, pp. 69–74; Pedro Lombardía in EUNSA, pp. 107–109; Pio V. Pinto in Urbaniana, pp. 54–58; James E. Risk in CLSA, pp. 64–68; Richard A. Strigl in *Handbuch,* pp. 107–109.

[31]For a discussion on one aspect of the pastoral implications of this power in regard to religiously mixed marriages, see Eoin de Bhaldraithe, "Mixed Marriages in the New Code: Can we now implement the Anglican-Roman Catholic Recommendations?" *The Jurist* 46/2 (1986).

To what extent is a bishop's power constitutive of his office, so that he cannot relinquish ultimate responsibility for it and still retain the office? This is a second implication of the theoretical question about the bishop's power. The question has been raised most pointedly in the celebrated case involving the Archdiocese of Seattle. The archbishop, acting on direct orders from Cardinal Gantin, prefect of the Congregation for Bishops, delegated "complete and final" authority in five aspects of diocesan life to his auxiliary bishop.[32] The authority here pertains not just to incidental issues, but to critical areas for which a diocesan bishop is responsible: for example, the liturgical life of the diocese,[33] the diocesan tribunal,[34] and the training of priests.[35]

The diocesan bishop was not suspended in this case. If he had been, he could not have delegated those powers from which he was suspended. The delegation was not made by the Apostolic See in the appointment of the auxiliary bishop, although this is a possibility according to the code (c. 403, §2). The archbishop, however, was directed to delegate *final* authority so that he would no longer exercise the powers which are properly his by office. This could be an example of the Supreme Pontiff, acting through an official of the Roman curia, reserving to some other ecclesiastical authority (namely, the auxiliary bishop) certain cases as provided for in canon 381, §2. If so, the canon has not been specifically cited; moreover, the restriction was not done in the ordinary fashion, but by requiring the diocesan bishop himself to delegate elements of what, theoretically, is constitutive of his office.

The canonical questions this case raises will be studied for some time, but ordinarily in diocesan governance it is not possible for the diocesan

---

[32]Raymond G. Hunthausen, "Authority of Seattle's Auxiliary Bishop," *Origins* 16/14 (September 18, 1986) 251: his auxiliary bishop has been "delegated by me to have complete and final decision-making power" over the designated areas. This is confirmed in the "Chronology" released by the Apostolic Pronuntio through the N.C.C.B.: "The faculties, which were originally to be given by Rome, would be given instead by him as archbishop, but with the same effect. The archbishop of Seattle then petitioned the Holy See for an authoritative clarification. When this was given, the archbishop of Seattle granted the faculties. . . . " "Vatican Releases Chronology of Events in Seattle," *Origins* 16/21 (November 6, 1986) 364.

[33]For some of the specific responsibilities of the diocesan bishop (not merely a local ordinary) in liturgy, see cc. 838, §4; 839, §2; and 844, §4.

[34]The diocesan bishop is the judge in first instance in each diocese (c. 1419, §1), and the judicial vicar constitutes one tribunal with him (c. 1420, §2).

[35]It is the diocesan bishop, not a local ordinary, who admits students to the seminary (c. 241, §1) and who calls to orders and ordains (c. 1016).

bishop to delegate away his ultimate responsibility in matters which are required for the exercise of his pastoral office. A delegate, by definition, acts on behalf of another and not in his own name; the delegate is an agent of the one who granted the delegation. A diocesan bishop who delegates someone to do something remains ultimately accountable for what the delegate does in his name. This is even true when the diocesan bishops assigns a vicar the responsibility for some aspect of diocesan life (cc. 475–476). The law retains to the bishop the right to act in that area as well (c. 65, §3). In theory it has not seemed possible for the one who does the delegating to give up this ultimate responsibility, as seems to have been mandated by the prefect of the Congregation for Bishops in this case. Short of such mandate from the Apostolic See, this should not be the practice of diocesan bishops in other situations.

Power Sharing by the Bishop

Diocesan bishops normally share their powers with others. Before addressing specific issues about personal or collegial participation in the bishop's power, it may be helpful to recall some of the key distinctions in canon law which affect this sharing of power.

Normally power is structured according to the stable configuration of rights and duties which is termed an ecclesiastical office (c. 145). An office can be exercised in one's own name (e.g., the diocesan bishop), or in the name of another (as by a vicar). Vicarious power is "ordinary" in that it is attached to an office; but it is a sharing in the power of another, in the sense that it is exercised in that other's name and may even be tied to that other's power.[36] Vicarious power is interpreted broadly (c. 138), and carries with it a presumption in favor of the vicar's initiative.

While normally persons exercise power in virtue of an office, it is also possible to share in power by delegation—that is, by "power which is granted to a person, but not by means of an office" (c. 131, §2). This can be given to the person for an individual action or limited period and scope, an ad-hoc arrangement; or the person may be delegated "habitually," such that the delegation has a fairly stable or on-going quality. This latter is often done through "habitual faculties."

Delegated power is generally more restricted than ordinary power. The

---

[36]For example, the powers of vicars general and episcopal vicars who are not themselves bishops are closely related to the diocesan bishop; the vicars are suspended if the diocesan bishop is suspended, and cease when the diocesan see becomes vacant (c. 481).

burden of proving delegation rests with the person who claims to have been delegated (c. 131, §3); delegation is limited to the persons and matters contained in the mandate (c. 133, §1); unless delegation has been "for all cases," it is interpreted strictly (c. 138). However, a delegated person is considered to have in addition to the delegation itself, whatever is needed to exercise the delegated power.

The new code utilizes some additional distinctions which affect diocesan governance. Under the 1917 code ecclesiastical power was divided into the power of orders and the power of jurisdiction. The distinctions of ordinary and delegated power are taken from the law on jurisdiction. The teaching function in the Church was considered to fall under the rubric of jurisdiction. The new code organizes the mission of the Church into the three *munera* or functions of teaching, sanctifying and governing. Teaching is now recognized as a distinct function, not a species of governing, although maintaining good order even in the area of teaching is a governance responsibility.[37] It is not yet clear how apt the categories of ordinary and delegated power are to this renewed sense of the teaching function.

The code also reflects a distinction between administrative power and acts of administration. This is clearest in contrasting canon 1400, §2, which restricts tribunals from addressing controversies arising from an act of administrative power, with canon 1413, where a person may be brought before a tribunal for cases which concern administration. The first sense of administration (that of c. 1400, §2) appears to relate to the executive function which can issue administrative acts such as decrees, precepts, rescripts, and dispensations (cc. 35–93). The second sense (that of c. 1413) applies more to financial administration.

Where does sacramental administration fit? Sacraments may be administered by persons who have not been ordained (c. 230, §3), and this does not require that they exercise the power of governance. As with the teaching function, so with the sanctifying function: it is now presented in the law as a distinct *munus*. While the concepts of ordinary and delegated power have traditionally been applied to this function, it is not yet clear to what extent the category of "administration" applies here. For example, could one sue before a church tribunal in cases where the sacraments or other religious rites of the Church were not properly administered? If a

---

[37]See discussion in Giuseppe Damizia, "La funzione di insegnare nella Chiesa," in *Il Nuovo Codice di Diritto Canonico: Novità, motivazione e significato*, pp. 265–295.

person is denied access to the Eucharist by a Eucharistic minister, could the case wind up on the docket of the diocesan tribunal? What if it were the parish pastor who denied access? The answer is not yet clear.

These distinctions have a real bearing on sharing of power by a diocesan bishop. He is clearly an ordinary, who acts in his own name. He can act in the internal as well as the external forum, and exercises the teaching and sanctifying functions as well as the power of governance. He exercises legislative, judicial and executive authority; but he also carries out acts of administration which do not entail the power of governance.

He shares power with various vicars and on occasion with ad-hoc delegates. A number of dioceses have also instituted diocesan offices which are not held by vicars, but whose office holders exercise delegated power which is entrusted to them in habitual faculties when they are given the office; the office itself, however, may be only an administrative post and it is not always specified whether a share in the bishop's executive power has been granted to it.

Depending on the kind of authority delegated to these new office holders, their actions may or may not be subject to judicial review by the diocesan tribunal. If they are exercising delegated executive power, appeal must be made to the diocesan bishop; if they are exercising non-executive administration, it may be possible to cite them before the diocesan tribunal.

This is not to suggest that litigation should become the norm in American dioceses! However, it does illustrate the complexity of sharing the bishop's power. It also suggests that there may be other means, including the diocesan tribunal, which could help resolve difficulties in diocesan administration besides burdening the diocesan bishop directly.

PERSONS PARTICIPATING IN DIOCESAN GOVERANANCE

As noted above, the diocesan bishop is not alone in the governance of a diocese; he is aided by various people who participate in diverse ways in governance activities. Some of these people today are lay persons; others are clergy, as has been traditional. There are several issues to be examined here: the participation by laity in the governing functions of the diocese; vicars; delegates; and special developments related to the office of diocesan chancellor.

Participation by Lay Persons in Diocesan Governance

This has proven to be a much discussed topic in post-Vatican II canonical literature.[38] One school of thought, emphasizing the unity of power in the Church and its sacred character, holds that only clergy are capable of exercising the power of governance; lay people are excluded in principle. Another school of thought, pointing to historic examples of lay people actually exercising governing power in the Church, argue the Church could not have erred on such a significant issue for so many centuries, and that it is indeed possible for lay persons to exercise some governing power in the Church.

The new code represents a compromise between these views. Clergy are said to be "capable" of the power of governance (c. 129, §1). The law does not say lay persons are capable of it, but it also does not say they are *not* capable of it; it merely states they "can cooperate" in its exercise (c. 129, §2).

Offices which require the exercise of governing power are said to be limited to clergy (c. 274, §1); on the other hand, lay persons can be named to the office of tribunal judge (c. 1421, §2), an office which requires the exercise of the power of governance (c. 135, §2). Indeed, a variety of positions in the diocese are open to lay persons, although it is debated to what extent these offices in themselves entail the exercise of the power of governance.[39]

Several issues require further exploration by scholars; here they can only be identified, without attempting to resolve them. One issue concerns the validity of the appointment of lay persons to ecclesiastical offices, and another relates to the meaning of lay "cooperation" in the power of governance.

1. Valid Appointment to Office

If the person named to an office lacks the qualities required for that office, is the appointment invalid? The question is more acute today

---

[38]See, for example, the various studies cited in James H. Provost, "The Participation of the Laity in the Governance of the Church," *Studia Canonica* 17 (1983) 417–448; see also Julián Herranz, "Le statut juridique des laïcs: l'apport des documents conciliaires et du Code de droit canonique de 1983," *Studia Canonica* 19 (1985) 229–257; and Francisco Urrutia, "Delegation of the Executive Power of Governance," ibid., pp. 339–355.

[39]For a listing of positions open to lay persons under the new code, see Jorge Medina Estévez, "Notas sobre los ministerios de la Iglesia confiados a fieles laicos," *Teologia y Vida* 27 (1986) 167–172.

because of the broadened meaning of office,[40] and because of the potential for lay persons being named to ecclesiastical offices even if only because of the increasing shortage of clergy.

Unless the qualities were expressly required for the validity of the appointment, it is a valid appointment; but it can be rescinded by decree of the "competent authority or by the sentence of an administrative tribunal" (c. 149, §2).[41] This is an application of the general principle that "only those laws which expressly state that an act is null or that a person is incapable of acting are to be considered to be invalidating or incapacitating" (c. 10).

How does one determine if a specific canon "expressly" states that an act is null or a person is incapable? Commentators on the 1983 code do not address how this is to be done in practice.[42] However, canon 10 is practically the same as canon 11 of the 1917 code, so some clarification may be gained by consulting commentators on the previous code. Some of them held that nullity or incapacity could be "expressly" stated either explicitly or implicitly. Explicitly means that the canon directly states the invalidity or incapacity in positive or negative terms; implicitly means the words do not actually state the invalidating or incapacitating effect, but that this follows as a conclusion from principles, an effect from a cause, in light of what the canon does state.[43] Others held that "expressly" and "explicitly" meant the same thing, and that "implicitly" was really the same as the word "equivalently" which appeared in the 1917 canon.[44]

With the elimination of the term "equivalently," does the new code restrict "expressly" to "explicitly," or does it adopt the position that "expressly" includes both explicit and implicit expressions? The differ-

---

[40]In the 1917 code, c. 145 required a strict sense of office to be understood in canon law, one which entailed the exercise of the power of orders or jurisdiction, both of which were restricted to clergy (c. 118). The new code has dropped this requirement, so that only one meaning of ecclesiastical office is applied in church law, that which is based on *PO, 20*, and does not necessarily require the exercise of the power of orders or jurisdiction.

[41]For commentaries, see: Juan Ignacio Arrieta in EUNSA, pp. 141–143; Richard Hill in CLSA, pp. 98–102; Georg May in *Handbuch,* pp. 141–145; Julio Manzanares in BAC, pp. 112–117; Pio Pinto in Urbaniana, pp. 86–90.

[42]See: Teodoro Jiménez Urresti in BAC, pp. 20–21; Lombardía in EUNSA, p. 74; Ladislas Orsy in CLSA, pp. 30–31; Pinto in Urbaniana, p. 10.

[43]See, for example, Gommar Michiels, *Normae Generales Juris Canonici* 1 (Lublin: Universitas Catholica, 1929), p. 275.

[44]1917 code, c. 11: "expresse vel aequivalenter statuitur." The *vel aequivalenter* has been dropped in the 1983 code. For a review of authors on both sides and an argument for why "implicit" means the same as "equivalent," see A. Van Hove, *De Legibus Ecclesiasticis*, Commentarium Lovaniense 1:2 (Mechlin: H. Dessain, 1930), pp. 167–168.

ence between the two points of view is significant. The code seldom uses terms explicitly stating invalidity or incapacity when listing the qualifications for an office; but when it does, these are clearly the "expressly required" qualities of canon 149, §2.[45] But what of other statements of qualifications?

Sometimes the code introduces the qualifications by stating the office holder "must be."[46] At other times, a subjunctive of the verb "to be" is used.[47] The qualifications for the office of bishop in the Church are introduced with "it is required that he be . . . " (c. 378, §1), while qualifications for seminary faculty begin with "only those . . . who" (c. 253, §1). It is difficult to determine from the words whether these positive statements of qualifications are required for validity; they often include both canonical status (e.g., being a priest) and general moral qualities (good reputation, etc.). Could such canons still be "expressly" stating qualities required for valid appointment if those which are required for validity are introduced with the same words as qualities which are not?

The code has several canons which clearly exclude blood relatives of the diocesan bishop from certain offices.[48] They do not include explicit reference to the validity of the appointment; does the negative phrasing ("excluded are . . .") constitute an express requirement for valid appointment?

There are at least two practical ramifications from these theoretical questions. The first, which will be discussed here, is whether non-Catholics may be appointed to some ecclesiastical offices. The second ramification will be addressed later, for it concerns the possibility of appointing lay persons to some offices for which the quality of "cleric" is required, such as a vicar.

A general requirement for appointment to any ecclesiastical office is that the candidate be "in the communion of the Church" (c. 149, §1). Here is another interesting example of the difficulty in determining not only if this is for validity, but also the meaning of what is required. The wording of the canon makes this a "must" requirement (*debet esse*), although there is no explicit reference to "validity." Is this implicitly a requirement for

[45]See, for example, cc. 425, §1 (diocesan administrator), 521, §1 (parish pastor), 546 (parochial vicar), and 643 (novitiate).

[46]See, for example, cc. 483, §2 (chancellor and notaries), 1420, §4 (judicial vicar and adjutant judicial vicar), 1483 (procurators and advocates).

[47]See, for example, cc. 478, §1 (vicars general and episcopal vicars), 494, §1 (fiscal officer), 1421, §3 (diocesan judges).

[48]For example, cc. 478, §2 (vicar general and episcopal vicars), 492, §1 (finance council members).

validity, such that the appointment of one who is not "in the communion of the Church" would be invalid from the start, and whatever that person did in virtue of the office would be invalid? Or is it not for validity, so that the actions performed by an appointee who is not "in the communion of the church" would be valid but the appointment could later be rescinded?

Moreover, what does "in the communion of the Church" mean here? Several commentators take it to mean in the *full* communion of the Church.[49] Elsewhere the code distinguishes between being in the communion of the baptized (c. 204) and being in full communion with the Catholic Church (c. 205). "Full" communion is explicitly required by the code for certain positions; for example, members of a diocesan pastoral council must be "Christian faithful who are in full communion with the Catholic Church" (c. 512, §1), and advocates in church courts must be Catholics, unless the diocesan bishop permits otherwise (c. 1483). Since the law distinguishes communion and full communion both in principle and in practical application to qualifications for some offices, would it not be appropriate to respect these different degrees of communion? Only where "full communion" is specified is that degree of communion required by the law. This raises the question of whether it would be possible to appoint, for example, a baptized Protestant to the ecclesiastical office of diocesan fiscal manager.[50]

As indicated earlier, issues of this type cannot be resolved in the space of this article. Commentaries on the new code which have appeared to date have not been able to address them in depth either. Yet persons with responsibilities in diocesan governance would clearly benefit from some clarity in regard to a question as basic as what is needed for valid appointment to office. If there is a genuine doubt of law here, the law does not bind; if on the other hand there is a doubt of fact (do the qualities possessed by this person meet what is needed for validity in appointment to this office?), the ordinary may dispense, provided he respects the usual limitations in these matters (c. 14).

2. Lay Cooperation in Governance

In drafting the new code a deliberate effort was made not to resolve the still disputed questions around the nature of sacred power and who can

---

[49]See Manzanares, pp. 114–115, and Pinto, p. 88; while the term "full communion" is not used, that is the concept expressed in Arrieta, pp. 142–143. Hill, p. 100, does not address the issue; May, p. 144, states "kirchlichen Gemeinschaft" without specifying whether this means *full* communion.

[50]In practice, of course, the bishop has the power to dispense from this disciplinary law; the problem is, does he need to issue a dispensation in order to make such an appointment?

hold it in the Church.[51] The word "cooperate" was deliberately selected for this reason. The law itself specifies one example of such cooperation, when it permits lay persons to be named judges on diocesan courts (c. 1421, §2). But there is still some question about the extent to which a lay judge may act within the diocesan court.[52]

Short of an office for whose exercise the power of governance is required, is it possible for lay persons to be delegated to exercise the power of governance? As discussed above, this is a traditional way in which bishops share their power. In the United States a common practice developed whereby the diocesan chancellor by delegation exercised all the powers a vicar general enjoys by office. Under the new code particular law could even specify this as part of the office of chancellor (c. 482, §1); otherwise, it still would be through delegation.

Could a lay person be named to the office of chancellor, or some other office for whose exercise the power of governance is not required, and then be delegated to cooperate in the bishop's power of governance? The issue has most explicitly been addressed in terms of delegating a lay person to grant marriage dispensations.[53] But the issue has wider ramifications.

Finally, could a lay person be named to an office for which the law requires the quality of "cleric," especially when this quality is not stated as required for validity explicitly? This question brings us to certain practices regarding vicars, but to address them a broader consideration must first be given to those who vicariously share in the bishop's power.

Vicars

The code presents vicars general and episcopal vicars as local ordinaries (c. 134). They exercise executive power either throughout the entire diocese (for vicars general), or within the scope of their vicariate (for episcopal vicars); they also exercise the habitual faculties granted by the

---

[51]Rosalio Castillo Lara, "La communion ecclésiale dans le nouveau Code de Droit canonique," *Communicationes* 15 (1984) 259–260, note 69.

[52]See discussion in James H. Provost, "Role of Lay Judges," *The Jurist* 45 (1985) 327–334.

[53]Urrutia, in the article cited in note 38 above, is against this possibility on the basis of what he discerns as a *regula iuris* in the new code, namely that only clergy are considered to be able to dispense (pp. 346–350). For arguments in favor of the possibility of lay persons being delegated to issue marriage dispensations, see James H. Provost, "The Power of Lay Chancellors to Dispense," in *Roman Replies and CLSA Advisory Opinions 1986*, ed. William A. Schumacher and J. James Cuneo (Washington: CLSA, 1986), pp. 56–61, and J. James Cuneo, "Another Opinion," in ibid., pp. 61–64.

Apsotolic See to the diocesan bishop.[54] Excepted are those powers which the law reserves to the diocesan bishop, unless he delegates these by a "special mandate"; also excepted are those powers the bishop reserves to himself, or in the case of episcopal vicars, which the bishop also reserves to the vicar general (c. 479).

Vicars can place a variety of administrative acts in the diocese. The law recognizes that as a result, several people could take the initiative in the same matter; it expresses a concern that they act in a coordinated manner and in close communication with the bishop (cc. 473, §2; 480). But from the perspective of diocesan governance, it is important to emphasize that the law does foresee vicars acting not as delegates or only under specific directions from the bishop; they are, within the governance of the diocese, agents with initiative and the ability to exercise real executive responsibility on behalf of the people of God.

If effect, the law proposes a certain decentralization of diocesan authority, all within the overall supervision of the diocesan bishop. This constitutes a significant potential for adapting the governance style within an individual diocese to varying local conditions. It is not clear, however, whether dioceses in the United States have taken full advantage of these possibilities.

In addition to vicars general and episcopal vicars, two other types of diocesan vicars are mentioned in the code. While the vicar general is the "alter ego" of the diocesan bishop in pastoral and administrative matters, the judicial vicar serves that function in judicial affairs. While the bishop, as the first judge in the diocese, can reserve cases to himself (c. 1420, §2), he generally designates a judicial vicar to act with full initiative and responsibility in tribunal cases. In this regard the traditional practice in American dioceses has been much closer to the code's approach to vicars.

Vicars forane or deans may be appointed within a diocese, although the new code does not require deaneries (c. 374, §2). Vicars forane are not necessarily episcopal vicars, although a diocesan bishop could name them as such. Their responsibilities are not specifically executive, although they do include certain administrative tasks (c. 555). The new code includes several references to particular law or directives of the diocesan bishop, indicating it expects the function of vicar forane to be tailored to local pastoral conditions.

In addition to those vicars named in the general law of the Church, could

---

[54]Unless, of course, the diocesan bishop was selected because of some personal qualification, or other express provisions have been made (c. 479, §3).

there be other vicars in diocesan governance? For example, some dioceses have named lay persons as "vicars" for education, or even for religious. This raises first of all the question noted above about whether the qualifications listed in the code for "vicar" are for validity.[55] Moreover, is the position of vicar in these dioceses actually an episcopal vicar, or something else? Vicars for religious existed prior to the creation of the position of episcopal vicar, and apparently some dioceses consider them not to be episcopal vicars.

Without attempting to resolve the theoretical issue, a practical comment may still be in order. Whenever the code uses the term "vicar" in the context of the diocesan church, it explicitly refers to priests.[56] This seems to reflect a technical use for the term, and it would seem preferable not to use a technical term such as "vicar" with a less technical meaning than the law itself provides.

Delegates

In order to avoid the limitations on the choice of persons for diocesan governance positions which the restriction of vicars to priests seem to impose, a number of dioceses have adopted a different nomenclature, ranging from "delegate" (which clearly specifies the nature of the power exercised by the person), to "secretary" or "department head," etc.

The persons in these positions exercise delegated power. At first glance this may seem anomalous since these are offices and an office should involve "ordinary" power, not delegation. Is it the person or the office which exercises delegated power? It is not unknown, however, for an office to be based on delegated power; such seems to be the basis for many offices in the Church.[57] If the office exercises delegated power, what kind

---

[55]Episcopal vicars "are to be" (*sint*) priests, according to c. 478, §1. The canon continues by giving the minimum age (not less than thirty), academic requirements or equivalent expertise, and character standards such as sound doctrine, integrity, prudence, experience in managing affairs. Is the appointment *invalid* if the vicar lacks sound doctrine? Is it *invalid* if the vicar turns out to be imprudent? Is it *invalid*, then, if the person named a vicar is not a priest? The provision of c. 274, §1 restricting to clergy those offices for whose exercise the power of governance is required, would seem to rule out non-priests; yet as noted earlier, the law itself makes an exception to this norm when it permits lay persons to be named judges.

[56]See cc. 478, §1 (vicars general and episcopal vicars), 546 (parochial vicars), 553 (vicars forane), 1420, §4 (judicial vicars and adjutant judicial vicars); an exception is for religious (c. 620), but this is not within the context of diocesan governance.

[57]The offices of the Roman curia, for example, act with power delegated to them by the Roman Pontiff rather than as vicars.

of power—executive, or non-executive administrative—has been delegated? Delegated executive power is a form of the power of governance; if this is the basis for these diocesan offices which were created not as vicars but with other titles—specifically so that lay persons as well as clergy could exercise them—are they not still restricted to clergy in virtue of canon 274, §1? The question deserves careful consideration in the context of the theoretical discussions above, but which are beyond the scope of this paper.

In the meantime practical arrangements might be made as follows. Since in fact most of these offices are administrative, not executive, then if executive power were also involved it could be conferred through habitual faculties given to the office holder at the time the person is named to the office. Such a practice would seem to avoid the restriction in canon 274, §1, and would more clearly identify both the nature and extent of the powers to be exercised by the office holder.

As discussed above, the difference between vicars and delegates relates to the scope of their presumed authority: vicars are presumed to be able to take a variety of initiatives whereas delegates are restricted to the terms of their mandate, and must prove they have the power to do something. From a canon law perspective, delegates are under a tighter rein than vicars. For the sake of effective distribution of work, the law prefers office to delegation, so a system in which lay persons are delegated executive power is clearly an exceptional one even though circumstances may require it.[58]

Chancellor

The chancellor has become a powerful figure in United States dioceses. Originally the office of record keeper and notary, it took specific action by the councils of Baltimore to require a chancellor in each diocese in this country.[59] In itself the office of chancellor has no executive power, but given the close working relationship that developed between bishops and

---

[58]See Urrutia, p. 353: "Delegated power is not the normal power of governance in the Church, but a form of auxiliary and subsidiary power, not stable but rather circumstantial, in order to help those who, holding offices, possess power which is ordinary and proper. . . . Only when the holders of the various offices do not seem to be able to cope with all the pastoral needs for which the offices were instituted, will they call upon other persons to come to their aid, granting them the necessary delegated power." It should be noted that Urrutia prefers the bishop to exercise most of diocesan governance personally (p. 348).

[59]See John E. Prince, *The Diocesan Chancellor: An Historical Synopsis and Commentary,* Canon Law Studies, 167 (Washington: Catholic University of America, 1942), pp. 36–40.

chancellors over the years these latter have come to be delegated the powers of a vicar general in many dioceses.[60]

Traditionally chancellors have also exercised the functions now described for the diocesan fiscal manager (c. 494). The code clearly distinguishes the two, but they are not listed as two incompatible offices so conceivably the previous practice could continue. Indeed, the code foresees the possibility of particular law providing for different responsibilities in the office of chancellor itself (c. 482, §1). The current American practice could be regularized in this way, expanding the nature of the office so that it also entails the exercise of executive power of governance and fiscal management.

If this is done, would it still be possible to name lay persons to the position? The difficulties in interpreting the restrictions in canon 274, §1 would have to be resolved first. On the other hand, if particular law does not so expand the office of chancellor, it could be filled by someone not in sacred orders. The use of delegation could continue, providing the lay chancellor with a means of cooperating in the exercise of the power of governance. However, the code is wary of concentrating so much authority in the hands of someone other than the diocesan bishop, either by office or delegation—a caution which is well taken.

The appointment of a lay person as chancellor is not just a theoretical issue; several dioceses have already done this, and with the increasing shortage of sacred ministers the appointment of lay persons to such administrative positions may increase.

Consultative Bodies

The law now requires several consultative bodies in each diocese: a presbyteral council and college of consultors (cc. 495, 502), and a diocesan finance council (c. 492). Other consultative bodies are also encountered in the code and other church norms; for example, diocesan pastoral council (c. 511), episcopal council (c. 473, §4), commissions on liturgy, sacred music, sacred art (SC, 46), ecumenism.[61]

---

[60]This fact was given official recognition by Paul VI in 1964. The diocesan bishop had been granted special faculties, but could only delegate them to his coadjutor, auxiliaries and vicars general—see Paul VI, motu proprio *Pastorale munus*, November 30, 1963: *AAS* 56 (1964) 6. However, he acceded to the request of the bishops in the United States and granted them the power to delegate these faculties also to their chancellors. See letter of Apostolic Delegate, December 3, 1964: *CLD* 6: 385.

[61]Secretariat for Promoting Christian Unity, directory *Ad totam Ecclesiam* (*Directory for*

There are many practical issues relating to these bodies: how to select their membership, their relationship to each other, and the effective carrying out of their tasks. These issues have been and are dealt with elsewhere.[62] Here, attention is directed to a more theoretical question, namely their role in the governance of a diocese.

By definition these are "consultative" bodies. But consultation has several aspects. At times, the *advice* of a consultative body is required; at other times, its *consent* is needed. In the canonical system, initiative resides with the individual who exercises executive power (e.g., the diocesan bishop). Consultative bodies are intended to serve as a moderating influence on executive initiative, while respecting the executive's prerogatives.

Thus, at times the executive must listen to a consultative body before acting. For the validity of the executive's action the law (c. 127, §1) requires that the body be properly convened and that the advice of each person present be sought. It is possible for particular law or the statutes of the consultative group itself to provide for a telephone or written consultation, but one of the principal reasons for requiring consultation with a body rather than individuals (c. 127, §2) is that collective discussion has distinct advantages.

Once the advice has been given, the executive retains the initiative, may decide to act or not, and may decide which option of action to take. The law cautions, however, that the executive should not act contrary to the advice which has been given, especially when there is a consensus, unless the executive has an overriding reason.[63]

In a limited number of circumstances, the consent of the consultative body is required. The executive still retains the initiative but cannot exercise it without the body's consent. Here the executive cannot act against the body's decision if it is negative; but if the body affirms the

---

the Application of the Decisions of the Second Ecumenical Council of the Vatican Concerning Ecumenical Matters), May 14, 1967, n. 3: AAS 59 (1967) 574.

[62]See the commentators on diocesan governance cited above. Certain special questions have also been studied; see, for example, James H. Provost, "The Working Together of Consultative Bodies—Great Expectations?" *The Jurist* 40 (1980) 257–281; Robert T. Kennedy, "Shared Responsibility in Ecclesial Decision-Making," *Studia Canonica* 15 (1980) 5–23; Bertram F. Griffin, "Diocesan Church Structures," in *Code, Community, Ministry,* ed. James H. Provost (Washington: CLSA, 1983), pp. 53–62.

[63]C. 127, §2, 2°; while this provision is stated with specific reference to consulting with individuals, it is all the more applicable to consultation with a group where there has been the opportunity for collective discussion.

proposed course of action, the executive retains the freedom to determine whether to go through with it or not.

What if the members of the consultative group are divided on the matter? An absolute majority (fifty percent plus one) of those present is required for a decision (c. 127, §1). Only those with a deliberative vote within the group (i.e., with voice and vote) are counted in terms of "those present." If an absolute majority is not reached, consent has not been given. If there were a tie vote, could the executive break the tie? Some have argued that since the diocesan bishop presides over the college of consultors (c. 502, §2) and diocesan finance council (c. 492, §1)—the two groups whose consent is required by law on certain matters—he could break the tie as presiding officer. The law, however, does not permit this according to an authentic (i.e., binding) interpretation.[64] In effect, a tie vote does not give the required consent.

The presbyteral council must be consulted on various issues,[65] but its role in diocesan governance is not limited to these. It is to be like a senate for the bishop, aiding him in the governance of the diocese for the pastoral welfare of the portion of the people of God entrusted to them.[66] The bishop is supposed to consult the presbyteral council in regard to all significant matters in the diocese, even if these are not listed individually in the law (c. 500, §2).

Similarly, the finance council and college of consultors must be consulted on more important acts of administration, determined in light of the diocese's economic situation; they must give their consent before the bishop can perform acts of extraordinary administration (c. 1277). While the bishops' conference is to set the norms for determining what is extraordinary administration, there is a certain latitude left to the bishop in determining "more important acts of administration." The intent of the law is clear, however, that the bishop should readily seek advice in financial matters.[67]

---

[64]Commission for the Authentic Interpretation of the Code, July 5, 1985: AAS 77 (1985) 771. The commission replied in the negative to the query, "When the law requires that the superior must have the consent of the council or of a body of persons in order to act, in keeping with canon 127, §1, does the superior have the right of voting with the others, at least to break a tie?"

[65]For a list see Alesandro in CLSA, p. 405.

[66]C. 495, §1; cf. c. 369, where the diocese is defined as the portion of the people of God entrusted to "a bishop with the cooperation of the presbyterate."

[67]He must consult the finance council on several other matters. He consults the finance council together with the college of consultors in hiring or removing the diocesan finance officer before his term is up (c. 494); he needs the *consent* of both groups to alienate property

To term a body "consultative," therefore, is not to diminish its importance; rather, it inserts the body in the governance system of the diocese at a very crucial level. The same applies to other consultative bodies which may be optional in the new code, but which when they exist do have specific responsibilities—such as the diocesan pastoral council, which is charged with an important role in pastoral planning (c. 511).

Those involved in consultative groups are to offer their opinion seriously (c. 127, §3). Offering opinion, and even moreso the giving of consent, are juridic acts; that is, they are acts which have a juridic effect, for without the advice or consent the superior cannot act validly. As with all juridic acts, they must be free from external force (c. 125, §1). If grave fear or fraud were involved, or the person acted out of ignorance or error, the result is usually valid but can be rescinded (cc. 125, §2; 126). It is important, therefore, for members of consultative bodies to be fully informed; the law makes a specific point of this in regard to those who must give their consent to alienation of property (c. 1292, §4), but the principle obviously applies to other situations as well.

Personnel and Finances

Among the many issues addressed in diocesan governance, those relating to personnel and to finances deserve special attention from a canon law perspective. They have proven to be of special importance in the history of the Church in the United States, have been the source of a certain tension between some American bishops and the Apostolic See, and are two dimensions of diocesan life for which the law has developed a notable amount of detail.

Personnel

Traditionally "personnel" in a diocese meant the clergy. Today that picture is rapidly shifting, so that in many dioceses—even those with a notable number of clergy—lay persons and religious constitute important dimensions of diocesan personnel. Dioceses have responded with person-

above the minimum set by the conference of bishops (c. 1292, §1). The advice of the finance council together with the presbyteral council is needed to impose a tax in the diocese (c. 1277). The advice of the finance council must also be sought in setting the limits of extraordinary administration for entities subject to the bishop which do not already have a limit (c. 1281, §2); in investing endowments (c. 1305); in reducing obligations from foundations (c. 1310, §2); and in reviewing annual reports (c. 1287, §1).

nel policies. Some of these deal only with personnel in individual agencies (Charities, schools, etc.). Others are for all the personnel in central administration, although frequently clergy are excluded from such policies. Occasionally a diocese will propose to develop a comprehensive personnel approach, one which deals with all aspects of the work (from recruiting to retirement), and sometimes with all levels of personnel (central administration, agencies, and parishes) and all types (clergy, religious, laity). Such comprehensive plans, however, are generally still in the experimental stages.[68]

There are five aspects of the personnel process which are addressed in canon law: recruitment and training, placement, recognition and support, retirement, and disciplinary problems.

1. Recruitment and Training

The most developed area of the law on recruitment and training concerns the clergy (cc. 232–264). In addition, bishops are told to foster vocations to the different ministries and to consecrated life (c. 385), and general principles for the training of religious are given in the code (cc. 659–661), to be supplemented by the specific provisions of each institute's own law. Bishops (c. 394), parish pastors (c. 529, §2), and clergy generally (c. 275, §2) are to promote the role of lay persons in the mission of the Church. Those lay persons who devote themselves permanently or temporarily to some special service of the Church have an obligation to acquire the appropriate formation for their work (c. 231, §1).

The Church provides special training centers for future clergy (cc. 234–237) and religious (c. 647). No special centers are designated in the law for the preparation of lay people for ecclesiastical service although they have a right to pursue higher studies in the sacred sciences, including attending ecclesiastical universities, faculties and institutes (c. 229). By providing its own educational system (cc. 793–821) the Church offers structural supports to prepare lay persons for, among other options, service in the church in pastoral, educational, charitable and administrative work.

There is little specific preparation for governance work in the Church. Although some programs, ranging from seminaries to lay ministry formation programs, include some study of canon law, this is usually a general introduction and perhaps some specialized attention to the sacraments,

---

[68]See the various publications of the National Association of Church Personnel Administrators (NACPA), especially John Kinsella and Barbara Garland, *Church Personnel Research and Planning.*

usually marriage. There are few if any programs outside of formal study of canon law which are designed to train persons for their work in diocesan governance. This problem was highlighted over ten years ago by Robert Kennedy,[69] but there has been almost no improvement in the conditions he identified then.[70]

There is a special problem relative to training new bishops. There is no formal training provided, even though a new diocesan bishop has suddenly become the chief executive officer of what are in many cases multi-million dollar corporations. He is now responsible for that corporation's personnel, financial and property administration, public communication, and other policies. He has become the chief judge in the diocese, the chief teacher and catechist, the chief pastor. While many bishops cope remarkably well with these responsibilities, every bishop could be given greater assistance if executive training programs which have been developed in the private sector, and even for religious superiors, were made available on a regular basis to newly appointed diocesan bishops.

2. Placement

Placement of personnel in the diocese is subject to the bishop's determination. That is, he is the one who appoints those who exercise offices within the diocesan curia or central diocesan administration (c. 470), those who teach religion in Catholic schools (c. 805), and those who exercise pastoral care of a parish (cc. 517, 523, and 547). Frequently he delegates much of this responsibility to others for all but key positions. He can also set policy for the placement of personnel by others in the diocese, such as teachers in schools (c. 806, §1).[71]

This does not mean, however, that he can be capricious about appointments. His discretion is confined by the norms concerning appointment to office, including the requirement that the candidate be "suitable" (c. 149, §1). Even for offices created specifically within his diocese, and for which there are no qualifications listed by the general law of the Church, the

[69]Robert T. Kennedy, "Introductory Address," *CLSA Proceedings* 33 (1971) 1–10; idem, chairperson, report of CLSA Committee on Education in Church Government, *CLSA Proceedings* 34 (1972) 126–138.

[70]See Paul Golden and Richard A. Hill, "Report on Survey of Teachers of Canon Law," *CLSA Proceedings* 40 (1978) 117–124; also, "Statement on Education in Canon Law For Future Ministers of the Church in the United States," *CLSA Proceedings* 43 (1981) 314–316.

[71]These policies are a key means to implement the bishops' own teaching on the rights of employees to organize and bargain collectively, and to promote new creative models of collaboration even in the placement of personnel. See N.C.C.B., *Economic Justice for All,* November 13, 1986, nn. 353 and 295–304.

bishop (or other executive involved) must nevertheless specify the obligations and rights pertaining to the office (c. 145, §2) and thereby sets criteria for suitability in the exercise of that office. Placement which is the result of simony is invalid (c. 149, §3). As noted earlier, certain positions are closed to the bishop's blood relatives. In the appointment of the finance officer he must consult the finance council and council of consultors (c. 494, §1); otherwise the appointment is invalid. If he has a coadjutor bishop or an auxiliary bishop with special faculties, he must name him a vicar general (c. 406, §1). Other auxiliary bishops are to be named vicars—either vicars general, or episcopal vicars (c. 406, §2).

The key placement for diocesan governance in any diocese, of course, is the naming of the diocesan bishop himself. The current law of the Latin Church, operative in the United States without the restrictions which may still exist in other countries in virtue of concordat, places the full responsibility for this in the hands of the Roman Pontiff (c. 377, §1). However, he does not act in isolation. Through the pontifical legate he consults with the metropolitan, neighboring bishops, president of the bishops' conference, some members of the clergy, religious and laity of the diocese. Present norms require this to be done secretly and individually (c. 377, §3). Whether the current placement system is effective depends upon one's point of view in individual cases; the current norms have been in effect for nearly fifteen years, and an objective evaluation of experience under them might be beneficial.

3. Recognition and Support

Maintaining competent personnel in key positions is crucial to both effective ministry in the diocese and the effective running of diocesan governance systems. Too rapid a turn over in personnel can reduce parishes and even diocesan structures to chaos. The law recognizes this in reference to an office's stability.[72] Two factors which favor retention of key personnel are recognition and support.

Recognition is not just holding testimonial dinners or giving awards for so many years of service; recognition is the acknowledgement in practice of the expertise and competence of individuals. This is reflected in trust, in a climate of support and mutual collaboration, in encouraging initiative and shared responsibility. Working in an environment where one is conscious

---

[72]Vatican II emphasized the subjective stability of a person in the office—*stabiliter collatum* (*PO*, 20). The code adds reference to the objective stability of the existence of this particular office—*stabiliter constitutum* (c. 145, §1).

of being valued, of being entrusted with appropriate responsibility, is the kind of encouraging recognition that stimulates competent and dedicated persons. The law encourages this atmosphere by the initiative which goes with office, and a preference for structuring diocesan governance through offices rather than delegation.[73]

Support includes spiritual as well as material and programmatic support. Working for the Church should be the source of spiritual growth for anyone, in the same way that clergy themselves are to find the first element in their spirituality in the fulfillment of their pastoral duties (c. 276, §2, 1°). Those with responsibility in diocesan governance are involved in ministering not only to a larger public, but also to the persons who work with and for them. This can be accomplished by providing opportunities for spiritual growth, days of reflection on the spiritual meaning of the work being done, personal contacts, and various other ministries.

Material support is also required. This is guaranteed to clergy (c. 281) in virtue of their incardination and the resulting obligation which binds the diocesan bishop in their regard (c. 384). For religious, while their institute is to provide them with what is necessary to achieve the purpose of their vocation (c. 670), the institute itself is supposed to assure financial matters, among other concerns, through a written agreement with the diocese (c. 681, §2).

For lay persons, the teaching of the magisterium and the new code apply its own principles of social justice to the inner life of the Church.[74] A just family wage, adequate pension, social security and health benefits are to be provided to lay persons who devote themselves permanently or temporarily to some special service of the Church (c. 231, §2). Laborers employed by the Church at any level must be paid a just and decent family wage, and are to receive the full benefit of the civil laws which apply to their work and working conditions (c. 1286). If some wish to volunteer their services, or to donate part of their income to the Church, that must be a free, personal decision, not something forced upon them just because they work for the Church.

Personnel—clergy, religious and lay—deserve support in the work they do. This ranges from systematic reviews by which their performance is evaluated and improvements are suggested, to opportunities for continuing education and professional development. At the parish level the law foresees the bishop's regular visitation which could be one means to

---

[73] See Urrutia, p. 353.

[74] See statements by the 1971 and 1974 synods of bishops cited above, and the pastoral letter of the American bishops on the economy, *Economic Justice for All*, n. 351.

accomplish some of this support (c. 396). Various dioceses have policies which address performance evaluation in diocesan offices. Programs for continuing education of clergy and of other ministers are examples of other practical efforts already underway. A person who is employed for service in the Church deserves the support which will make that service effective and beneficial.

4. Retirement

Retirement has received increased attention in recent years. The Second Vatican Council took a new approach to the retirement of clergy, encouraging bishops and parish pastors to submit their resignation from office because of the burden of age, health or some other reason.[75] Particular law can set mandatory retirement ages for diocesan offices (cc. 184–186).

Since the council there has been a developing awareness of the need to provide for all who work for the Church in this regard. The condition of religious has become a source of major concern.[76] Programs to provide for the retirement of lay persons have existed in some dioceses, and are gradually being adopted in others. As noted above, the new code mandates that provisions be made for this. Special diocesan or interdiocesan funds are recommended as one means to fund these benefits (c. 1274).

The term "retirement" has carried with it the connotation of ceasing from all service; yet a Christian does not "retire" from participating in the mission of the Church. "Senior status," "emeritus" (c. 185), and similar terms have been adopted to clarify this fact. But funding and titles are not the only elements in a personnel policy on retirement; preparing people for this situation in their life is equally important. Some programs have been developed to assist dioceses and pre-retirement of clergy,[77] and various secular sources have developed similar programs which could be of benefit to all who work for the Church.

---

[75] *CD*, 21 and 31; these have been incorporated in subsequent legislation, and are reflected in cc. 401 and 538, §3.

[76] The Conference of Major Superiors of Men, the Leadership Conference of Women Religious and the National Conference of Catholic Bishops have begun a two year project to address the $2.5 billion unfunded retirement liability of religious institutes; see "On File," *Origins* 16/4 (June 12, 1986) 78.

[77] See John F. Kinsella and Walter H. Jenne, *Fullness in Christ: A Report on a Study of Clergy Retirement* (Washington: USCC, 1982).

5. Disciplinary Problems

Disciplinary problems have occasioned the development of notable portions of canon law in regard to the clergy. The law reflects a pastoral approach, beginning with the need for the bishop to have a special concern for the presbyters in his diocese (c. 384). If the diocese has deans, these vicars forane are not only to be vigilant over the work and life style of clergy in the deanery (c. 555, §1), but also to promote their spiritual support and provide help to those in difficulty (c. 555, §2, 2°). Religious superiors have a similar responsibility of support toward the members of their institutes (cc. 618–619). Good personnel practices of recognition and support are also examples of setting a climate in which disciplinary problems are forestalled from the outset.

When a breach of discipline does occur, the code calls first for fraternal correction, rebuke and other ways of pastoral care to repair scandal, restore justice and reform the accused (c. 1341). Only when it is clear these will not work should penalties be considered.

If it appears necessary to take more serious disciplinary actions, the law recognizes several types. It distinguishes administrative actions such as transfer (cc. 190–191) and removal from office (cc. 192–195), from penal actions such as deprivation of office (c. 196). Penal action requires that a crime have been committed and that the procedural safeguards be observed which are provided in the law (cc. 1341–1353, 1717–1728). The diocesan bishop, for example, cannot simply decree a penalty when suspicion of a crime or immoral action is reported to him; he is bound to observe the procedures set forth in law. This is not a mere legalism; it is an historic concern to protect both the ecclesiastical authority from capricious and unfounded action, and the rights of individuals in the Church.

Administrative actions must also provide at least basic procedural safeguards. For example, administrative transfer when the officeholder is unwilling requires a grave cause, the right to present arguments against the transfer, and the observance of whatever procedure has been set in law.[78] Administrative removal from office must respect the rights which have been acquired by contract (c. 192). It requires a due cause (c. 193) which must be stated at least in summary form when the removal is decreed (c. 51), and must observe procedures specified in law if the office was

---

[78]The code sets such a procedure only for the transfer of pastors (cc. 1748–1752); particular law on personnel matters should specify the procedures to be followed in other transfers in a diocese.

conferred for an indefinite term or if removal is taking place before the expiration of a limited term (c. 193, §§1 and 2). The person involved has the right to be heard (c. 50). Attention must be given to termination pay if the office was the source of the person's livelihood (c. 195). Given the broader meaning of office, these safeguards apply not only to removing clergy from ecclesiastical offices, but also to firing lay persons from them. Religious, however, are not afforded the same protection individually (c. 682, §2), and the termination of workers who do not have an ecclesiastical office is governed by applicable civil laws (c. 1286, 1°).

The problem discussed above concerning adequate remedies for vindicating rights has a special importance here. Personnel issues have formed the bulk of "due process" activities in those United States dioceses where such procedures are active. Conceivably they could be brought to the diocesan tribunal in cases where the disciplinary action did not entail the exercise of executive administrative power. Care must also be taken that whatever disciplinary action is applied be done with equity and respect for the rights of persons; there is a growing willingness of the civil courts to accept cases where such safeguards were not observed.[79]

Finances

The canon law on financial matters has been reorganized in the new code, although in many ways it continues the traditional approach of church law.[80] Diocesan governance in the United States is faced with three key areas of concern in regard to finances: structural questions, procedural questions, and accountability.

1. Structural Questions

There is a difference between the civil law and canonical structures for ownership in many dioceses. In canon law, the diocese, parishes, and other entities within a diocese are juridic persons. A juridic person in canon law is analogous to corporations in civil law, although there are differences which are beyond the scope of this paper.[81]

---

[79]See William W. Bassett "Christian Rights in Civil Litigation: Translating Religion into Justiciable Categories," *The Jurist* 46/1 (1986).

[80]See Book V, The Temporal Goods of the Church, cc. 1254–1310; for commentaries, see: Lamberto de Echeverría in BAC, pp. 597–623; Mariano López Alarcón in EUNSA, pp. 745–788; John J. Myers in CLSA, pp. 859–890; Francesco Salerno in Urbaniana, pp. 711–747; Winfried Schulz et al. in *Handbuch*, pp. 859–919.

[81]See cc. 113–123; for commentaries, see: Jiménez Urresti in BAC, pp. 87–99;

In civil law in the United States, the property of the Catholic Church is held according to the laws of the various States. Several systems are in use.[82] Under corporation sole, a religious corporation is established in which the sole member of the corporation is the diocesan bishop; title to all property is held in the name of the corporation sole. When a new diocesan bishop takes possession of the diocese, he files as the new sole member of the corporation. In the system of corporation aggregate, each parish, institution, and the diocese itself are separately incorporated, with a distinct board of trustees for each. The diocesan bishop is always a member of the board, frequently its head, and usually the by-laws of each corporation give the bishop the same powers in the corporation that he has according to canon law. Other members of the board are often the vicar general, the pastor or other canonical agent for the entity, and two other incorporators, frequently lay persons. When a new diocesan bishop takes possession of the diocese he automatically succeeds to the position assigned the bishop in each of these corporations. There has also been a system of "fee simple" ownership in which the property is held in the name of the bishop personally; church property is passed on not to his personal heirs but to his successor in office. Some dioceses have no civil incorporation, and operate as associations.

The corporation aggregate system comes closest to reflecting in a civil law structure the distinct juridic personalities in canon law. In more centralized systems, where all property is held in the name of a diocesan corporation, it is possible to neglect the fact that ecclesiastical goods pertain not to the bishop but to the juridic person which legitimately acquired them (c. 1256). Careful bookkeeping is needed to respect the canon law requirements.

2. Procedural Questions

There are three issues here: taxation by the diocese, the dinstinction of ordinary and extraordinary administration, and "alienation."

The new code grants increased taxation powers to the diocesan bishop. He can impose a moderate tax on public juridic persons subject to his authority (for example, parishes) provided the tax is proportionate to the juridic persons' income, is for diocesan needs, and he first consults the

---

Ellsworth Kneal in CLSA, pp. 80–87; Eduardo Molano in EUNSA, pp. 118–125; Pio Pinto in Urbaniana, pp. 67–73; Franz Pototschnig in *Handbuch,* pp. 118–121.

[82]See the description in Chester J. Bartlett, *The Tenure of Parochial Property in the United States of America,* Canon Law Studies, 31 (Washington: Catholic University of America, 1926).

diocesan finance and presbyteral councils. The practices which American dioceses have followed for some time are now regularized in law.[83] These include the diocesan assessment, diocesan-wide fund raising drives with mandatory quotas (i.e., when the difference between donations and the quota is to be made up with parish funds), deposit and loan funds which impose a lower interest on parish funds deposited with the diocese, to name the major ones. It is noteworthy, however, that consultation requirements are now in effect for the valid imposition of such taxes; this has not always been the practice in the past.

The distinction of ordinary and extraordinary administration existed in the former code (1917 code, c. 1527) but the law did not specify the difference between them. Under the new code, this determination is to be made by particular law—adopted by the conference of bishops for dioceses (c. 1277), contained in its own statutes for other juridic persons or, if these do not determine this, then made by the diocesan bishop for juridic persons subject to him (c. 1281, §2).[84] A second distinction exists within ordinary administration, some of which are "more important" matters in light of the economic situation of the diocese (c. 1277).

The distinctions have practical results. For a diocesan bishop to perform (or authorize) more important acts of ordinary administration, he must consult the finance council and the college of consultors; failing this, the actions would be invalid (c. 127, §1). The law does not specify who determines what is a "more important" matter of ordinary administration; presumably, this would be the decision of the bishop himself. Yet to avoid possible civil as well as canonical difficulties in financial dealings, it would be well for the bishop to confine his discretion by working out with these two bodies the practical criteria for how these "more important" matters for the diocese are to be identified.

Acts of extraordinary administration require that an administrator obtain someone else's consent. For the bishop, this consent comes from the diocesan finance council and college of consultors (c. 1277). For other administrators within the diocese, the written permission of the ordinary is necessary (c. 1281, §1). There are several "ordinaries" who could be involved; for religious institutes and societies of apostolic life which are pontifical right and clerical, it may be their major superior (c. 134, §1).

---

[83]See Donald J. Frugé, "Taxes in the Proposed Code," *CLSA Proceedings* 44 (1982) 274–288.

[84]This is another instance when the diocesan bishop must first consult the diocesan finance council (c. 1281, §2).

Vicars general and episcopal vicars are included as well as the diocesan bishop. But lacking this written persmission, the action is invalid.

What is the result of such an invalid action? This is primarily a canon law concept; the action lacks binding legal force under canon law. It may also have civil effects depending on the wording of the statutes or corporate papers of the juridic person, or the extent to which civil courts will consider an organization's own norms in determining the authorization needed for a legitimate business transaction. Remedies can be sought in canon law against the individual administrator who violates these norms (cc. 1281, §3; 1377).

Alienation is another traditional concept which receives renewed attention in the 1983 code. Alienation is "the transfer of property or of rights over property from one person to another."[85] The norms on alienation apply to the alienation of a juridic person's stable patrimony (c. 1291) and to any transaction which could worsen the patrimonial condition of a juridic person (c. 1295).[86]

The code requires the bishops' conference to set minimum and maximum values for alienation purposes. Providing the statutes of the juridic person are observed, an administrator needs only obtain the consent of the parties concerned to alienate below the minimum amount. Between the minimum and maximum levels, juridic persons subject to the diocesan bishop need his permission; above the maximum level and for goods which were donated to the Church through a vow or which have special artistic or historical value, the permission of the Apostolic See is required (c. 1292). The bishop is subject to the same requirements for goods above the maximum level. Moreover, he cannot alienate goods of the diocese or give permission for alienation above the minimum level without first obtaining the consent of the diocesan finance council, the college of consultors, and the parties concerned.

The provisions in the new code about consultation and consent are quite clear. One area which may lead to further discussion is determining who are "the parties concerned" who must also consent before the bishop can

---

[85]Myers, p. 879.

[86]Examples include pledging, mortgaging, renting for a notable period of time, or entering into a perpetual lease (basically, a lease with option to buy); see Paul VI, motu proprio *Pastorale munus*, p. 10. A widely-used commentary on the 1917 code, where c. 1533 made a similar provision, also listed annuity obligations, compromise or arbitration in financial matters, renunciation of active easements, allowing passive easements, and acting as security for others; see T. Lincoln Bouscaren, Adam C. Ellis and Francis N. Korth, *Canon Law: A Text and Commentary* (Milwaukee: Bruce, 4th rev. ed. 1966), p. 839.

permit an alienation. The previous code also required their consent;[87] however, it was not considered necessary for the validity of the alienation.[88] Who are included as concerned (or "interested") parties? Commentators on the new code generally do not discuss this issue. Myers, who does, draws on interpretations of the previous code and presents "parties concerned" as "the beneficiaries." He explains: "The administrator would speak for any juridic persons which are beneficiaries. Several persons might need to be consulted if a collegial juridic person were the beneficiary. A patron or his or her family might be consulted, but this does not seem to be required always and necessarily."[89]

"Beneficiaries" in the former code, however, did not mean those who would benefit from a transaction, but the person who held a benefice. If the alienation would affect the stable patrimony of a benefice, clearly the benefice holder (beneficiary) would have an interest in the matter. Commentators on the previous code did not attempt to give an exhaustive list of who would be included under "parties concerned," but often listed the benefice holder (beneficiary), rector of a church building, patron, the college for a collegiate moral person, the administrator for a non-collegial moral person, etc.[90]

In the case of an ecclesiastical institution established for the good of a group of believers, if the alienation were such as to deny them the services

[87]1917 code, c. 1532, §§2 and 3. Even in cases where the cathedral chapter and council of administration only needed to be consulted rather than give consent, the consent of concerned parties was required.

[88]See Eduardus Regatillo, *Institutiones Iuris Canonici,* 2nd ed. rev., 2 (Santander: Sal Terrae, 1946), p. 161. This was part of a general *dubium iuris* about when consent was required for validity; see Clement V. Bastnagel, "The Requirement of Consultation for Valid Action," *The Jurist* 9 (1949) 365–395. Under the new code such consent is required for validity (c. 127, §2).

[89]Myers, p. 881. For the restriction on patrons he refers in a note to Felix M. Cappello, *Summa Iuris Canonici* 2 (Rome: Apud Aedes Pontificiae Universitatis Gregorianae, 1951), p. 585, and M. Conte a Coronata, *Institutiones Iuris Canonici,* 3rd ed., 2 (Rome: Marietti, 1948), p. 489. The common opinion was that patrons need be consulted only if this were included in the right of patronage for this patron.

[90]See, for example, Christophorus Berutti, *Institutiones Iuris Canonici,* 4 (Turin: Marietti, 1940), p. 515; Matthaeus Conte a Coronata, *Institutiones Iuris Canonici* 2 (Turin: Marietti, 1931), p. 486; Marius Pistocchi, *De Bonis Ecclesiae Temporalibus* (Turin: Marietti, 1932), pp. 407–408; Regatillo, p. 161; A. Vermeersch and J. Creusen, *Epitome Iuris Canonici,* 4th ed., 2 (Mechlin: H. Dessain, 1930), p. 529; Joseph Wenner, *Kirchliches Vermörgensrecht* (Paderborn: F. Schöningh, 1940), pp. 212–213.

to which they had become entitled then they, too, would need to consent.[91] Moreover, as always the will of the donor must be respected (c. 1300).

If effect, to be a "party concerned" would seem to require some claim in law, some right to what is being alienated. But determining the extent to which various people have claim to such an interest is not so easy today as in an earlier time when only wealthy individuals provided the goods of the Church. When parishioners donate to a special project, such as the purchase of land for a cemetery, the building of a school, or even the furnishings of a church, they express not only their generosity; they are also giving for a specific purpose. Does this include them under the category of those who are "concerned"?

In practice, it would seem advisable for dioceses to adopt policies whereby they confine their discretion through clear procedures for alienation, including adequate consultation of the consultative bodies which have now been established. For example, consulting the parish pastoral and finance councils could help avoid problems when goods belonging to the juridic person of the parish are involved. But even so, it appears the issue of those "concerned" may require ongoing attention by canon lawyers and persons in positions of diocesan governance.

3. Accountability

Accountability in financial matters is a constant concern. The requirements of consultation are one process the new code reinforces to assure some sense of accountability even prior to major financial transactions. Another is the requirement of regular reporting. The code requires that annual reports be submitted to the diocesan bishop by all juridic persons subject to him (c. 1287, §1). An annual report on diocesan operations must also be drawn up (c. 493).

There is no requirement in the code for financial reporting by dioceses to any external authority, even to the Apostolic See. The law does not even mandate an external audit. But the new code does set up the diocesan finance council as an agency for internal audits, including a careful study of all the reports submitted to the diocese and by the diocese. The code has also introduced a requirement that an accounting be given to the faithful

---

[91]See Wenner, p. 213. In effect, this applies the principle of acquired rights to the issue of alienation.

concerning their offerings to the Church, and calls for particular law to specify norms for doing this.[92]

Who enforces these requirements of consultation and reporting? For the juridic persons subject to him, the diocesan bishop is the enforcing agent (c. 392). But what of the consultation and reporting to which the diocesan bishop is obliged? Here the law is not so specific. In regard to consultation, those who are to be consulted have a right to be consulted; if a diocesan bishop fails to consult, could members of a consultative body such as the diocesan finance council or college of consultors appeal to higher authorities to vindicate this right? What of a "party concerned"?

Since every right is safeguarded by an action (c. 1491), certainly some recourse must be available. In regard to the goods of the diocese as such, for which the bishop is the legal agent in canon law (c. 393), a suit could be brought before the appellate tribunal (c. 1419, §2). Otherwise recourse to a tribunal would have to be at the Roman Rota (c. 1405, §3). Of course, hierarchical recourse could also be attempted.

Is recourse to the civil courts a possibility? This is a very complex question, and currently is in a state of development in the United States.[93] The code asserts a proper and exclusive right of the Church to judge violations of ecclesiastical law (c. 1401, 2°). Yet the previous code's automatic excommunication for taking a bishop to court[94] has not been retained in the current code. Clearly Catholics should attempt to resolve disputes by making use of church procedures rather than having recourse to civil processes. Yet this presumes ecclesiastical avenues of recourse are effective; making sure they are may be the most effective way to avoid civil suits.

Some Rules for Diocesan Governance

To conclude these limited reflections on canon law issues relating to diocesan governance, it may be helpful to draw on the Church's tradition to sketch twelve "rules" or guidelines which may assist those in positions of diocesan governance.

1. *Be always vigilant for the spiritual purpose of diocesan governance.*

---

[92]C. 1287, §2; see N.C.C.B., *Principles and Guidelines for Fund Raising in the United States by Arch/Dioceses, Arch/Diocesan Agencies and Religious Institutes,* November 14–17, 1977: *CLD* 8: 415–421.

[93] See Bassett, "Christian Rights in Civil Litigation: Translating Religion into Justiciable Categories," *The Jurist* 46/1 (1986).

[94]1917 code, cc. 120, 2341.

The salvation of souls is the supreme law of the Church. This is not only a literary device with which the legislator concluded the new code (c. 1752, at the end); it reflects the very purpose of diocesan governance, which is ultimately spiritual. Effective governance requires constant vigilance to the spiritual dimension of being Church.

2. *Think with the Church.*

Church law is to be interpreted in light of the teaching and new way of thinking characteristic of the Second Vatican Council.[95] *Sentire cum Ecclesia* is to resonate with the mystery of Christ as this is presented through the teaching, witness and tradition of the Church. Diocesan governance steers not by the isolated lights of those currently at the helm, but by the wisdom of God made manifest in the Catholic communion as it carries out the mission entrusted to it.

3. *Serve if you would lead.*

Hierarchical authority is a service, directed toward the spiritual welfare of God's people.[96] This service of leadership implies the development of the personality of the leader, attention to the common good, and commitment to the spiritual goal for which the Church exists.

4. *Use the power you have.*

The bishop has all the power needed to exercise his pastoral office (c. 381, §1). There is no need, nor is it appropriate, to refer matters to a higher authority which properly pertain to the diocesan bishop as vicar and ambassador of Christ in the particular church. Failure to use power may not only be irresponsible, but damaging for the welfare of all the Church.

5. *Empower the Church.*

All the Christian faithful, in virtue of Christ's action through the sacraments of initiation and charisms, participate in the mission which Christ gave the Church to accomplish in the world (c. 204, §1; *AA*, 3). To govern is to foster the common good; that is, to empower others to reach their potential, and thereby build up the Body of Christ.

---

[95] Paul VI, allocution to Code Commision, p. 988; John Paul II, allocution to Roman Rota, pp. 645–646.

[96] See John Paul II, *Sacrae disciplinae leges*, p. xii; see also the discussion in Agnes Cunningham's article above.

6. *Promote and protect rights.*

The obligations and rights of Christians are the context in which the hierarchical structure of the Church performs its Christ-given ministry of service. They highlight the responsibility for which diocesan governance empowers Catholics in the communion and mission of the Church.

7. *Consult when making decisions.*

What touches all ought to be considered by all.[97] There is a standard pattern in the new code calling for consultation in coming to significant decisions. Sometimes this is required for validity (c. 127); otherwise, it is a general counsel for prudent action. Consulting also involves reminding those who have something to offer that they have an obligation to speak up (c. 127, §3), especially if they disagree.[98]

8. *Interpret the law as it is meant to be interpreted.*

Laws are made for God's people, not the people for laws. Indeed, no one is held to the impossible.[99] The laws are therefore not meant to be interpreted in such a way as to make Christian living impossible, or to defeat the purpose of the salvation of souls. Any one who administers the law interprets it; a number of guides are available to help in this.[100]

9. *Be generous.*

The law itself is generous, even to an accused person: when there has been a change in the law, the law which is more favorable to the accused is to be applied (c. 1313, §1). Traditionally, favors are to be expanded and burdensome matters restricted.[101] Moreover, laws which establish a penalty, restrict the free exercise of rights, or which contain an exception to the law are to be interpreted strictly (c. 18). On the other hand, the law is generous in situations of doubt.[102]

---

[97]*RJ* 29 in VI°: "Quod omnes tangit debet ab omnibus probari"; cited in Urbaniana, p. 1031. See Yves Congar, "Quod Omnes Tangit, Ab Omnibus Tractari et Approbari Debet," *Revue historique de droit français et étranger* 35 (1958) 210–259.

[98] *RJ* 43 in VI°: "Qui tacet consentire videtur"; cited in Urbaniana, p. 1031.

[99] *RJ* 6 in VI°: "Nemo potest ad impossibile obligari"; cited in Urbaniana, p. 1031.

[100]See, for example, the studies by James A. Coriden, Richard A. Hill, Ellsworth Kneal and Ladislas Orsy, *The Art of Interpretation* (Washington: CLSA, 1982).

[101]*RJ* 15 in VI°: "Odia restringi et favores convenit ampliari"; cited in Urbaniana, p. 1031.

[102]When there is a doubt of law, even nullifying and disqualifying laws do not bind; in a doubt of fact, the possibility of dispensation exists (c. 14). In legal or factual common error, or a probable doubt about law or fact, the Church supplies executive power (c. 144, §1).

10. *Be consistent.*

Effective governance is governance people can count on. What once seemed proper ought not suddenly to be presented as improper,[103] nor should an opinion once adopted be changed to the detriment of another.[104] Indeed, legal consistency is a characteristic of the Church's legislation,[105] and should mark the service of those in diocesan governance.

11. *Be timely.*

If justice delayed is justice denied, so unnecessary delay in any aspect of governance can be harmful to people.[106] The code sets various time limits to enforce timely governance; even where no limits are specified, sensitivity to the rights of persons calls for prudent timeliness.

12. *Be forthright.*

The Church exists to bear witness to the gospel, to be a light to the nations. As with its teaching on social justice, so with forthrightness, the Church must practice what it preaches if it is to be a credible witness. Respecting proper confidentiality (c. 471) and preserving the privacy of others (c. 220) is important, but it cannot be an excuse for obscurantist practices or secretive governance. There is a standard pattern in the code encouraging forthrightness: norms require the promulgation of laws (c.7), publication of judicial acts (c. 1598, §1) sentences (c. 1610), administrative acts (c. 37). The truth, after all, has nothing to fear from being proclaimed.

---

[103]*RJ* 21 in VI°: "Quod semel placuit amplius displicere non potest"; cited in Urbaniana, p. 1031.

[104]*RJ* 33 in VI°: "Mutare quis consilium non potest in alterius detrimentum"; cited in Urbaniana, p. 1031.

[105]See c. 21, and John Paul II in *Sacrae disciplinae leges,* p. xii where he describes the new code as faithful in its newness and new in its fidelity.

[106]*RJ* 25 in VI°: "Mora sua cuilibet nociva est"; *RJ* 37 in VI°: "Utile per inutile non debet vitiari"; cited in Urbaniana, p. 1031.

APPENDIX

Representing the Canon Law Society of America
    Rev. James K. Mallett
    Rev. Msgr. William Varvaro
    Rev. James H. Provost
    Rev. John J. Myers
    Rev. Charles L. Torpey
    Rev. Msgr. Roy M. Klister
    Rev. John E. Lynch, C.S.P.
    Rev. John M. Huels, O.S.M.
    Rev. James A. Coriden
Representing the National Catholic Education Association
    Rev. J. Stephen O'Brien
Representing the National Conference of Catholic Charities
    Rev. Thomas Harvey
    Rev. Edwin Conway
Representing the National Pastoral Planning Conference
    Rev. James Picton
Representing the Diocesan Fiscal Management Conference
    Rev. Msgr. Vincent A. Tatarczuk
Representing the National Organization for Continuing Education of
Roman Catholic Clergy
    Rev. Jerome Thompson
Representing the National Federation of Priests' Councils
    Rev. Richard Hynes
Representing the National Association of Church Personnel Administrators
    Sister Barbara Garland
Representing the Center for Applied Research in the Apostolate
    Dr. Edward M. Sullivan
Other Participants
    Sister Agnes Cunningham, S.S.C.M.
    Rev. George Sarauskas
    Rev. Philip Murnion

Rev. Thomas Curry
Rev. Michael A. Fahey, S.J.
Rev. Gerald P. Fogarty, S.J.
Rev. Eugene Hemrick
Dr. Robert J. Willis

AGNES CUNNINGHAM, S.S.C.M., holds a doctorate in theology and is professor of patristics at Saint Mary of the Lake Seminary, Mundelein, Illinois. A past president of the Catholic Theological Society of America, she has also contributed to previous Canon Law Society of America projects, including a study in the permanent seminar book, *The Church as Mission.*

THOMAS CURRY, a priest of the Archdiocese of Los Angeles, is currently Director of Continuing Education for Clergy for the archdiocese and has served as chairman of its Senate of Priests. He holds a Ph.D. in American History, specializing in church-state relations, from Claremont Graduate School. Oxford University Press has recently published his book, *The First Freedoms.*

MICHAEL A. FAHEY, S.J., holds a doctorate in theology from the University of Tübingen. He serves as dean of the faculty of theology, University of Saint Michael's College in Toronto, Canada. He has contributed to previous Canon Law Society of America projects, including a study in the permanent seminar book, *The Church as Communion.*

GERALD FOGARTY, S.J., Ph.D., is associate professor of history at the University of Virginia, Charlottesville. A specialist in the history of the Church in the United States, he has contributed to various Canon Law Society of America conferences and conventions.

EUGENE HEMRICK, Ph.D., is a priest of the Diocese of Joliet. A member of the research staff of the Center for Youth Development at The Catholic University of America, he also serves as director of research for the National Conference of Catholic Bishops.

JOHN M. HUELS, O.S.M., is a priest of the Servite Order who holds a J.C.D. from The Catholic University of America. He teaches canon law at Catholic Theological Union in Chicago and has contributed studies to numerous journals and to the commentary on the new code sponsored by

254

the Canon Law Society of America, *The Code of Canon Law: A Text and Commentary.*

JOHN E. LYNCH, C.S.P., Ph.D., is professor of the history of canon law at The Catholic University of America. He has published widely, including several studies in ecumenism, and has contributed to a number of Canon Law Society of America projects including the permanent seminar book, *The Church as Communion.*

JAMES K. MALLETT is a priest of the Diocese of Nashville. He received his S.T.L. from the Gregorian University and the M.Ch.A. degree from The Catholic University of America. He has served as chancellor, vicar general, moderator of the curia, and officialis of the Diocese of Nashville. A past treasurer of the Canon Law Society of America, he directed the Society's Symposium on Diocesan Governance from 1981 to 1985.

JAMES H. PROVOST, J.C.D., is a priest of the Diocese of Helena. Associate professor of canon law at The Catholic University of America, he has also served as executive coordinator of the Canon Law Society of America and directs the Society's permanent seminar projects.

ROLAND-BERNHARD TRAUFFER, O.P., J.C.D., is chancellor and canonical consultant for the Diocese of Basle, Switzerland. A member of the Canon Law Society of America, he participates regularly in Society activities.

ROBERT J. WILLIS, Ph.D., is a psychologist in private practice in Kingston, New Jersey. He serves as consultant in organizational development issues to health care and religious organizations, and has contributed to several books and periodicals on issues of religious psychology.